Acting
Jewish

Acting Jewish

Negotiating Ethnicity on the American Stage & Screen

Henry Bial

The University of Michigan Press
Ann Arbor

Copyright © by the University of Michigan 2005
All rights reserved
Published in the United States of America by
The University of Michigan Press
Manufactured in the United States of America
⊚ Printed on acid-free paper
2008   2007   2006   2005   4 3 2 1

A CIP catalog record for this book is available from the British Library.

Library of Congress Cataloging-in-Publication Data

Bial, Henry, 1970–
    Acting Jewish : negotiating ethnicity on the American stage and
screen / by Henry Bial.
       p.   cm.
    Includes bibliograpical references and index.
    ISBN-13: 978-0-472-09908-5 (cloth : alk.paper)
    ISBN-10: 0-472-09908-6 (cloth : alk. paper)
    ISBN-13: 978-0-472-06908-X (pbk. : alk.paper)
    ISBN-10: 0-472-06908-X (pbk. : alk. paper
       1. Jews in the performing arts—United States.   2. Jews in motion pictures.
3. Jews on television.   4. American drama—20th century—History and
criticism.   5. Jews in literature.   I. Title.

PN1590.J438B53   2005
791'.089'924073—dc22   2005014439

For Anna Sophia and Emily Margret

Acknowledgments

THIS BOOK WOULD NOT have been possible without the intellectual and emotional support of many wonderful people. First among these is Barbara Kirshenblatt-Gimblett, a true teacher and master, who guided this project through its first incarnation as a doctoral dissertation in the Department of Performance Studies at New York University. Along with Barbara, Richard Schechner and Carol Martin have taught me virtually everything I know about scholarship, teaching, and writing for publication; without their personal and professional support, this book would have taken twice as long to write and been half as enjoyable to read.

As members of my doctoral committee, Una Chaudhuri, Robert Vorlicky, Jeffrey Shandler, and Brooks McNamara each contributed to this project at different times and in different ways; the influence of their scholarship is, I hope, visible in my own. I especially thank Jeffrey Shandler for his challenging questions and suggestions on how to deepen my analysis, and Robert Vorlicky for introducing me to LeAnn Fields at the University of Michigan Press. LeAnn's enthusiastic support and insightful editing have been instrumental in shaping the final form of this book. I thank also those anonymous readers for the press who pushed me to address deficiencies in the original manuscript to the greater good of the book you now hold.

Cindy Brizzell read every draft of the manuscript with a keen eye and offered many valuable insights that made the book better. Stephanie Marlin-Curiel, Dan Bacalzo, David Gerstein, and Rabbi Lawrence Kelemen all read portions of the manuscript at various stages and offered helpful suggestions. My sister, Amy Bial Heavenrich, also read an early draft and helped me with some of the finer points of *halacha* discussed herein. Dorothy Chansky, Leonard Dinnerstein, Shimon Levy, Julius Novick, Gershon Shaked, and Rabbi Gerald M. Kane were among the many scholars who gave generously of their time and energy to offer advice, leads, and research materials. Aviva Weintraub at the Jewish Museum in New York City and Andy Ingall at the

National Jewish Archive of Broadcasting went above and beyond their job descriptions to assist me in researching their collections.

Portions of this book (in significantly different form) were presented at various scholarly meetings, including the Mid-Atlantic Popular Culture Association, Society for the Study of Multi-Ethnic Literature in the United States, Association for Theatre in Higher Education, Northeast Modern Language Association, Modern Language Association, American Literature Association, and the American Society for Theatre Research. I thank the organizers of these conferences for the opportunity to discuss my work with like-minded colleagues. I also thank my students at the University of New Mexico and New York University for their questions, enthusiasm, and patience.

My former colleagues in the Department of Theatre and Dance at the University of New Mexico have provided invaluable support and encouragement, especially those faculty in theater: Digby Wolfe, Jim Linnell, Denise Schulz, Susan Pearson-Davis, and Eugene Douglas. My department chair, Judith Bennahum, helped provide the time and resources needed to complete this project. Graduate students Gabrielle Johansen and Clareann Despain were of great assistance in the final preparation of the manuscript.

On a personal note, I wish to thank my parents, Ernest and Martha Bial, for making sure that their son attended both Hebrew school and Broadway theater with regular frequency and for never failing in their support and encouragement of my academic career. My greatest thanks are due Christine Dotterweich Bial for her enduring patience and love, which sustained me before, during, and after the writing process.

Finally, for my daughters, Anna and Emily, to whom this book is dedicated: though neither of you was born when I started this book, it's you I've been writing for all along. May you each find your own way of acting Jewish.

Contents

CHAPTER I

Performance Studies, Mass Culture, and the Jewish Problem

*A*T 8:00 P.M. ON the evening of Thursday, 14 May 1998, the Jewish Museum in New York City hosted a panel discussion entitled "Young Jewish Writers" featuring novelists Allegra Goodman (*The Family Markowitz*), Marcie Hershman (*Tales of the Master Race*), Thane Rosenbaum (*The Golems of Gotham*), and Aryeh Lev Stollman (*The Illuminated Soul*). The conversation, moderated by Ellen Pall (*Among the Ginzburgs*), focused in part on how the writers' perceptions of their own Jewish identity did or did not affect their professional craft. As part of the museum's inaugural "Live at the JM" series, the event was specifically intended to attract a younger, "hipper," Jewish audience than the institution's typical public programs. Although the discussion was lively, the hall was sparsely filled. Many spectators left early. The real interrogation of contemporary Jewish American identity was taking place elsewhere.

At 9:00 p.m. Eastern Daylight Time on that very same evening, the National Broadcasting Company (NBC) broadcast the final episode of its top-rated comedy *Seinfeld* (1989–98). The self-billed "show about nothing" features comedian Jerry Seinfeld as a comedian named . . . Jerry Seinfeld. The character of Jerry is explicitly identified as Jewish in selected episodes, and this identification is reinforced through a variety of visual and linguistic performance codes: Jerry has dark hair, dark eyes, and a stereotypically Semitic profile. His accent (especially in the early episodes) betrays his real life upbringing in Queens and Long Island. He resides on Manhattan's Upper West Side, a largely Jewish neighborhood. His last name, Seinfeld, is unmistakably "different" from the Anglo-Saxon norm and is recognizable to a Jewish audience as German-Jewish in origin.

Yet, while Jewish critics and viewers alike identify Jerry Seinfeld as unambiguously Jewish, his religious and ethnic background is essential to the narrative in only a handful of episodes scattered over the show's nine-year run on NBC. The vast majority of episodes contain no

explicit reference to Jews or Jewishness. The episodes that do acknowledge his Jewishness tend to downplay its importance. For example, in
one episode Jerry suspects that his dentist has converted to Judaism so
that he can tell Jewish jokes without being labeled a bigot. When a
priest asks Jerry, "This offends you as a Jewish person?" he replies, "No
it offends me as a comedian."[1]

Other elements of the show, such as Jerry's relationship with his
family, that might be read as Jewish are not explicitly connected to religion or ethnicity; the viewer is thus free to miss or ignore any implied
Jewish message. Yet Mary Kaye Schilling and Mike Flaherty of the
mainstream magazine *Entertainment Weekly* labeled *Seinfeld* "quintes-
sentially Jewish."[2] And within the Jewish community, as film and television critic Vincent Brook reports, there is an ongoing conversation
about the Jewishness of the series and its characters that has spanned
and outlived the series' original nine-year run in prime time.[3] Indeed,
Seinfeld's relentless exegesis of quotidian reality can itself be seen as a
humorous and self-deprecating indicator of Jewishness. As Jon Stratton, who devotes an entire chapter to *Seinfeld* in his recent book *Coming Out Jewish*, writes:

> The underlying narrative issue of *Seinfeld* is, I will argue, intrinsi-
> cally Yiddish, though ultimately a function of many other migrant
> groups and their descendants in the United States. This issue is
> usually addressed by describing *Seinfeld* as "a show about noth-
> ing."[4]

As Stratton implies, the description of *Seinfeld* as a show about nothing
is as provocative as it is misleading. It suggests that *Seinfeld* resists interpretation, that any meaning the audience ascribes to Jerry's Jewishness,
or any other element of the series, is purely unintentional. But, as the
title of Stratton's volume suggests, the nothing that *Seinfeld* is about is
really something: something ambiguous, closeted, hidden—something
Jewish.

This book analyzes the work of Jewish American writers, directors, and
actors in theater, film, and television in the United States from 1947 to
the present. Performances created by Jews for consumption by a mass
audience are prime sites for analyzing what I call *acting Jewish*, a critical
formulation of Jewish American identity in the latter half of the twentieth century. I use the term *acting Jewish* to indicate the liminal, fluid,
and multi-real nature of this formulation, as well as to emphasize the
importance of the performer-spectator interaction in generating it.

The provisional and contested quality of acting Jewish distinguishes it on the one hand from *performing Judaism*, a concept based on the assumption of an "authentic" Jewish culture, and on the other hand from *representations of the Jew*, a concept that locates the generation of meaning exclusively in the performance text. My argument is based on the concept of *double coding*, the specific means and mechanisms by which a performance can communicate one message to Jewish audiences while simultaneously communicating another, often contradictory message to gentile audiences.

As the late performance theorist Dwight Conquergood explained, "Subordinate people do not have the privilege of explicitness, the luxury of transparency, the presumptive norm of clear and direct communication, free and open debate on a level playing field that the privileged classes take for granted."[5] Jewish American artists in theater, film, and television, while certainly enjoying access to the "means of production" at a level far from subordinate, nonetheless have tended to approach their creative work from just such an outsider's point of view. Because of real or perceived anti-Semitism, Jewish characters and themes are frequently "reformed" for performance. David Zurawik, for example, writes in *The Jews of Prime Time*, "'Too Jewish' is an expression that echoes all too loudly across the history of Jewish characters on network television in its use—most often by Jewish programmers and network executives—as a tool to distort, disguise, or altogether eliminate depictions of Jewish identity from American prime-time television."[6] Yet this does not stop audiences from attempting to "decode hidden Jewish identity,"[7] a pastime that I will argue is itself a source of community formation for many American Jews.

Acting Jewish takes the form of a dialectic tension between the specific ("Jewish enough") and the universal (not "too Jewish"). Yet despite the connotations of the term *double coding*, the distinction between *Jewish* and *gentile* is neither essentially determined nor strictly binary; rather, I use these terms to indicate two "ideal" reading positions around which most interpretations of a performance coalesce. I will further suggest that over the course of the last half century the ability to decode Jewishness in performance, to *read Jewish*, has itself become an indicator of in-group status, a strategy for acting Jewish in the United States, offstage and offscreen.

Beginning with the film *Gentleman's Agreement* (1947), I will trace, chronologically, the shifting formulation of acting Jewish as a response to an ongoing crisis in the construction of Jewish American identity in the postwar era. By analyzing selected plays, films, and television programs, I will demonstrate how double coding functions to negotiate between the desire to assert the specificity of the Jewish experience and the apparently competing desire to speak to the universal human condition. While this basic dynamic remains the same throughout the period under consideration, the apparent thrust of double coding shifts significantly in response to the ever-changing relationship between Jews and mainstream American culture.

Program Notes

This first chapter sets out the boundaries and terms of our inquiry. The analysis of Jewish-created American popular culture in an academic context faces many disciplinary obstacles. Jewish studies as a discipline tends to dismiss popular and/or nonreligious performances; theater, ethnic, and cultural studies are often tied to theoretical and rhetorical structures inadequate to the situation of Jews in American entertainment. Using the tools of performance studies, an emerging "interdiscipline," I explain how and why acting Jewish can function as a more useful model for understanding Jewish American identity in the latter half of the twentieth century.

Chapter 2, "Acting Jewish, 1947–1955," focuses on three responses by the American entertainment industry to the crisis of Jewish identity in the immediate postwar era: *Gentleman's Agreement* (1947), the first major Hollywood film to seriously address the question of anti-Semitism; *The Goldbergs* (1949–55), the first television series built around the life of a Jewish family; and Arthur Miller's *Death of a Salesman* (1949), a Broadway hit regarded by many as the single best play in the history of American drama. The canonical status of *Death of a Salesman* in twentieth-century drama is unassailable, and the play's Jewishness, or lack thereof, has been hotly debated over the last half century. The universality to which *Gentleman's Agreement, The Goldbergs,* and *Death of a Salesman* all aspire demonstrates the initial emphasis in the double coding of Jewishness in American popular performance.

Chapter 3, "Fiddling on the Roof, 1964–1971," further develops the model of double coding and applies it to the Stein, Bock, and Harnick musical *Fiddler on the Roof* on stage (1964) and screen (1971). What gentile audiences liked about *Fiddler* and what Jewish audiences liked about *Fiddler* were significantly different. Further, the stage version of the musical—directed by the Jewish Jerome Robbins and starring Zero Mostel as Tevye—presents a very different model for acting Jewish than does the film version—directed by the non-Jewish Norman Jewison and starring Topol.

A more sophisticated example of double coding appears in chapter 4, "How Jews Became Sexy, 1968–1983." This chapter juxtaposes the stage and screen work of Barbra Streisand and Woody Allen, arguably the two most recognizably Jewish actors of the last half century. Their work both drove and benefited from a change in the way the sexual attractiveness of the Jewish body was perceived by both Jews and gentiles. During this period, the Jewish body not only came to be recognized as sexually appealing, it also helped redefine sexual attractiveness in American culture more generally.

Chapter 5, "The Desire to Remember, 1989–1997," addresses a different type of Jewish identity crisis. Where the Jewish artists of the 40s and 50s were most urgently concerned with universalism and defining acting Jewish for a non-Jewish audience, the period focused on the desire of a later generation to define acting Jewish as something particular and essential to Jews themselves. A look at three key works by the most critically acclaimed Jewish American playwrights of the 1980s and 1990s is instructive: *Angels in America* (Los Angeles 1992; Broadway 1993) by Tony Kushner, *The Sisters Rosensweig* (Lincoln Center 1992; Broadway 1993) by Wendy Wasserstein, and *The Old Neighborhood* (1997) by David Mamet. As Jewish artists born after the Holocaust, Kushner, Wasserstein, and Mamet self-consciously look to history as a guide to acting Jewish at the millennium. Even more importantly, these plays portray this desire to reconstruct a lost or forgotten Jewish culture, the *desire to remember*, as itself an essential element of acting Jewish.

Chapter 6, "You Know Who Else Is Jewish? Reading and Writing Jewish in the Twenty-first Century," examines the recent increase of scholarly attention paid to Jewish popular culture and explores the possibility of reading Jewish as a means of creating an "imagined community" that is defined in the interaction between the spectator and the performance.[8] It is in this possibility of imagining community via performance-reading strategies that the model of double coding has the most potential applicability to identity groups other than Jews.

The significance of this project is twofold. Its primary purpose is to demonstrate that "mainstream" American entertainment is a crucial site for understanding the relationship between Jews and American culture. As Jeffrey Shandler writes, "The search for Jews on TV is . . . a very important and legitimate part of an approach to Jewishness in the modern age as a question in constant need of investigation."[9] However, while this book focuses specifically on acting Jewish, it also offers a model for theorizing the representation of other minority groups in

American mass culture—a model based neither on questionable essentialisms nor on a politics of victimhood.

The "Jewish Problem" in Studying Mass Culture

In 1922, President A. Lawrence Lowell of Harvard University penned a now infamous memo on how the university should deal with the "Jewish Problem."[10] Lowell's remarks concerned the enforcement of admissions quotas intended to prevent Jews from being disproportionately overrepresented at America's oldest university. The Jewish reader might take some satisfaction in asking what President Lowell would think of today's Harvard, with a Jewish president, Lawrence Summers, who has made headlines by defending the university's investments in Israeli corporations. The Jewish reader who is also an academic might further wonder what Lowell would think of the rapid rise of ethnic studies programs on our nation's campuses.

Ethnic studies as it has developed in the United States owes its greatest debt to African American studies and Marxist epistemology. A by-product of this genealogy is that ethnic studies, or in some departments cultural studies, tends to assume that there is an adversarial relationship between the ethnicity under consideration and the so-called dominant culture. In other words, to be a minority, whether ethnic, racial, or religious, is to be by definition marginalized, oppressed, victimized. Ella Shoat writes:

> The marginalization of "ethnicity" reflects the imaginary of the dominant group which envisions itself as the "universal" or the "essential" American nation, and thus somehow "beyond" or "above" ethnicity. The very word *ethnic*, then, reflects a peripheralizing strategy premised on an implicit contrast of "norm" and "other," much as the term *minority* often carries with it the implication of minor, lesser, or subaltern.[11]

The politics inherent in this formulation are deeply emotional and have led to a significant backlash against "politically correct" multiculturalism in the academy. On one side, members of minority groups cry out against a theory that posits them as seemingly helpless victims. On the other, members of ethnic groups usually considered to be part of the "white majority," have begun to recognize the political and intellectual potential of interrogating their own ethnic subjectivity or (more cynically) of claiming a seat at the multicultural table. Hence, a literature of "whiteness" has been generated, one that strives to assess and celebrate the culture and heritage of white peoples.[12] Amid all this hue and cry there has emerged a new Jewish Problem: how does one analyze popular culture with regard to American Jews?

After all, Jews are anything but marginalized in American theater, film, and television. Indeed, the success of Jewish writers, actors, and directors (not to mention producers, agents, and network executives) is legion, to the point where "Jewish control" of America's entertainment media has achieved almost mythic status among both Jews and anti-Semites: a source of pride for the former, an instrument of demagoguery for the latter.[13] Numerous theories have been put forward to explain this preponderance of Jews in the performing arts. Those seeking an origin in religious practice point to the *Purimshpilim*, traditional plays put on by Jews in celebration of the Purim holiday. The chaotic, inverted, and therefore potentially subversive nature of Purim is thought to provide a foundation for theatrical innovation.[14] Historians of stand-up comedy have looked to the *badchen*, or wedding jester, a designated entertainer in Ashkenazic weddings. Still others have argued that Jews' success in the performing arts is a natural result of their distaste for representational arts such as sculpture and painting. As the argument goes, Jews interpreted the Second Commandment, "Thou shalt not make unto thee any graven image," as an injunction against representational art, so artistically inclined Jews were forced to channel their creativity into performance. It might even be argued that Judaism is a particularly *performative* religion; that is, unlike most forms of Christianity, Judaism is more concerned with process than product, more concerned with actions than interior reiterations of faith.[15]

Theater historian Brooks McNamara suggests, on the other hand, that Jewish dominance of Broadway is largely a historical accident. Popular entertainment, he argues, has always been looked down on by so-called respectable people. In the nineteenth century, the Irish, the largest working-class ethnic group, dominated theater and vaudeville. With the vast immigration of eastern European Jews to the United States around the turn of the century, the Jews became the new underclass and moved into the performing arts largely because no other group was willing to humiliate itself.[16] But, as one of the many Jewish stand-up comics of the 1950s might have put it, a funny thing happened on the way to the theater. As Jews experienced upward mobility throughout the twentieth century, they did not leave the performing arts behind; rather, theater and film also climbed the social ladder. This was partly due to the emergent technologies of radio, film, and television. Mass market entertainment turned the performing arts into a cash crop, and executives such as Louis B. Mayer found themselves playing in the same league as Knickerbocker bankers. Celebrity opened the door to so-called polite society for Jews such as Harpo Marx and Al Jolson.

There is also the issue of geography. While Jews account for less than 4 percent of the U.S. population, in the New York and Los Angeles metropolitan areas, the historical centers of theater, film, and television, Jews make up closer to 25 percent of the population. One might therefore suggest that the large number of Jews in the entertainment industry is analogous to, for example, the large number of Lutherans in the dairy-farming industry: an accidental confluence of immigration patterns and the economic topography of the nation. Still, even the percentage of the urban, coastal population that is Jewish is significantly lower than that reported for the representation of Jews in the ranks of the entertainment industry, suggesting that Los Angeles and New York became media centers, at least in part, because of their relatively high Jewish populations.

Whatever the cause of this "overrepresentation," the binary, dominant versus oppressed paradigm of ethnic and cultural studies lacks a vocabulary that can address the phenomenon of a dominant minority. As a result, Jews as an ethnic group are frequently left out of the ethnic/multicultural studies conversation. This is especially true in theater and performance studies. Contemporary performance theory holds that performance's political potential lies largely in its power to disrupt the existing social order.[17] Therefore, it is the responsibility of the minority performer (female, gay, ethnic, communist) to use performance to call attention to the inequities of late capitalism and/or present a rehearsal for social change. The former usually means a sort of Brechtian alienation or estrangement, which often finds its expression in performance art that explicitly critiques the so-called dominant or hegemonic culture.[18] The latter implies a grassroots empowerment project similar to that outlined by Brazilian director and politician Augusto Boal in *Theatre of the Oppressed.*[19]

But the Jewish minority, which we might call a dominant minority, is not looking to overturn the entire applecart. Its political activism as played out in theater is limited largely to addressing issues of racial or ethnic discrimination. The Jews are decidedly not planning the revolution. In fact, as Neal Gabler points out, Jewish artists are largely responsible for—some critics would say complicit in—the promotion of the myth that America is a meritocracy.[20] While there have been many self-identified leftists among Jewish theater, film, and television artists (e.g., Lillian Hellman, Zero Mostel, Tony Kushner), their political messages have always been wrapped in the audience-friendly trappings of well-constructed emotional drama. Is this protective coloration? Is this part of the secret plot to control America that is alleged by anti-Semitic hate groups? Or is it a genuine belief that the system works? After all, the so-called meritocracy in America has worked out better for Jews than for almost any other definable ethnic group over the last century.[21]

Yet any consideration of Jewishness in the academy necessarily involves coming to terms with the so-called dominant culture. Although we refer to it as a known, or a least a knowable, entity, the dominant culture has never been adequately and clearly defined. This is not an oversight but rather a recognition that the structures and forces that maintain the existing social order are to some degree indefinable. Indeed, as the French philosopher Michel Foucault has argued, it is power's resistance to definition that allows it to shift and evolve, to turn back any attempt to delegitimize it.[22] Despite this lack of a clear definition, it is commonplace for scholars to identify performers and performances as standing either inside or outside the mainstream. Often the distinction is made implicitly by negation. The dominant culture is not black, brown, or yellow, not gay, not female, not poor, not ethnic. However, the distinction between the "dominant" and the "oppressed" or "subversive" is not as simple as a single line dividing the ins from the outs. Television programming, for example, is nearly always assumed to originate from and serve as a tool of the dominant culture. So it is fitting to cite a television theorist, John Fiske, as representative of the prevailing paradigm.

> As those with social power are, amongst other things, white, male, middle-class, of conservative religion, middle-aged, and living in an economically and politically powerful region, we may expect the metadiscourse of television realism to originate from that social point where these discourses intersect, and therefore to naturalize that point of view and to work towards establishing it as the common-sense consensus of the nation.[23]

This approach to popular entertainment can be very useful, but it tends to break down when we try to address the work of Jewish artists. Where in the discourse, for example, can we locate *The Goldbergs*, a performance written by and featuring Gertrude Berg, a Jewish American woman? Gabler has gone so far as to suggest that the dominant culture of Hollywood is in fact a product of the Jewish imagination, suggesting of the Jewish movie studio founders that "They would fabricate their empire in the image of America as they would fabricate themselves in the image of prosperous Americans. They would create its values and myths, its traditions and archetypes."[24] The familiar Hollywood narratives of rags to riches, taming the frontier, and suburban domestic bliss, argues Gabler, reflect not a self-satisfied gentile culture but the fantasies of Jewish artists seeking an escape from the literal and metaphorical ghettoes of early-twentieth-century urban Jewish communities.]

If the idea of a dominant culture—or what the German Marxist critic Theodor Adorno called the "culture industry"—does not seem to apply to the "Jewish Problem," then neither does the idea that visibility in the popular media is a measure of cultural influence. Many feminist scholars have productively challenged this notion by pointing out that the preponderance of media depictions of women's bodies as spectacle has impeded rather than advanced the cause of women's rights.[25] Yet most scholars still suggest that the equation can work the other way, that access to the means of mass cultural production by members of minority groups leads to increased, and more positive, portrayals of those identities in popular entertainment. As Zurawik explains:

> In media studies, one hypothesis that has become conventional wisdom without the benefits of rigorous testing or historical examination is that as membership by a given minority group increases in a particular community of production, so will images of that minority group tend to become less stereotyped and more representative of social reality. . . . but that is not what happened with Jews and television.[26]

On the contrary, suggests Zurawik, the high concentration of Jews in the American television industry has led to Jews "policing each other's visibility and, in some cases, striving for invisibility."[27] Hence, we have seen the entrance into popular usage of the phrase "closet Jews," which stands as a more sympathetic and strategic reading of what others have called "self-hating Jews."[28] To put the matter in colloquial terms, it seems to be Jews, rather than an anti-Semitic culture industry, who are most concerned about performances that are "too Jewish."

If cultural studies does not know how to address this Jewish Problem, then Jewish studies has also balked at analyzing popular culture. Forays into "Jewish cultural studies" tend to focus on past history, for it is there that Jews clearly fit the role of the oppressed and victimized minority.[29] Holocaust studies is the most widespread example, legitimized within the Jewish community by the dual injunctions of "never forget" and "never again." But there are other histories of Jewish oppression: the pogroms of nineteenth-century Russia, the poverty of New York's Lower East Side, the development and execution of Zionism. Even studies of contemporary social phenomena tend to focus on the vestiges of European anti-Semitism that lurk in language, law, and mass culture.

It is not my intent to deny or devalue the systematic oppression Jews have endured throughout history, from the biblical enslavement in Egypt to the Roman occupation of Jerusalem, the Crusades, the Inquisition, and the Holocaust. Nor is it coincidental that resistance to oppression has become a leading trope in American entertainment. The importance not just of justice but of freedom to be oneself is a particularly American theme, one that many critics have cited as at least partially Jewish in origin. Andrea Most, for example, suggests that musicals written by Jews such as Rodgers and Hammerstein strategically championed civil liberties as an American value to counter both anti-Semitism and the suspicion that, as Jews and theater artists, the authors were communist sympathizers.[30] It is clear however that narratives that portray the Jews as outsiders and underdogs are more easily interjected into scholarly conversations about race, ethnicity, and performance in the United States.

Yet these narratives are not without perils of their own. In the early 1990s, the French writer Alain Finkielkraut proposed the term *imaginary Jews* to refer to those Jewish children of the post-Holocaust years who identify themselves as an oppressed people yet suffer no genuine oppression. He writes: "They are unwavering Jews, but armchair Jews, since, after the Catastrophe, Judaism cannot offer them any content but suffering, and they themselves do not suffer."[31] Finkielkraut does not condemn the imaginary Jews; indeed, he identifies himself as one and attempts to address the reasons for this. But in critiquing this phenomenon Finkielkraut calls attention to an inevitable problem with the dominant versus oppressed paradigm: a politics of identity grounded in oppression is unattractive to all but the most stalwart. Or, as Tevye says to God in *Fiddler on the Roof,* "It's true we are the Chosen People. But once in a while, can't you choose someone else?"[32]

Jonathan Boyarin in his book *Thinking in Jewish* seeks a new formulation of Jewish identity, one that is based neither on religion nor on a history of oppression: "I wish to avoid a likely first impression according to which the Jewishness of secular critics is merely a tag of identity, an inert or nostalgic name to which these 'imaginary' Jews are not really entitled."[33] This disclaimer can be understood as a response to both Finkielkraut's critique of the imaginary Jew and the Orthodox argument that debating Jewish identity is simply a way for secular Jews to rationalize their lack of faith. Boyarin then proposes the idea of a *critical post-Judaism.*

> I mean to name an already-existing but unidentified commonal-
> ity, a way of being Jewish "otherwise than Being.". . . This kind of
> identity formation is not enabled solely through its own intellec-
> tual passion and inventiveness, but on the contrary, only within or
> at the margins of academic institutions and academic culture (and
> even then generally outside the boundaries of "Jewish Studies"),
> and certainly at the margins of Jewish institutional life in the
> United States.[34]

Boyarin calls his formulation post-Judaism to signal that it is not meant to identify an ideal and monolithic Jewish community. The term *criti-cal*, he explains, signals an engagement with an existing academic dis-course as well as an opposition to the prevailing epistemology. Because of the historical link between "Jewish institutional life" and Jewish studies within the academy—specifically that those foundations, orga-nizations, and individuals that have been most financially and publicly supportive of Jewish studies have tended to be those with more rigid definitions of Jewish identity—Boyarin expresses little hope that a crit-ical post-Judaism can gain widespread acceptance.[35]

Hypothesis: Acting Jewish

It is not easy to speak of a "Jewish American identity" or even of "American Jews." As Arnold Eisen writes:

> The "American Jewish community"? We immediately see the
> problem: who precisely would those members be? There is no
> unanimity as to definition of group boundaries among Jews in the
> United States. . . . Still less is there unanimity among the various
> subgroups that constitute American Jewry concerning what one
> needs to know or believe or do, if anything, in order to belong to
> those groups or to the "American Jewish population" as a whole.[36]

Yet Jewish studies as a discipline often proceeds as if it were possible to define an "authentic" Jewish culture.[37] Expressions of Jewish identity can therefore be measured against a fixed standard. Alternatively, with the rise of postmodernism many scholars have adopted a pluralistic view of Jewish identity in which all formulations of Jewishness are equally authentic.[38] Both points of view are limited by a discipline that for historical reasons has a strong tradition of text-based inquiry.

We should remember however that, although Jews are often called the "people of the Book," Jewish identity is also closely linked to the concept of performance. While any child born of a Jewish mother is a Jew, the process of making oneself fully Jewish in a religious sense requires action: the performance of religious ritual and the performance of everyday life in accordance with *halacha* (Jewish law).[39] For Jews in the diaspora, however, especially in the postwar United States, where barriers to assimilation and intermarriage are lower than ever before, the traditional approach to performing Judaism has been destabilized. As Haym Soloveitchik notes:

> To the immigrants and to those raised in immigrant homes, identity was fixed. . . . The next generation, the first one to be raised in American homes, found identity to be anything but a given. . . . The mimetic religiosity came to an end soon after the twentieth century rounded the halfway mark.[40]

In communities with strong religious affiliations, writes Soloveitchik, the yeshiva (Jewish religious school) became the focal point for imparting Jewish religion and culture to new generations. In less affiliated homes, popular drama has become increasingly more important as a source of information on how to act Jewish. Stephen Whitfield, for example, in *In Search of American Jewish Culture*, writes, "No epicenter of American Jewish culture exists. . . . But if there were such a locale, it would be Broadway."[41] Egon Mayer, expressing optimism about the future of American Jewry writes, "We see this longing for Jewishness reflected time and again in Jews who flock to Woody Allen movies."[42] Literary critic Arnold Band perhaps sums up the proposition best:

> [O]nce we ask the basic question: What shapes the identity (in the sense of self-image) of a Jew in the post-Enlightenment period?, we are compelled to treat *Exodus, Marjorie Morningstar,* and *Fiddler on the Roof*—and dozens of other works of this genre—with the same scholarly respect as a truly epic work like Graetz's *History of the Jews*, which reached a select audience both in its German original and in its translations.[43]

Following Band, this book shows how a performance-based analysis of significant performances created by Jews in American theater, film, and television over the last half century is essential to understanding the shifting formulation of Jewish American identity over the same period. Furthermore, I suggest that the influence of mass culture is magnified by the fact that the power of parental and community influence on Jewish identity formation has diminished in the last half century.

While the transmission of cultural information through theatrical performance is, like ritual performance, mimetic and instructional, it lacks the authenticating power of traditional religious or academic structures. Perhaps this is why, to paraphrase Jonathan Boyarin, Jews are not marginal in either theater or the academy, yet Jewish performance criticism is at home in neither theater nor Jewish studies.44 Of the handful of book-length critical studies of Jewish American performance, most are the product of scholars working across traditional disciplinary boundaries. Michael Rogin, a professor of political science, authored *Blackface, White Noise*, which explores how Jewish performers used blackface minstrelsy to negotiate their own relationship with whiteness; Neal Gabler, author of *An Empire of Their Own: How the Jews Invented Hollywood*, began his career as a journalist; Norman Kleeblatt, the editor of *Too Jewish? Challenging Traditional Identities*, is a curator at the Jewish Museum in New York.45 More recent scholarship in conventional academic departments, much of it cited within these pages, has been influenced significantly by the boundary-crossing scope and rhetoric of queer theory. Significantly, most attempts to come to terms with the Jewish presence in American entertainment still focus primarily on the period prior to World War II.

This book takes as its starting point the conviction that if a critical formulation of contemporary Jewish identity is possible performance studies is where and how it must happen. Performance studies is itself a marginal, cross-disciplinary project. It exists, as Boyarin would have it, "within or at the margins of academic life."46 According to Conquergood, it is "a border discipline, an interdiscipline, that cultivates the capacity to move between structures, to forge connections, to see together, to speak with instead of simply speaking about or for others."47 In his view, the interdisciplinarity, marginal status, and mobility of the field reflect the qualities of performance itself.48 Couldn't we also apply these terms to Jewish Americans? Like the tortured spirit in S. Anksi's classic Yiddish drama *The Dybbuk* (1914), the modern American Jew is trapped between two worlds: the "Old World" of our ancestors and the "New World" of America. This is perhaps the most commonly cited metaphor in the field of Jewish sociology.49 But a deeper and more positive understanding of performance suggests that, rather than being *trapped* between these two worlds, Jewish American writers, directors, and performers have the potential to *move*, and even *circulate*, between the two environments. "Jewish" and "American" need not be mutually exclusive because they are not fixed, static identities.[50] The transformative potential of theatrical performance allows these concepts to evolve into something less than essentialisms and something more than flags of convenience.

The concept of performance also allows us to bring together two disparate discourses of Jewish difference: on the one hand, the Jewish body, a genealogical or descent-based understanding of Jewish identity; and, on the other hand, Jewish behavior (ritual or social), an elective or consent-based model.[51] Sander Gilman, perhaps the foremost historian of Jewish images (and self-images), writes:

> What I hope to demonstrate is how this "becoming-Jewish" is a less fixed locus of difference than Deleuze and Guattari ever imagined because the common wisdom after the Shoah about the power of assimilation to annihilate Jewish identity is not only false, but also a simplistic attempt to deal with the complexity of identity formation both in the Diaspora and in contemporary Israel—for Israeli identity is in part a reflex of Diaspora Jewish identity.[52]

Performance studies offers a mode of inquiry for understanding this process of *becoming Jewish* as something more than an internal, individualized desire for identity. Jewish and American are akin to what philosopher Judith Butler calls "a continual materializing of historical possibilities" that are performatively reinscribed through "a stylized repetition of acts played out on the body."[53] Following Butler, this book explores acting Jewish on the stage and screen with an eye toward how it affects questions of acting Jewish in everyday life.

The concept of acting Jewish is based on the idea of identity as performance. This does not, however, mean that Jewish identity is simply a matter of individual choice. The production of meaning in a performance is a matter of negotiation between the performer and the audience.[54] The audience can only interpret what the performer gives; the performer cannot completely control the terms of that interpretation. Yet, since both are required for the performance to exist, the needs and desires of each must be satisfied. Nor should the term *acting* suggest that this formulation of Jewish identity is somehow inauthentic. Rather, acting Jewish displaces the question of authenticity away from an appeal to a fixed textual authority (whether the Torah or some other formulation). Instead, the authentic is constantly in motion, circulating in an ongoing conversation between performance and audience. Acting

Jewish as a formulation of identity should thus be understood as a processual, provisional, and always already contested performance that circulates between the two worlds of essentialism (insistence on the authentic) and postmodernism (all authenticities are equal, which is to say that nothing is authentic).

A Mechanism: Double Coding

Throughout the history of anti-Semitism, Jews have been accused of two contradictory offenses against gentile sensibilities. On the one hand, Jews are considered so vulgar, deformed, and unpleasant to look at that they must be other than human. On the other, Jews are considered so crafty, cunning, and imbued with devilish power that they can appear to look just like everyone else. How does a group, or an individual, respond to such a dual accusation? Gilman writes: "It may be internalizing and self-destructive (self-hating) or it may be projective and stereotyping; it [may] take the form of capitulation to the power of the image or the form of resistance to the very stereotype of the Jew. But there is the need to respond, either directly or subliminally."[55]

When considering the performance of Jewishness in mass culture, then, it is necessary to address the way the work speaks to at least two audiences: a Jewish audience and a general or gentile audience. This is what I mean by the term *double coding*. Many elements of a performance, from simple aural and visual signs to complex affective impressions, are open to multiple readings. While theoretically there are as many variant readings of the performance as there are spectators, in practice readings tend to coalesce around certain culturally informed subject positions: a "Jewish" reading and a non-Jewish or "gentile" reading. Selective attention to these two admittedly idealized and imaginary reading positions is itself a strategic choice.

The concept of double coding is similar to but nonetheless different from the phenomenon of *double-consciousness*, first articulated by W. E. B. Du Bois in 1903 as an explanation of the betwixt and between status of the "American Negro."[56] Du Bois's "sense of always looking at oneself through the eyes of others, of measuring one's soul by the tape of a world that looks on in amused contempt and pity"came, as theater historian David Krasner writes, "to dominate analytical conditions of identity."[57] Double consciousness meant that African American performers were caught between loyalty to the black community and the compromises necessary to succeed in a white-dominated society. To speak simultaneously to white and black audiences, African American minstrels in the late nineteenth and early twentieth century often used parody and "signifying" as encoded forms of resistance, frequently co-opting racist terms and stereotypes in the service of a race-conscious agenda. The white audience laughed at the Negro's antics without realizing that whites were the butt of the joke.[58] Thus, in this form of performance the in-group and out-group codes are directly opposed.

While Jewish American theater, film, and broadcast artists may have felt a similar double pull between the Jewish and the American parts of their identity, the performance strategies engendered by this doubling have taken significantly different forms. While some Jewish performers (most notably Mel Brooks) have parodied anti-Semitic stereotypes of Jews in their work, most have chosen to deemphasize their "difference" from the non-Jewish population. This is due, in large part, to the ability of Jews to blend in with and succeed in the so-called dominant culture, a possibility not available to most artists of color.[59] Yet when such "passing" is successful, as when a Jewish actor becomes famous playing non-Jewish roles, it brings increased scrutiny regarding the authenticity of one's Jewish identity. As the playwright Tony Kushner has noted, being Jewish "offered, at various points, a sort of false possibility of a kind of an assimilation that demanded as one of its prerequisites that you abandon your identity as a Jew. The possibility of passing which is not, let's say, available to people whose oppression stems from racial difference or gender difference."[60]

For Kushner, the "possibility of passing" is "false" and abandoning one's identity is clearly too high a price to pay for acceptance. Yet assimilation and identity (or American and Jewish) are not binary opposites in the way that white and black seem to be. The double-coded performance of Jewishness, then, does not typically carry meanings that are opposed to one another, nor does it usually imply hostility of the performer toward the audience or (vice versa). Rather, in my formulation of double coding, the Jewish reading of a performance is most commonly *supplemental* to the dominant or gentile reading. It offers an alternative story line but one that does not contradict the primary narrative. Andrea Most's reading of *Oklahoma!* for example, suggests that this 1943 Rodgers and Hammerstein musical expresses the "Jewish desire to assimilate and escape discrimination," a reading not inconsistent with the "celebration of American statehood and American democratic values" that Most identifies as the primary appeal of the play for a general audience.[61]

Such supplemental readings arise from a shared awareness between the writer/performer and the audience, a mutual act of memory that is intrinsic to performance itself.[62] Analyzing how certain performances evoke such a selective application of memory is often a slippery task, akin to that of performance itself. As Richard Schechner tells us in his definition of *performance* as "restoration of behavior":

> The field is precarious because it is subjunctive, liminal, transitional: it rests not on how things are but on how things are not; its existence depends on agreements kept among all participants, *including the audience*. The field is the embodiment of potential, of the virtual, the imaginative, the fictive, the negative, the not not. The larger it gets, the more it thrills, but the more doubt and anxiety it evokes, too.[63]

It is this "subjunctive" space in which the "Jewish reading" of popular culture is played out. Quite frequently, what a spectator identifies as Jewishness is equivocal, affective, and not exclusively Jewish. It is Jewishness by proxy: an absence, but a palpable one. To paraphrase Schechner, a character or situation may be "not Jewish" but it is also frequently "not not-Jewish."

In analyzing the double-coded performance of Jewishness, certain questions come to the fore. How do the artists' assumptions about the two audiences differ? Is the performance interpreted differently by a Jewish audience than by a general audience? And, perhaps most importantly, how does the mimetic nature of performance transmit information about acting Jewish even when the performance does not deal explicitly with Jewish characters or themes?

This last question is especially fascinating. In *Staging the Jew*, Harley Erdman identifies a shift toward less visible ethnic representation in the early years of the twentieth century. Among the specific performance practices he highlights is the fact that the beard, a sine qua non of Jewish characters in the English and American popular theater of the nineteenth century, began to be used less frequently. For Erdman:

> Performing oneself as a Jew-without-a-beard is, after all, the first requisite step towards performing oneself as no-Jew-at-all. Indeed, this new type of Jewish body signaled the beginning of an era where ethnic visibility in general and Jewish visibility in particular were no longer desirable. In its place came invisibility, as Jewish characters became less frequently seen on major American stages.[64]

In Erdman's formulation, "invisibility" is equivalent to erasure; it is an act of violence, a forced conformity to the melting pot ideal. The Jew who is not visually recognizable is "no-Jew-at-all." But while there is no doubt that in many cases the decision to "reform" one's Jewishness for the stage (or, for that matter, for the street) is an action taken "under duress," that does not necessarily mean that its end is the complete erasure of Jewish difference. A Jew without a beard is still a Jew.[65] His parents or grandparents or neighbors might consider him a *bad* Jew, and strangers might assume that he is a Christian, but he is still a Jew. Moreover, he may still be visually identifiable as a Jew, depending on who's looking at him.

How can we tell that Jerry Seinfeld is Jewish? His beard is missing.

Knowing the Codes

In the early 1960s, Jewish American comedian Lenny Bruce performed a routine in which he divided the world into Jewish and goyish (Yiddish for "not Jewish"):

> Dig: I'm Jewish. Count Basie's Jewish. Ray Charles is Jewish. Eddie Cantor's goyish. B'nai B'rith is goyish; Hadassah, Jewish.
>
> If you live in New York or any other big city, you are Jewish. It doesn't matter even if you're Catholic; if you live in New York, you're Jewish. If you live in Butte, Montana, you're going to be goyish even if you're Jewish.
>
> Kool-Aid is goyish. Evaporated milk is goyish even if Jews invented it. Chocolate is Jewish and fudge is goyish. Fruit salad is Jewish. Lime jello is goyish. Lime soda is *very* goyish.[66]

Though performed with tongue firmly planted in cheek, Bruce's routine represents a playful attempt to isolate some of the many signs that can be decoded as Jewish. That is, Bruce is giving a mock lesson in how to be a Jewish reader of American culture. His itemized list, when analyzed, reveals at least some general characteristics of Jewishness: difference from the norm, urbanity, and a raw, flavorful, or unrefined quality (extrapolating from his choice of foodstuffs). Yet attempting to lay out Bruce's rationale in words sounds faintly ridiculous because all of these characteristics are affective, more suited to communication through performance than through text.

Equally important, Bruce's routine reinforces the idea that the true key to acting Jewish is whether one possesses—or, more appropriately, demonstrates—these qualities. Religion and ethnicity are irrelevant to his distinction between Jewish and goyish: Count Basie, Ray Charles,

Catholics living in New York, chocolate, and fruit salad are Jewish, while even people who identify themselves as Jewish, who in fact are Jewish in religious or ethnic terms, may be goyish: Eddie Cantor, B'nai B'rith (a Jewish fraternal organization), Jews living in rural areas. In other words, Bruce's definition of *Jewish* is not about *being* as much as it is about *performing*. And this performance of Jewishness is not linked directly or necessarily to religious observance but is instead associated with what we might call the aesthetics of everyday life.[67]

Furthermore, as Bruce's routine makes clear, one does not have to identify as Jewish to recognize Jewishness in performance. One simply needs to be literate in the requisite cultural codes. But these codes, while not exclusively or essentially Jewish, are nonetheless connected to an ideal of Jewishness that is neither wholly individual nor wholly arbitrary. Therefore, if a reader *is* Jewish by descent or consent, or if he or she has had extensive exposure to Jewish culture (for example, having grown up in a Jewish neighborhood), then they will be much more likely to have the requisite cultural literacy to recognize what is Jewish and what is goyish.

In this sense, Bruce's routine itself provides the real litmus test for his standard of Jewishness: if you get it, if you nod, if you understand without being told why Count Basie is Jewish and Eddie Cantor is goyish, then you are Jewish. Double coding is not simply a means of communicating Jewish continuity through performance. Double coding is itself a means of acting Jewish. Knowing the codes, reading Jewish, can be a way to affirm one's membership in an imagined community of American Jews.

While Bruce's performance plays with the idea of Jewish decoding, the analytical use of double coding as a model for understanding acting Jewish requires an awareness that the Jewish-goyish, or Jewish-gentile, binary is both constructed and unstable. It is constructed because *goyish* and *gentile* are terms that are meaningful only as they represent the Other of Jewish. Except under extraordinary circumstances, non-Jewish audiences do not perceive themselves or their reading strategies in these terms. Therefore, this construction is significant primarily because it offers those who employ it a means of recentering the conversation, of eliding the double bind, in which the Jew is always already Other. The danger is that in so doing we may forget that the goyish or gentile audience is no more homogeneous (and probably a good deal less so) than the Jewish audience.

Because this book is primarily concerned with the ways that Jews decode performances that they experience as multiply encoded, and because part of reading Jewish is imagining Jewishness as opposed to an equally imaginary and undifferentiated gentile culture, I have chosen to treat many of the performances discussed herein as if there are only two sets of codes in operation. That the particular spectrum of encodings and decodings at work in any given performance does not conflict with the strategic and provisional adoption of such a binary model is a point which I have tried, throughout, not to take for granted. *a problem*

Terms: Judaism *and* Jewishness

Soloveitchik argues that through the first half of the twentieth century Judaism was essentially a mimetic tradition. Jews learned how to act Jewish by following the examples set by their parents and their local communities. Such a mimetic tradition, argues Soloveitchik, "mirrors rather than discriminates;"[68] it makes little or no distinction between religion and culture. But as barriers to interethnic and interreligious interaction have broken down much of everyday life has been "emptied of religious meaning."[69] It is now possible, as the sociologist Stephen M. Cohen has proposed, to speak of a distinction between "Judaic content" and "Jewish continuity."[70] Judaic content may be defined as situations or references directly involving Jewish ritual practice or religious observance. Jewish continuity, on the other hand, is defined as any instance by which Jews identify as Jewish—and therefore different from the culture at large.

Extending this idea to the realm of entertainment, Felicia Herman draws a similar distinction in her essay "The Way She *Really* Is: Images of Women and Jews in the Films of Barbra Streisand":

> Because her films are so nearly devoid of Jewish religious content, it is more appropriate to speak about their images of Jewish*ness* than of Juda*ism*. This Jewishness arises out of an idea, popularized in the interwar period in America, that Jewish identity encompassed more than religious observance and could, in fact, exist in the absence of religion.[71]

This book mirrors Herman's use of the term *Jewishness* to refer to the instances of Jewish continuity in performance, while resisting her implied scorn for Jewishness as somehow a lesser (or less authentic) mode of acting Jewish than is performing Judaism.

Jewishness, in this usage, is similar to the early-twentieth-century concept of *Yiddishkeit* (literally, "Jewishness"), which, as Samuel Freedman writes, was less an organized movement than a sensibility. And that sensibility, as the historian Gerald Sorin put it, "had to do with language, style, values, and behavior much more than belief." *Yiddishkeit* did not reject Judaism as much as appropriate it, treating religious tradition not as the ultimate expression of Jewish identity but as part of the raw material for it.[72]

But whereas *Yiddishkeit*, which was decidedly European in origin, looked backward to an idealized and authentic Jewish past, the postwar American idea of Jewishness explored in the performances discussed here is both more forward looking and more malleable.

Beyond Yiddishkeit: *A New Tradition of Performance*

Between 1880 and 1930, more than twenty-three million immigrants arrived in the United States, the largest population movement in recorded history; roughly 10 percent (well over two million) of these newcomers were Jews.[73] By 1920, New York had a larger Jewish population than any other city in the world.[74] This mass immigration was driven primarily by an equally unprecedented economic expansion caused by the growth of industrialism. America's new factories needed laborers, and the depressed agrarian nations of Europe (primarily Italy, Ireland, and Russia) provided the source.

Not coincidentally, this same period witnessed the growth of professional entertainment from a leisure activity reserved for a wealthy few to a thriving nationwide industry offering live entertainment (and later films) to middle- and working-class audiences at a reasonable price. Both economics and immigration were responsible for the expansion in dramatic entertainment. An increasingly urbanized populace, gainfully employed in a time-clock-driven industry, provided a rich new market for theater. More importantly, the high percentage of Jews and Catholics among the new immigrants also contributed to the growth of the theater because they did not share the antitheatrical prejudices of America's Protestant majority.

In the nineteenth century, theater was considered immoral by many Protestants and was often prohibited by local ordinances.[75] In 1835, the French commentator Alexis De Tocqueville wrote that

as yet a very small number of them [Americans] go to the theatre at all. Although playgoers and plays have prodigiously increased in the last forty years, the population indulge in this kind of amusement only with the greatest reserve. This is attributable to peculiar causes, which the reader is already acquainted with, and of which a few words will suffice to remind him.

The Puritans who founded the American republics not only were enemies to amusements, but they professed an especial abhorrence for the stage. They considered it as an abominable pastime; and as long as their principles held sway, scenic performances were wholly unknown amongst them.[76]

When Americans did go to theater in the first half of the nineteenth century, it was most frequently to enjoy classical works, which might be rationalized as "educational," or patriotic historical dramas, which promoted national pride. The first widely produced Jewish American playwright, Mordecai Manuel ("M. M.") Noah (1785–1851), specialized in the latter. A politician, journalist, and early Zionist, Noah penned several pageant-style works based on American military engagements, including *The Siege of Tripoli* (1820) and *The Siege of Yorktown* (1824). His *She Would Be a Soldier* (1819), based on the Battle of Chippewa, was a popular choice on national holidays for several decades.[77]

By the end of the nineteenth century, however, the religious balance of the nation had begun to swing away from the Puritans; moreover, the Protestant establishment itself, under the influence of economic changes that allowed more leisure activity, began to relax its antitheatrical stance. It was no longer necessary for theater to wrap itself in the flag or assume the guise of education to meet the approval of a conservative establishment.

As the American theater began to grow, it moved beyond the revivals or adaptations of European plays and the patriotic pageantry that had characterized its infancy. While Shakespeare, Sophocles, and Racine remained frequent choices, audiences began to demand entertainment that spoke more directly to their own situation. As a significant portion of these audiences was of immigrant origin, a number of late-nineteenth- and early-twentieth-century American dramas dealt with the struggle to adapt to the New World. David Belasco's *The Music Master* (1904) told the story of a Viennese musician who gives music lessons in America while trying to find his long-lost daughter. *The Melting Pot* (1905) by English-born Jewish playwright Israel Zangwill won modest success with a plot about Jewish-Catholic intermarriage, a precursor to the runaway hit of the 1920s, Anne Nichols's *Abie's Irish Rose* (1922). J. Hartley Manners's *Peg o' My Heart* (1912), the rags to riches success story of a good-hearted Irish girl, played for over a year to packed houses in New York's Cort Theatre.[78]

During these early years, the focus of plays (and eventually films) dealing with immigrants was almost invariably on the ways in which newcomers to America could achieve success by giving their allegiance to their new home. The 1926 film *Private Izzy Murphy*, for example, featured George Jessel as a Jewish delicatessen worker, Izzy Goldberg, who changes his name to Murphy when he enlists in the army to fight in World War I. While overseas, he meets a gentile girl, falls in love, and brings her home to New York to marry her and live happily ever after.

Perhaps the most representative performance of this era, and certainly the most influential, was Samson Raphaelson's 1925 play *The Jazz Singer*, which in 1927 became the basis for the first feature-length motion picture to include synchronized sound, the first "talkie." Inspired by the life of Al Jolson (born Ayesha Joelson to Orthodox Jewish parents), *The Jazz Singer* tells the story of a cantor's son, Jakie Rabinowitz, who runs away from his Lower East Side home and becomes a professional singer, changing his name to Jack Robin. When Jack returns to New York for his Broadway debut, his father refuses to acknowledge the validity of his career choice. The climax of the play comes when Jack, who is scheduled to open on Broadway on the eve of Yom Kippur, must choose between "going on with the show" or singing *Kol Nidre* in the Orchard Street Synagogue as a replacement for his father, who lies near death. Despite his overwhelming desire to be a singing star, Jack succumbs to his father's dying wish and forsakes his opening so that he can attend the service. The play ends with the sound of Jack, offstage, leading the Orchard Street congregation in the traditional prayer that begins the Yom Kippur observance.

Raphaelson's preface to the 1925 Brentano's edition of *The Jazz Singer* suggests that he sees Jack's forfeiture of a show business career as a tragedy.

> I have used a Jewish youth as my protagonist because the Jews are determining the nature and scope of jazz more than any other race—more than the negroes, from whom they have stolen jazz and given it new meaning. Jazz is Irving Berlin, Al Jolson, George Gershwin, Sophie Tucker. These are Jews with their roots in the synagogue. And these are expressing in evangelical terms the nature of our chaos today.[79]

For Raphaelson, it seems, jazz is morally equivalent to prayer, and perhaps more relevant to modern society. This is the view expressed by Jack, who is unequivocally the hero of the play. In contrast, Jack's father, Cantor Rabinowitz, is portrayed as a stern and outdated patriarch; as the film version tells us, he has "his face turned toward the past" and he has "stubbornly held to the ancient traditions of his race."[80]

Raphaelson's preface is also of interest because he not only acknowledges the predominance of Jews in jazz, the quintessential "American" musical form, but he even goes so far as to suggest that there is something about being Jewish that causes the success of Berlin, Jolson, et al. This sentiment is reflected in the play (and subsequent film); Jack Robin, a.k.a. Jakie Rabinowitz, is a superior entertainer, the play suggests, precisely because he is a Jew, imbuing songs such as "Mammy" with the intensity his father the cantor brings to "Kol Nidre." Viewed in this light, we might see Jack (and *The Jazz Singer*) as promoting a kind of Jewish cultural continuity, even while rejecting Judaic religious observance.

The Jazz Singer ends with Kol Nidre, a prayer in which Jews ask God to be released from all vows they made under duress during the past year. This is a holdover from the days of forced conversion to Christianity in Europe. In "Kol Nidre," Jews express their desire to be released from promises they have made that go against Jewish law. For Jack, his singing of "Kol Nidre" is apparently his repentance, his plea to be released from his "conversion" to the secular world of Broadway. Yet even as he sings it his gentile girlfriend Mary remarks on how performing is clearly "in his blood . . . he'll have to come back [to theater]."[81] The lingering message, then, is that it is Jack's return to the synagogue that is a false conversion; show business is his true faith. This is underscored by the additional scene that Warner Brothers added to the film version of *The Jazz Singer*. In the film's finale, we see Jack back in the theater, singing "Mammy" in blackface before a sold-out house.[82] With his father now dead, he has his mother's blessing; she is sitting proudly in the front row, granting Jack's choice to become a showman a legitimate connection to his Jewish heritage.

By the time *The Jazz Singer* revolutionized the film industry in 1927, Jewish American writers, directors, actors, and producers had already achieved a predominant position within the entertainment industry. In musical theater, for example, Kathryn Bernheimer notes that "In the first half of the twentieth-century, the only major gentile composer was Cole Porter."[83] In film, Jews headed most of the major Hollywood studios, and their dominance of the industry had begun to attract the attention of anti-Jewish figures. The *Dearborn Independent*, owned by Henry Ford, reported in 1921 that the film industry was "Jew-controlled, not in spots only, not 50 per cent merely, but entirely; with the

natural consequence that now the world is in arms against the trivializ-
ing and demoralizing influences of that form of entertainment as
presently managed."[84]

Yet, despite this type of dire warning, Hollywood was hardly turning
out pro-Jewish propaganda. In fact, between *The Jazz Singer* and
World War II, there were few, if any, Hollywood films that dealt with
explicitly Jewish characters or themes. The Jews who ran the studios
(Mayer, Fox, Zukor, et al.) chose to devote their attention to more
generic characters and stories. Because of the Depression, studios could
only afford to make films with broad-spectrum appeal, and the prevailing wisdom was that audiences would have a hard time accepting
and/or identifying with Jewish protagonists.[85] Moreover, many Hollywood Jews had chosen to follow the lead of Jack Robin, pursuing entertainment first and keeping religion and ethnicity in the background.[86]
On the stage, the same phenomenon held true, with a few notable
exceptions produced in little theater, such as Clifford Odets's *Awake
and Sing!* (1935) and Elmer Rice's *Street Scene* (1929) and *Counsellor-at-
Law* (1931), and a few less notable plays targeted at New York's large
Jewish audience, such as Silvia Regan's *Morning Star* (1941).

In the aftermath of World War II, the importance of cultural difference began to reassert itself. For American Jews, this movement was
given added impetus by the Holocaust, which annihilated most of
European Jewry, and rising intermarriage rates, which threatened to
dilute the American Jewish community beyond recognition. These two
assaults on Jewish cultural continuity raised new fears about "assimilation" and the future of American Jewry. From the 1940s through the
1960s, Jews began to move in large numbers out of predominantly Jewish neighborhoods and into suburban areas. "In this situation," wrote
Nathan Glazer, "the religious behavior of the Christian neighbor
began to impinge on the consciousness and conduct of the Jewish sub-
urbanite," and "the second generation had to become self-conscious
about religion."[87] The self-conscious "repackaging" of Jewishness for
consumption by non-Jewish audiences was central to films such as *Gentleman's Agreement* (1947) and television series such as *The Goldbergs*
(1949–55). The emphasis was on creating performances that were not
"too Jewish"—that is, they would not alienate non-Jewish audiences.
These performances depended on the ability of Jewish audiences to
recognize culturally specific aural and visual performance codes as indicators of Jewishness and then "fill in the blanks" with their own experience of the Jewish-specific cultural and religious practices that are not
depicted in the performance. This predominantly universalist mode of
acting Jewish reached its apotheosis in the 1971 film version of *Fiddler*

on the Roof, directed by the non-Jewish Canadian director Norman Jewison.

Beginning in the late 1960s, the melting pot ideal of American culture began to lose influence in the face of the civil rights and ethnic pride movements. Jewish fears of anti-Semitism, both real and imagined, began to ease slightly.[88] As Barry Gross wrote, "Most American Jews admit to no real conflict in their hyphenated identity; it is possible to be American *and* Jewish, the terms are not mutually exclusive, not even contradictory."[89] Perhaps because it was now more acceptable to act Jewish in mainstream American entertainment, performances created by Jewish American artists in this period show a shift toward the Jewish-specific end of the spectrum. While still seeking to appeal to a general audience, performances such as *Play It Again, Sam* (1969), *The Way We Were* (1973), *Manhattan* (1979), and *Yentl* (1983) seem more concerned with communicating a specific message of Jewish continuity to a Jewish audience. However, the Jewishness that is communicated in these performances is still encoded in subtle and affective ways, allowing these performances to embrace Jewishness while simultaneously questioning whether Jewish is still a meaningful designation.

By the late 1980s and 1990s, Jewish acceptance in American society had reached unprecedented levels, and the question of whether a mainstream audience would accept explicitly Jewish characters and themes was largely settled in the affirmative.[90] This period, however, saw increasing concern within the Jewish community about the future of Jewish identity. Glazer formulates the problem thus: "What is the nature of Jewish life in the United States; and how, and in what form, will it continue?"[91] This was no doubt driven in part by a renewed emphasis on ethnic identity in American culture as a whole. Hence, while the explicit depiction of Jewishness in popular performance had become commonplace by this time, the 1990s for the first time saw a greater assertion of Jewish particularism. If the 1970s and 1980s were characterized by the growing acceptance of acting Jewish, the 1990s were distinguished by works such as *The Sisters Rosensweig* (1992), *Angels in America* (1993), and *The Old Neighborhood* (1997), which interrogated more explicitly than ever before the moral, ethical, and historical responsibilities incumbent on those who would so act. Even *Seinfeld,* as Stratton, Brook, and others have suggested, can be understood as a parodic exegesis of Jewish ethical and social imperatives.[92] Yet even within these explicitly Jewish performances, elements of acting Jewish are still couched within a double-coded framework. Audiences still respond differently depending on whether they apply Jewish-specific expectations, assumptions, and reading strategies to the performance.

Overall then, the change in acting Jewish in American entertainment from *Gentleman's Agreement* to *Seinfeld* and beyond should be seen as a shift in emphasis rather than a complete reformulation.

This book is structured to trace the history of the various codes and concepts employed in acting Jewish on the American stage and screen in the period from 1947 to the present. In selecting performances for analysis from the vast range of work created by Jewish American artists, I have been guided by Band's criteria for similar analyses in literature: "Did the work become a cultural event that elicited discussion and perhaps action? Did it modify the reader's notions about a certain aspect of contemporary Jewish life? Did it seek to confirm or subvert certain 'Jewish values' held by the audience?"[93] Additionally, all the performances discussed in this book have two characteristics in common: (1) the performance generated, immediately or eventually, a critical discourse among writers and critics for whom Jewishness is a major concern; and (2) the performance achieved significant commercial and critical success.

The former criterion is important because it demonstrates that interpretation of the performance according to a Jewish reading strategy is warranted by more than my own desire to "read Jewish." I am not the first critic to recognize, rightly or wrongly, double-coded indicators of Jewishness in *Death of a Salesman* or *Zelig*. Nor is this book an exercise in the "recovery" of a lost or hidden Jewishness that lies undiscovered in the source material. While readers may make some discoveries of their own in the pages that follow, my intention is not to "out" Jewish artists, characters, or themes. Rather, this book aims to theorize and interrogate such strategies of outing or recovery as a means of constructing an "imaginary community" of American Jews.

The second criterion is equally important. Since Jews, by any definition, constituted no more than 3.5 percent of the U. S. population throughout the period under consideration,[94] this book considers as axiomatic the proposition that a performance that attains unusual commercial success must appeal to a significant portion of the non-Jewish audience. This proposition is not without caveats: *Seinfeld*, for example, consistently earned higher ratings in coastal urban centers than in rural or middle-American media markets.[95] The Jewish audience for Broadway theater, by accounts both statistical and anecdotal, is disproportionate even to the Jewish numerical representation in the population of the New York metropolitan area.[96] But if *Seinfeld* was not the top-rated show in, say, Butte, Montana, it was certainly in the top 10, and if the audience at a given performance of *Fiddler on the Roof* or

The Old Neighborhood was largely Jewish, it was not exclusively so. Nor could an exclusively Jewish audience sustain such a show over an extended Broadway run, let alone in subsequent regional and international productions. This is important because it is the interaction with a non-Jewish audience that creates the particular context in which double coding operates.

The resulting bricolage of case studies makes no claim to encyclopedic thoroughness. Rather, it attempts to isolate the brightest stars in a constellation that stretches over literally hundreds, if not thousands, of performances that have wrestled, one way or another, with the question of acting Jewish. Werner Sollors, in the introduction to his epic study *Beyond Ethnicity: Consent and Descent in American Culture*, reasons:

> If I tried to discuss my subject by narrowing it down, for example, to "Consent and Descent in American Culture: The Case of the Chicago South Side Writers Workshop from 1925 to 1934," I might be in better company with currently practicing ethnic historians. However, with such a procedure I would have lost the wider view, and I might have felt tempted to structure such a study along melodramatic lines.[97]

Like Sollors, I am convinced that the phenomena examined here are significant precisely because they are so commonplace as to be nearly invisible. While the details of each case study are certainly important, the "wider view" is necessary as well, both to understand the larger significance of the project and to avoid the impression that these performances were produced independent of the larger conversation. To paraphrase Sollors, to prevent the elusive creature that is the postwar Jewish American identity from escaping our grasp, we must cast a broad net.[98] Toward this end, the performance examples are presented chronologically, with particular emphasis on the ways in which each subsequent portrayal of acting Jewish responds to and refines the mechanisms of double coding employed by performances that came earlier. The history of acting Jewish can thus be seen as an ongoing conversation between Jewish artists, Jewish audiences, and American culture.

CHAPTER 2

Acting Jewish, 1947–1955

*I*N THE IMMEDIATE aftermath of World War II, Jews in the American entertainment industry were faced with an identity crisis. It was no longer possible to ignore one's Jewishness in the face of the annihilation of European Jewry; nor was it possible to take comfort in the apparently secure position that Jews had established in the United States. At the same time, "assimilation" had been very good to the Jews in terms of social mobility, especially in the realm of theater and film.[1] In fact, the widespread perception among anti-Semites that Jews controlled the American entertainment industry caused many Jewish actors, directors, and playwrights to feel deeply ambivalent about publicly acknowledging their Jewishness.[2] The "Jewish double bind" had resurfaced with a vengeance. In the face of persistent anti-Semitism—both real and imagined—there was, as Sander Gilman writes, "the need to respond, either directly or subliminally."[3]

This chapter addresses three responses by the American entertainment industry to the postwar crisis of Jewish identity: *Gentleman's Agreement* (1947), *The Goldbergs* (1948–55), and *Death of a Salesman* (1949). Although each performance employs different representational strategies, all three seek to negotiate the double bind, acknowledging the value of Jewish difference while simultaneously stressing the universal brotherhood of all peoples. This is accomplished by reformulating Jewishness as a mode of *acting* rather than a mode of *being*.

Gentleman's Agreement, written by a Jew but produced and directed by gentiles, presents Jewishness as a matter of religious choice and that choice as a matter of self-labeling; some people call themselves Jews and others call themselves Christian, but all share a fundamental humanity. Acting Jewish is distinguished from acting Christian only by the Jew's experience of anti-Semitic persecution.

In *The Goldbergs*, by contrast, Jewishness is much more than a label; it is a way of life, a source of both humor and warmth. Yet over the life of the series the religious specificity of the Goldberg family was significantly minimized, self-consciously positioning the show as representative of an immigrant experience that is universal and generic. In fact, most of what is specifically Jewish about *The Goldbergs* is encoded in performance practice: accents, rhythms of speech, and emotional affect. Yet the presence of these cultural codes allows a Jewish audience to infer the religious and cultural practices that the program itself rarely depicts.

In *Death of a Salesman*, virtually everything that an audience might recognize as Jewish is implicit. Miller's protagonist, Willy Loman, is in fact distinguished by his lack of a clearly defined identity, exacerbated by his desire to fit into modern American culture. Yet almost from its premier, the Loman family's Jewishness (or lack thereof) has been a source of conversation and contention within and without the Jewish community.[4] Although the written text of the play reveals few clues to the characters' religion or ethnicity, its performance history strongly suggests that the identity Willy lacks is Jewishness. *Death of a Salesman* thus demonstrates the importance of acting Jewish through its palpable absence.

Gentleman's Agreement

In 1947, Hollywood addressed anti-Semitism in America in two feature films: *Crossfire*, a low-budget crime drama directed by Edward Dmytryk; and *Gentleman's Agreement*, a high-profile drama featuring several major stars and directed by Elia Kazan. While both films were clearly made in response to the Holocaust, neither was directed or produced by Jews (though Jewish playwright Moss Hart wrote the screenplay for *Gentleman's Agreement*). Dmytryk said that because both he and producer Adrian Scott were gentiles they could make their controversial film without being accused of self-interest.[5] Similarly, the Jewish-run studio Twentieth Century-Fox employed the Greek American Kazan to direct and the Methodist Daryl F. Zanuck to produce *Gentleman's Agreement*. Both Kazan and Zanuck might be termed, as Neil Gabler suggests, "Jewish fellow travelers."[6] Kazan was a veteran of the largely Jewish Group Theater, and Zanuck was a Hollywood veteran who had previously produced one of the few overtly pro-Jewish war dramas, *The Purple Heart* (1944).[7] The prerelease responses to *Crossfire* and *Gentleman's Agreement* underscore the ambivalence of Jewish American artists and American Jews generally toward the explicit depiction of Jewish characters and themes in the aftermath of the Holocaust.

Gabler reports that many Jews in and out of Hollywood were against the films, for fear that open discussion of anti-Semitism would backfire. Rabbi Edward Magnin of the B'nai B'rith synagogue in Los Angeles said of the studio heads, "All they talk about is the Holocaust and all the sufferings. The goddamn fools don't realize that the more you tell gentiles that nobody likes us, the more they say there must be a reason for it."[8] Perhaps in response to these fears, neither film overtly mentions the Holocaust. Promotional trailers for *Gentleman's Agreement* do not mention the words *Jew, Jewish,* or *anti-Semitism,* though the controversial nature of the subject matter is invoked for its presumed sales value. In one such trailer, an unseen narrator reads "reviews" of the novel on which the film is based: "No story of the last decade has hit the literary world with such impact. . . . The author has deftly treated a taboo topic to give it excitement, exhilaration, and entertainment."[9] The voice-over goes on to inform us that "In selecting the cast, the roles were filled with unusual care"; this is followed, however, not by an explanation of why such care was necessary but by a recitation of the leading players, accompanied by brief clips in which each actor appears. These clips are too short (perhaps three seconds each) to communicate any information about the film's narrative.

Both *Crossfire* and *Gentleman's Agreement* enjoyed wide commercial and critical success. Both were nominated for Academy Awards for Best Picture and Best Director, with *Gentleman's Agreement* winning in both categories, along with a Best Supporting Actress nod for Celeste Holm. Of the two films, *Gentleman's Agreement* has become a classic. Its star-studded cast and Oscar-winner status ensured that it would be shown around the country, not just in the coastal urban centers. Moreover, while *Crossfire* is essentially a detective story focused on a murderer motivated by anti-Semitism (a fairly obvious case of good and bad), *Gentleman's Agreement* is much more complex, dramatizing a wide range of responses to anti-Semitism by both Jews and gentiles.

A half century later, it may be hard to see why *Gentleman's Agreement* was controversial. *Leonard Maltin's 2001 Movie and Video Guide,* for example, comments that the film's "Then-daring approach to subject matter is tame now."[10] But the long-term significance of *Gentleman's Agreement* lies in the curious way in which it delivered its anti-anti-Semitic message. Based on Laura Z. Hobson's award-winning novel (serialized in *Life* magazine, which assured it widespread attention), the film was scripted by the celebrated Jewish American playwright Moss Hart.[11] It features Gregory Peck as a gentile journalist assigned to write a series on anti-Semitism. But the story should not be, his editor warns him, the same old boring facts and figures story that's been done so many times. During the early part of the film, Peck's character, Skyler Green, wrestles with how he can write about the personal side of anti-Semitism, since he is not Jewish. Finally, he tells his mother:

> I got it! The lead, the idea, the angle. This is the way, it's the only way. I'll—I'll be Jewish! I'll—well, I—all I gotta do is say it. Nobody knows me around here. I—I can just say it. I can live it myself for six weeks, eight weeks, nine months, no matter how long it takes.

In order to get the story he wants, Green must "be Jewish." To accomplish this, he simply tells everyone he meets that he *is* Jewish; the way people's reactions to him change on learning that he is Jewish becomes the basis for his story—"I Was Jewish For Eight Weeks"—and ultimately for the film.

Asked by his young son Tommy (played by Dean Stockwell) to define *Jewish*, Green explains it as a religious choice.

> Remember how we passed that church, and I explained to you that some people go to one kind of church, and they're called Catholics, and some people go to another kind of church, and they are called Protestants? . . . Well, some people go to still another kind of church, and they're called Jews; only, they call their church a synagogue.

Lester Friedman writes of this scene that this reduction of religious differences between Catholic, Protestant, and Jew to a simple matter of denomination "represents the dominant ideology of the commercial film industry."[12] If so, then we should not be surprised that Green does not set foot in a synagogue or make any attempt to learn about Jewish religious practice as part of his attempt to put himself in the place of a Jew. He doesn't try to order kosher food in a restaurant; he doesn't refuse to work or ride on the Sabbath; he doesn't cover his head. So by his own terms Green does not try to *be Jewish* as much as he *acts Jewish*. Moreover, this acting Jewish is not based on *performing Judaism* (ritual observance).

Nor is the film's definition of acting Jewish based on ethnic or racial characteristics, though Green judges his own ability to pass for Jewish in these terms. Examining his reflection in the mirror, Green searches his face for characteristics that will distinguish him from the one Jew he knows well, his boyhood friend Dave Goldman (John Garfield).

Dark hair, dark eyes. Sure, so has Dave. So have a lot of guys who aren't Jewish. No accent, no mannerisms, neither has Dave. Name: Phil Green, skip the Skyler! Might be anything . . . Phil Green. . . .

Because Green has the stereotypically Jewish features of "dark hair, dark eyes" but is not Jewish, the discourse of Jewish racial difference is dealt a small blow. As Barry Gross writes, "the point of *Gentleman's Agreement* seems to be that anti-Semitism is silly because Jews are no different from anyone else, that is, if Gregory Peck could be mistaken for one."[13] Yet even as Green rejects some forms of ethnic stereotyping he acknowledges the validity of the name as a reliable indicator of ethnicity. He assumes that no Jew would be named Skyler, or rather he assumes that no one he meets would accept the idea of a Jew named Skyler. This is an ironic moment, because in an earlier scene Green has explained to the film's love interest Kathy (Dorothy McGuire) that his real name *is* Phil and he adopted Skyler as a pen name when he began his career as a journalist.

Gentleman's Agreement is, in a sense, forced to regard names as reliable predictors of ethnicity because much of the anti-Semitism that the film targets takes the form of discrimination based solely on one's name. This is illustrated through the character of Green's secretary, played by June Havoc. She has changed her name to Elaine Wales because the magazine's personnel manager, Mr. Jordan (Harold Vermilyea), summarily rejected her job application when she submitted it under her real name, Estelle Walofsky.[14] When Green reports this to the publisher, Mr. Minify (Albert Dekker), Minify confronts the personnel manager, asking, "Do you mean to say that we haven't one secretary named Finkelstein or Cohen? In the city of New York?"

But when Jordan is directed to place a new "help wanted" ad, including the phrase, "religious preference is a matter of indifference to this office," Miss Wales is aghast. "Well, I mean, just let them get one wrong one in here, and it will come out of us," she says. "It's no fun being the fall guy for the kikey ones." Green's impassioned rebuttal of Miss Wales's attitude anticipates Jean-Paul Sartre's distinction (made a year later in *Anti-Semite and Jew*) between the authentic Jew—whose visible pride in his Judaism may bring about persecution but never defeat—and the inauthentic Jew—who "repudiates his liberty as a man in order to escape the sin of being a Jew . . . in order to seek the repose and passivity of a thing."[15] The inauthentic Miss Wales is for Green (and for the film) as much a contributing factor to anti-Semitism as are outwardly bigoted gentiles.

But *Gentleman's Agreement* actually paints a much more sophisticated picture than the simple binary offered by Sartre, in part because the film's protagonist is not a Jew but a gentile who chooses to pass as Jewish. Because Green is not Jewish in the sense of *being*, he is able to flirt with the idea of *selective visibility*.[16] This selective visibility is inextricably bound up within a psychoanalytic framework that positions the Other (in this case, the Jew) as negative—not only in the pejorative sense but also as something that can only be defined by what it is not. Because the dominant subject perceives the Other as, by definition, negative, the Other can never be perceived on its own terms. This dilemma is expressed comically in *Gentleman's Agreement* through the character of Professor Lieberman (Sam Jaffe).

You see, my young friends, I have no religion, so I'm not Jewish by religion. Furthermore, I'm a scientist, so I must rely on science, which tells me I'm not Jewish by race, since there's no such thing as a distinct Jewish race; there's not even such thing as a Jewish type. Well, my crusade will have a certain charm. I will simply go forth and state frankly: I am not a Jew. With my face, that becomes not an evasion, but a new principle.

Lieberman recognizes that he is not in control of how he is perceived. The world, he assumes, will identify him as Jewish by his face. By stating that he is not a Jew, his "crusade" strikes a blow for self-identification. If Lieberman, who is stereotypically Jewish looking, were able to pass as a non-Jew, the visual codes that demarcate Jewishness in the anti-Semitic imaginary would be exposed as meaningless. But Lieberman does not want to pass as a non-Jew, for to do so would be a statement of inauthenticity (in the Sartrean sense)—a statement he is not prepared to make. Lieberman continues:

There must be millions of people nowadays who are religious only in the vaguest sense. I've often wondered why the Jewish ones among them still go on calling themselves Jews. Can you guess why, Mr. Green? . . . Because the world still makes it an advantage *not* to be one. Thus, for many of us it becomes a matter of pride to go on calling ourselves Jews. So you see, I shall have to abandon my crusade before it begins. Only if there were no anti-Semites could I go on with it.

As Lieberman's pride in the disadvantage of being Jewish shows, the subject who is different from the unmarked norm *by choice* can recognize this difference as positive. The catch is that in valorizing the position of the Other, we reinforce the same-Other binary. To claim pride in being a Jew is a form of resistance but also of capitulation, for it acknowledges that "Jewish" is a meaningful designation. Professor Lieberman may playfully syllogize that "only if there were no anti-Semites" could he feel comfortable discarding the label of Jew, but as a practical matter *Gentleman's Agreement* seeks to counter anti-Semitism, at least in part, by asserting the fundamental right to label oneself in whatever way one chooses.

The success of Green in passing as Jewish is proof that "passing" can and does move in both directions: not only can the Jew pass for a non-Jew, but the gentile can pass for a Jew. This is not the gentile actor donning the Jew's beard in parody, as in nineteenth-century burlesque, but rather an acknowledgment of the possibility of bidirectional passing. It firmly establishes the category of Jewish as something nonessential, primarily a matter of labeling. Literary critic Elaine K. Ginsberg writes in her introduction to *Passing and the Fictions of Identity* that the "possibility of passing challenges a number of problematic and even antithetical assumptions about identities, the first of which is that identity categories are inherent and unalterable essences: presumably one cannot pass for something one *is not* unless there is some other, pre-passing, identity that one *is*."[17] Green is not Jewish, yet he is able to pass as Jewish in a way that convinces both the Jewish (Miss Wales, Professor Lieberman) and the gentile characters in the film. *Gentleman's Agreement* takes advantage of this misrecognition to make its case against anti-Semitism. As Green declares to Miss Wales after he has admitted to his ruse, "The only difference between me yesterday and me today is the word Christian." The absurdity of this scene—with Green, who passes as a Jew, "coming out" as a Christian to Miss Wales, the Jew who passes as a Christian—highlights the film's contention that neither Jewish nor Christian are fixed, essential identities.[18]

Green's Jewishness is not something that he is, nor is it something that he does; it is something that he calls himself. But this self-appellation is not without meaning. If there were *no* difference between Jews and gentiles, Green wouldn't have had to "be Jewish" in order to understand the emotional response of the Jew to anti-Semitism. On the other hand, the film shows Green's experiment to be successful. His experience of anti-Semitism is emotionally equivalent to the experience of his Jewish friend, Dave Goldman. "Now you know it all," Goldman tells Green. "You can quit being Jewish now, there's nothing else."

Goldman's own character, however, represents a peculiarly negotiated form of acting Jewish. Although the plot of *Gentleman's Agreement* figures Goldman as the film's only "authentic" Jew, the only character explicitly marked as Jewish and unabashedly proud to be so, it is not immediately clear what, other than the label, makes him so. He has, as we heard Green say, "no accent, no mannerisms." Goldman's physical appearance could perhaps be an indicator of ethnicity, but even as Green mentions it ("dark hair, dark eyes") he undercuts its significance, noting that he himself has dark hair and dark eyes. Goldman's Jewish status is repeatedly noted by various characters in the film. In terms of the filmic narrative, "his Jewishness," as Samuel J. Rosenthal writes, "is central to his presence."[19] Yet it is a Jewishness seemingly devoid of ethnic or religious content.

In fact, the film goes to great lengths to demonstrate that Goldman's Jewishness presents no obstacle to his Americanness. When we first see Goldman, he is dressed in his military uniform, having just returned from service in World War II. Normalizing an ethnic character through veteran status was an established dramatic strategy by 1947, having been used in such classic intermarriage stories such as *Abie's Irish Rose* (1923, stage; 1928 and 1946, films) and *Private Izzy Murphy* (1926, film). We also learn that Goldman is a native of California, which associates him with an idea of modernity and the American West, in stark contrast to the stereotype of the New York Jew. Goldman is also presented as an ideal father and family man who has come to New York to seek honest work so he can provide for his wife and three children. Although we never see his family in the film, he offers sagely paternal advice to Green's son Tommy, and frequent references to his wife provide an interesting contrast to Green's status as a single parent. The only way, it seems, in which Goldman's Jewishness affects his life is that anti-Semitic prejudice prevents him from obtaining housing for his family, reinforcing the circular logic that characterizes Green's own attempt to act Jewish. Why is Goldman victimized, spurned by potential landlords? Because he is a Jew. But what, besides the label, makes him one? His victimization.

Given the problematic status of American Jews, particularly in Hollywood in 1947, Goldman's particular way of acting Jewish is perhaps not surprising. As one Jewish critic of the era noted, "The stated purpose of the film is to destroy that lethal commonplace which categorizes the Jews in special ways apart from others. . . . Garfield [wasn't] supposed to betray any traits commonly labeled as 'Yiddish.'"[20] This quotation, argues Rosenthal, "suggest[s] an awareness both of the film's significance as a watershed in the public presence of American Jewry and of the problematic nature of acceptance into the cultural mainstream at the price of concealing difference."[21] But this quotation also indicates the degree to which a Jewish audience may have recognized that concealment as strategic. Note the use of the word *betray*, as if the Jewish actor Garfield contained within himself a kind of innate *Yiddishkeit*, which he actively repressed in the service of the film's "stated purpose." Certainly Garfield was known to be Jewish, at least by readers of the Jewish American press, where Warner Brothers frequently directed publicity for his films. One typical advertisement from the *B'nai Brith Messenger* began with the tagline "Another Jewish Actor Rises to Stardom."[22] Yet his Jewishness was "completely ignored by the mainstream press,"[23] which chose instead to focus on his tough, rebellious screen persona, established in films such as *They Made Me a Criminal* (1939) and *The Postman Always Rings Twice* (1946). So, while Goldman's (and Garfield's) Jewishness was largely immaterial to a gentile audience, the knowledge that Garfield's "birth name was Garfinkle, that he spoke and read Yiddish, and that he was born and raised on New York's Lower East Side may have given the character an additional layer of authenticity with which a Jewish audience could identify.

Still, it is not Goldman but Green, the righteous gentile, on whom the story of *Gentleman's Agreement* turns. Experiencing anti-Semitic discrimination is a choice for Green because he can choose to reject the label Jew. Goldman, Professor Lieberman, and even Miss Wales cannot "quit being Jewish," regardless of their actions. Yet Green's example in the fight against anti-Semitism carries an important message. As a practical matter, *Gentleman's Agreement* argues against anti-Semitism on the grounds that Jews *are* exactly the same as everyone else, even if they call themselves something different. But on another level the film offers a model for acting Jewish in which Jewishness is treated *as if* it were a choice, not an obligation. Jewishness becomes, in Werner Sollors's terms, an issue of consent rather than descent.[24]

Gentleman's Agreement, then, portrays Jewishness as a matter of nomination—one does or does not call oneself a Jew—to advance the universalist message that Jews and gentiles are essentially the same. But ironically the film's extensive discussions around the issue of naming (and the names of the characters themselves) show the persistence of the opposite view, of Jewishness as an issue of descent. Character names, in fact, are often the last holdout of Jewish essentialism in an otherwise universal performance. How do you know a character is Jewish? Because they are named Marosky or Goldman or Finkel. The character name is always spelled out in the script or screenplay, but its implications go beyond the textual realm. If the character's name is Ginsberg or Hirsch, the actor or director might assume that the part calls for some sort of aural or visual indication of the character's ethnicity.

Furthermore, because the history of Jews (as well as other immigrant groups) in the United States is in part a history of "changing one's name for business purposes," even apparently generic "American" names can signify ethnicity. Hence, names that appear to be Anglicized German, such as Loman, Kramer, and Rose, provoke debate.[25] And because so many Jewish immigrants gave their children Anglicized approximations of Hebrew or Yiddish names, first names such as Irving (Isaac), Mort (Mordecai), and Bernie (Baruch) can signify Jewishness, despite having only a tenuous connection to traditional Jewish culture. In *Gentleman's Agreement*, for example, the character played by June Havoc has not only changed her last name from Walofsky to Wales but she has also changed her first name from Estelle (Esther) to Elaine.

The name of an actor can also communicate the Jewishness of the character he or she plays, especially in the case of a "star" whose name appears above the title on a theater marquee or before the title in the opening credits of films or television shows. In the first half of the twentieth century, when anti-Jewish sentiment was both more prevalent and more openly expressed in American culture than it is today, Jewish actors frequently sought to erase indicators of Jewishness from their public images for fear that they would be stereotyped exclusively into explicitly Jewish roles, of which there were very few available. Hence, Ayesha Yoelson became Al Jolson, Emmanuel Goldenberg became Edward G. Robinson, Issadur Danielovitch became Kirk Douglas. John Garfield was born Jacob Garfinkle, though his parents later amended his first name to Julius. As a young actor in New York's Group Theater, he billed himself as Jules Garfield; he changed the Jules to John under pressure from the Jewish studio head Harry Warner in 1938.[26]

By the 1950s, however, the studios' and stage producers' hold on the industry had begun to loosen (due in part to federal antitrust legislation, which may or may not have been anti-Semitically motivated). Moreover, the one-two punch of the Holocaust and the House Un-American Activities Committee (HUAC) investigation into Hollywood had awakened Jewish American entertainers to the anti-Semitic double bind: if actors did not acknowledge their Jewishness (and risk alienating part of their audience), they would be vulnerable to charges of hiding their identities. For example, on 24 November 1947, Representative Jon Rankin of Mississippi made the following statement to HUAC.

Here is a petition condemning the Committee. I am going to read some of the names on that petition. One is June Havoc. Her real name is June Hovick. Another is Danny Kaye. We found his real name was David Daniel Kaminsky. Another is Eddie Cantor, whose real name is Edward Iskowitz. There is one who calls himself Edward G. Robinson. His real name is Emanuel Goldenberg. There is another one here who calls himself Melvyn Douglas, whose real name is Melvyn Hesselberg.[27]

Rankin did not explain the significance of this information, nor did he need to. His statement clearly implies that the subversiveness of these actors' Jewish heritage is surpassed only by their subversiveness in trying to hide it.

The committee's hearings, which began just weeks before the release of *Gentleman's Agreement*, caused liberals throughout New York and Hollywood to run for cover. Among the major Jewish American artists to refuse to testify, and who were subsequently blacklisted, were John Garfield of *Gentleman's Agreement*, Edward Dmytryk of *Crossfire*, and Philip Loeb of *The Goldbergs*. And, while a widespread tolerance toward religious and racial difference characterized much of American theater, film, and television in the 1950s, the specific issue of anti-Semitism was not explicitly raised again in a major popular performance until Dmytryk's *The Young Lions* in 1958.

The Goldbergs

On 17 January 1949, less than ten months after *Gentleman's Agreement* was honored by the Academy of Motion Picture Arts and Sciences, the Columbia Broadcasting System (CBS) premiered the first television series to feature a Jewish family: *The Goldbergs*. The name Goldberg would seem to remove any ambiguity about the characters' ethnicity; it is understood both positively and negatively in many circles to be synonymous with the word *Jew*. While the emerging medium of television tried, like film, to reach the broadest possible audience, several early dramas focused on ethnically identifiable families. Cultural historian George Lipsitz suggests that the popularity of such ethnically themed television shows as *Amos and Andy* (African American), *Mama* (Norwegian), *Life with Luigi* (Italian), and *Life of Riley* (Irish) between 1949 and 1957 indicates a negotiation of postwar tensions in urban, working-class ethnic communities. These shows used a patina of ethnic authenticity to legitimize the promotion of the capitalist American Dream, mining the immigrant experience for humor while simultaneously teaching hyphenated Americans how to become part of the dominant culture.[28]

The Goldbergs was the Jewish entry in this category. It featured Gertrude Berg (who was also the show's head writer) as Molly Goldberg, an immigrant wife and mother who presides over her husband Jake and children Sammy and Rosalie with warmth and wit. The show was adapted from a radio series of the same name that premiered in 1929 and ran more or less continuously until it made the transition to television twenty years later. Donald Weber suggests that:

> Gertrude Berg's career in radio and television amounts to a gigantic effort to bridge the space between [the] dual ethnic and American identities, to soften the jagged edges of alienation through the figure of Molly Goldberg and her special accommodating vision—a vision of a loving family, of interdenominational brotherhood, of middle-class ideals, of *American* life.[29]

On radio, where speech patterns take on greater importance in the creation of character, *The Goldbergs* developed initially as a dialect comedy. Molly and Jake's greenhorn malapropisms were its stock in trade. But with the shift to television the Goldberg family's misuse of English became less important as a central trope.[30] While it was still a staple of the show, Molly's misuse of language was softened. This was aided by the fact that the half-hour format of the television *Goldbergs* allowed for more sophisticated plotting than the fifteen-minute time slot the show filled on the radio.

A typical episode of *The Goldbergs* begins with a commercial for the program's sponsor, the decaffeinated coffee product Sanka. Berg, already in character as Molly, addresses the camera directly through the window of her apartment, explaining how relaxing it is to have a cup of Sanka, "the coffee that leaves the sleep in. And if it costs a few pennies more, it's worth it."[31] After the commercial, the camera follows Molly through the window into the family living room. Vincent Brook suggests that this "integrated commercial" (which was reversed as a means of closing each episode) served to enhance the audience's identification between the spokesperson/character and product. This identification served a dual purpose: first, to associate the product (Sanka in 1949, later RCA television sets and Rybutol vitamins) with the feelings of identification the audience has with Molly; and, second, to legitimize new, technologically developed consumer products (decaffeinated coffee, television sets, vitamin pills) in the minds of viewers through the associative link to an exemplar of "Old World" values and practices. Brook notes that "the ethnic working-class family, as a link between modern and traditional values, provided an ideal vehicle for the transmission of the consumerist ethos."[32]

David Zurawik, noting that Berg wrote the commercial copy herself and always tried to link it to the subject of the particular episode, further suggests that Molly's success at pitching products indicates a degree of empowerment rarely associated with women or ethnic minorities in early television.[33] In part, he suggests, it was Berg's ability to sell Sanka (and to sell that ability to Sanka's parent company, General Foods) that enabled her to get *The Goldbergs* on television in the first place, the sponsor's desires trumping Jewish network executives' concern that the show was too Jewish. According to him, "the Jewish president of CBS resisted putting *The Goldbergs* on the air despite the fact that it fit the very model for the kind of ethnic sitcoms with a history of radio success that his network was looking to add. Meanwhile, a major advertising agency—often described as WASP (White Anglo-Saxon Protestant)—put *The Goldbergs* on the air."[34] As we will see, however, the perceptions of all three players (the networks, the sponsors, and Berg) about how much explicit Jewishness a mass audience would accept definitely influenced the show's manner of acting Jewish.

When the opening commercial ended, the audience would be invited to join Molly in the family living room, which was occupied, as always, by Molly's husband Jake (Philip Loeb, later replaced by Harold J. Stone and then Robert H. Harris), her son Sammy (Tom Taylor), her daughter Rosalie (Arlene McQuade), and her Uncle David (Menasha Skulnik, later replaced by Eli Mintz). After a few moments of exposition, a crisis becomes apparent. In one episode, Molly's aunt, "Tante" Elke, is depressed because she feels her new daughter-in-law doesn't like her. In another, Jake, a modest clothing retailer, must prepare for an appointment with an important dress manufacturer. Typically, Molly makes everyone else's business her own and then proceeds to make a mess of the situation. In the end, she is able to resolve the situation happily through honesty and compassion, as well as a cleverness uncommon in female characters of her day. Zurawik notes, for example, the contrast between Molly and her contemporary Lucy Ricardo (Lucille Ball) of *I Love Lucy:* "Unlike the schemes of Lucy Ricardo, Molly's schemes always work. She never has to beg her husband's forgiveness; he is the one tearfully thanking her for once again saving the day."[35]

The major source of comedy in *The Goldbergs* is Molly's inability to understand the "modern American" way of doing things, emphasized

reading of the Goldbergs solidit the Goldbergs — too surface + derivative

by her comic misuse of English. Some examples of these "Molly-propisms" include:

"When we get to the bridge, I'll burn it."

"Rosalee, the guests are here. Bring in the raw-derves [hors d'ouvres]."

"Rosie, don't talk smart. I don't like your latitude one bit, young lady."

"Sit down. Take your feet off."[36]

Yet while Molly may have been laughed at by her audience she was also loved and respected, as evidenced by the correspondence the show received, as well as by Berg's success at translating Molly's Old World wisdom into a variety of print media incarnations, including interviews, advice columns, and even recipes. Zurawik even suggests that Molly's *Yiddishe mama* dialect enhanced audience respect, noting, "Language is one of several ways that Molly is linked to a tradition of American humor dating back to the eighteenth century and seen in such forms as the wise fool and the commonsense philosopher."[37]

Viewing the taped performance of *The Goldbergs*, one certainly does get a sense of a family deeply grounded in tradition and what today we might call "family values." In contrast to other popular situation comedies of the period, such as *The Honeymooners* or *I Love Lucy*, Molly and Jake rarely yell at each other. They argue, of course, but their arguments are good-natured battles of wits and physical violence is never a factor. Nor do the Goldbergs yell at or hit their children. And whatever else happens in the episode Molly always find a way to ensure a happy ending for her family. Jewish author and essayist Francine Klagsbrun sees the Goldberg family's behavior as a recognizable, though comically exaggerated, mode of acting Jewish. She writes:

Jewish audiences cherished the Goldberg clan precisely because it did mirror our own unease in American society. With the Goldbergs' overdone cadences and excessive emotions, they made us laugh at ourselves, and in laughing find comfort. And we loved them because, in the warmth and aspirations of their family life, they portrayed to the outside our own values of family and education.[38]

Klagsbrun specifically highlights the aspects of *The Goldbergs* that are performance based: the "overdone cadences and excessive emotions"

and "the warmth . . . of their family life." It is in these affective qualities, as much as in any narrative situation, that the Goldberg family's
Jewishness is communicated. Brook describes this aspect of *The Goldbergs* as a "less quantifiable, but no less distinctive, Jewish ambience."[39]

The comments of Klagsbrun and Brook illustrate the degree to
which portraying Jews "to the outside"—that is, to the non-Jewish
audience—was essential to the construction of *The Goldbergs*, especially
in its televisual incarnation. Berg self-consciously sought to reach a
universal audience and certainly felt the pressure of openly acting Jewish for audiences all across America. In a visual display of universalism
(and a carnivalesque inversion of the Jewish immigrant's relationship
with America), Molly literally opened her window each week and
invited Americans inside. When they got there, they found it to be a
warm and welcoming place. This was a side of "us" that the Jews of the
early 1950s were comfortable showing "them." The Jewish comedian
and television writer Sam Leven'son, in a *Commentary* essay condemning Jewish dialect humor as "bad for the Jews," nevertheless acknowl-
edged that "on the other hand, there is Molly Goldberg, who speaks
with an accent yet teaches love, kindliness, honesty, respect for culture,
and decency on a high level."[40]

Levenson further derided "inside" or "between me and you" jokes
that denigrate Jews, because "Between me and you I think we are a
magnificent people and I prefer to talk about ourselves that way."[41]
Perhaps it is a similar motive that leads the contemporary critics cited
herein to remember, and maybe even recuperate, *The Goldbergs* in an
era when cultural stereotypes are often taboo subjects. *The Goldbergs*
represents that rarest of constructions, the unequivocally positive eth-
nic-minority stereotype. As Zurawik writes, "Cutting dead against the
conventional wisdom of 1950s' popular culture as a time of laughably
repressive images of women on television, Molly Goldberg is one of
the most empowered images ever of a Jewish woman in prime-time
network television."[42]

Still, as the show evolved from radio to television, and even more
over its six-year television life, the Goldberg family became more and
more Americanized.[43] By 1955, the family had moved out of their
Bronx apartment and into the mythical suburb of Haverville. Molly
brought her "values of family and education" with her, but by now they
had come completely unmoored from their roots in either Jewish religious practice or Ashkenazic Jewish culture. The Goldbergs speak no
Yiddish in their home. They do not observe a Saturday Sabbath or keep
a kosher kitchen. In most episodes, in fact, the words *Jew* and *Jewish* are
never mentioned. Even in situations in which the Goldbergs' religion

or ethnicity would seem to have a direct bearing on the plot, the subject is never broached. When Sammy gets married, a ceremony conspicuously not shown on the air, we hear ten minutes of discussion about the caterer but no mention of the rabbi. When Rosalie wants to have her nose bobbed, Molly dissuades her with guile and the aid of a gentile doctor, not with talk of religious law or ethnic pride. In other words, the Goldberg family's mode of acting Jewish in these later episodes does not include the performance of Jewish religious practice, at least not on the air.

By avoiding the representation of specifically Jewish rituals and acting Jewish as opposed to performing Judaism, the Goldberg family could more easily be accepted by a non-Jewish audience as representative of its own experience in acculturation. The CBS public relations staff, for example, trumpeted that "the Bronx neighbors of *The Goldbergs* will be introduced to the television audience when the classic family series of 17 years standing in radio makes its bow over the CBS-TV Network, Monday, January 17 at 9:00 PM EST."[44] The release goes on for an entire page, and the words *Jew* and *Jewish* never appear. In subsequent press releases, the Goldbergs' ethnicity is also conspicuously absent, though they are frequently referred to as "the immigrant family."

Yet, if *The Goldbergs* were generic immigrants to much of the nationwide CBS audience, they were identifiably Jewish to their "Bronx neighbors" and any other audience for which *Jewish* was a significant identifier. Today, to anyone who is Jewish or familiar with Jewish American culture, the Goldbergs are almost too Jewish.[45] All the Goldbergs have dark hair and eyes and speak with accents. Members of the older generation, Molly, Jake, and Uncle David, have Yiddish accents. The children, along with most of the younger guest characters, have equally thick Bronx tones. They live at 1038 East Tremont Avenue in the Bronx, a nonexistent building in a (then) predominantly Jewish neighborhood.

This is not to say that a gentile audience would fail to recognize that the Goldbergs are Jewish. But for an audience without the specifically Jewish cultural context in which to interpret the Goldbergs' behavior their Jewishness is simply a label, similar to the Jewishness of the characters in *Gentleman's Agreement*. Moreover, because the label Jewish is not foregrounded explicitly by the script, the relevance of the Goldbergs' religious and ethnic identity is likely to remain *unmarked* and *unremarked upon* unless and until the question is consciously raised.

One notable (and clearly exceptional) moment in which *The Goldbergs* did raise the question was the so-called Yom Kippur episode,[46]

which aired on 5 October 1954 on the now defunct DuMont Network.[47] This episode, one of the last to be set in the Bronx, not only
refers to the Jewish High Holiday but actually includes an extended
scene in an Orthodox synagogue.[48] On that night, the television audience *did* get to see the Goldberg family participate in religious ritual.
Significantly, the scene includes a cantor singing "Kol Nidre," the
prayer of atonement, evoking a similar scene in *The Jazz Singer*, and
implying, perhaps, a kind of atonement on Berg's part for the show's
usual absence of explicit religious observance.[49] Much as we saw with
Jack Robin in *The Jazz Singer*, the requirements to fit Jewish culture to
the expectations of the American entertainment industry are
configured, in this reading, as a forced religious conversion from which
the artist desires God's permission to be released.

But this reading was likely lost on most of the audience that night
due to the simple fact that the episode aired on Erev Yom Kippur, the
evening the holiday began. Certainly, viewers who would understand
and attach significance to "Kol Nidre" in this context would be at a synagogue themselves, not home watching television. Perhaps Berg's
intent in creating the episode was to draw nonobservant or assimilated
Jews (the kind that would watch television on the Day of Atonement)
back to the fold. But it seems more likely that the episode was calcu-
lated to provide the larger, gentile audience with a positive and educational image of Jewish religious practice, what we might call a "teachable moment." Zurawik, for example, calls the Yom Kippur episode
"the most Jewish episode of any series in the history of network television," noting, "It is the same kind of treatment for a Jewish holiday that
we have seen hundreds of times on television for Christmas with
fictional families like *The Waltons* wishing us a happy holiday from their
house to ours and God's blessings."[50]

While this assertion of "equal to Christmas" mass cultural status for
the Jewish High Holidays may generate a sense of pride or pleasure for
a Jewish audience, it is the very sameness of treatment that makes Jewish ritual practice, in this context, both understandable and "safe" for a
gentile audience. Any anxiety that audience may have about the Jew as
Other is defused by the warm, humorous, nonthreatening nature of the
Goldbergs themselves, reinforced by the episode's plot, which emphasizes the easily translatable virtues of forgiveness, piety, charity, and
family.

Family, and especially Molly Goldberg's dedication to hers, proved
to be the clearest and most apparently universal of the series' strengths.
In her autobiography, *Molly and Me*, Berg writes of the many letters she
received from Jews and non-Jews alike, seeking advice for help with

their family troubles.[51] "Dear Mrs. Goldberg," reads one, "Say a few words, please, to my son Harold. He's hanging out and my husband is worried he will fall into bad hands."[52] The CBS public relations department considered the Goldberg family a universal paragon of domestic bliss. One press release reads:

> Although the series provides comedy in the minor crises arising in every episode, it long has been accepted for its values beyond the field of entertainment. Psychiatrists, pathologists, educators, judges and ministers have written letters of praise and requested copies of scripts to study as an aid in better understanding human nature.[53]

While we may dismiss some of this as public relations hype, it is clear that for much of *The Goldbergs'* audience, the characters' Jewishness was not a significant identifying characteristic—or if it was it did not present a barrier to identifying with the Goldberg family and its adventures. Why not? Weber suggests that *The Goldbergs'* overt patriotism and unironic commitment to what contemporary critics would call "family values" made the show palatable to a mass audience.[54] Other critics cited here, including Lipsitz, Brook, and Zurawik, further argue that Molly's desire to achieve modernity, in the form of using (and shilling for) new consumer products, made her sufficiently representative of the postwar American middle class to overcome her Jewish "difference," especially because of the degree to which it was downplayed in the attempt to reach that mass audience.

For a Jewish-literate audience, however, *Jewish* signifies an identity position, implying a wealth of cultural and ideological information that is often conspicuously absent from the dramatic text. And for this audience the series takes on added resonance. Klagsbrun, for example, writes that Jews "could identify easily with Molly's attempts at matchmaking (whose mother or grandmother did not relish such activity?), with Rosalie's desire to have her nose fixed (not an uncommon wish in our circles), and with Jake's incessant anxiety about his clothing business."[55] Klagsbrun identifies the Goldberg family as Jewish not because gentile mothers do not engage in matchmaking or because gentile fathers don't worry about their businesses but because, as a Jewish reader, her associations with these themes and traits are linked to her own experience of Jewishness. The sociologist David Schneider writes:

> Because we assume others are like us in important ways, we infer that they possess attributes which, unlike size and behavior, we

cannot observe directly, but which we are aware of in ourselves. [. . .] Not only do we use knowledge about how our own goals and intentions produce behavior to infer something about the inner workings of other people, but we may even project our characteristics onto others.[56]

Hence, for a Jewish audience the "lovable immigrant family," the Goldbergs, is the quintessential Jewish family. Zurawik, for example, argues that the show depicted Jewish identity "first and foremost through language, but also through the body (Rosie's nose), objects (the menorah on the mantel in the family living room), geography (the Bronx), surname (Goldberg), food (blintzes and gefilte fish), and occupation (Jake as a dress cutter in the garment industry)."[57] It may seem odd, or at least inadequate, to locate Jewish identity—a formulation with thousands of years of history and significance—in such apparent trivia as an accent, a nose, a neighborhood, or a meal. Perhaps the fear of the nonconforming Other we associate with Eisenhower era conservatism explains why the show was thought by many to be too Jewish in the 1950s, yet why, fifty years later, do some Jewish writers feel that it was too extreme in its stereotypes?[58] Perhaps, I suggest, it is because the more esoteric cultural aspects of the Goldberg family's life, though rarely shown onscreen (and even more rarely discussed explicitly), can be inferred by an audience familiar with the requisite cultural codes. As Brook writes, "Viewing the series nearly fifty years after its original airing, the show still resonates with distinctly Jewish odors, textures, and tastes."[59] They resonate for Brook, certainly, and for many other Jewish observers. But do they resonate in the same way for an audience unfamiliar with these coded indicators of Jewishness? How many non-Jewish viewers, for example, would remark on dress cutting or blintzes as specifically Jewish? Note also that these codes are temporally specific: a character who cuts dresses in the Bronx today would be more likely to "read" to an audience as Dominican. But for those who do know the codes, *The Goldbergs'* positive portrayal of Jewish American family life implicitly sanctions Molly's religiously informed but less than religiously orthodox mode of acting Jewish.

It seems, then, that *The Goldbergs'* mode of acting Jewish represents an important shift from the representation of Jewishness in *Gentleman's Agreement*. While both performances achieved crossover success, appealing to both Jewish and gentile audiences, *The Goldbergs* appealed to a Jewish audience *for different reasons and in different ways* than it appealed to a gentile audience. As such, the CBS comedy is one of the earliest examples of the phenomenon I call double coding.

Death of a Salesman

On 10 February 1949, eleven months after *Gentleman's Agreement* received its Best Picture Oscar, and barely three weeks after the television debut of *The Goldbergs*, Arthur Miller's *Death of a Salesman* opened on Broadway. Unlike *Gentleman's Agreement* or *The Goldbergs*, *Death of a Salesman* is not overtly Jewish in any sense of the term. The characters do not identify themselves or anyone else as Jewish. The play's protagonist, Willy Loman (played in 1949 by Lee J. Cobb), is an aging garment salesman from Brooklyn who has been frustrated and beaten down by his attempts to live out the American Dream of economic and social advancement. Willy's religion and ethnicity are never specified in the play, and he is widely accepted as a universal character. Indeed, some have even suggested that Willy is "too anonymous" or "falsely universal."[60]

Yet there are many things about Willy Loman that lead a Jewish audience to identify strongly with him, including his situation, speech patterns, and mannerisms. George Ross, in a 1951 review of a Yiddish-language production of *Salesman* directed by Joseph Buloff (*Toyt fun a Salesman*), wrote:

> What one feels most strikingly is that this Yiddish play is really the original, and the Broadway production was merely Arthur Miller's translation into English.
>
> The vivid impression is that in translating from his mixed American-Jewish experience, Miller tried to ignore or censor out the Jewish part, and as a result succeeded only in making the Loman family anonymous . . . Buloff has caught Miller, as it were, in the act of changing his name.[61]

Julius Novick expressed similar sentiments four decades later in his review of the 1984 production of *Salesman*, which starred Dustin Hoffman as Willy, suggesting that "*Death of a Salesman* is the sequel to *Fiddler on the Roof*."[62]

This linguistic strategy may be considered another form of double coding. By presenting Jewishness in a way that is only recognizable to those who know the codes, a performance can acknowledge the value of Jewish difference within the community of readers who decode it thus while challenging the terms of the discussion without. The Yiddish-inflected English of Willy Loman can be seen as a way to incorporate the heteroglossic nature of Miller's own background into a "mainstream" artistic enterprise, gesturing toward his Jewish heritage for those who recognize, consciously or subconsciously, the underlying Yiddish grammar, while not calling attention to the characters' Jewishness in a way that might alienate a gentile audience. It is the linguistic equivalent of passing and carries with it the same double-edged potential.

Ross's review of the Yiddish production notes, for example, that "Willy speaks and behaves in Jewish idiom much more comfortably and eloquently than in American—and note that the translation is almost literal."[63] Willy Loman's repeated claim that his son has failed to find himself "for spite,"[64] notes Ross, sounds much richer as the Yiddish lament "*af tsuloches.*" Linda's declaration that "Attention must be paid"[65] is much more visceral in Yiddish: "*gib achtung.*" "Here, and in many places" writes Ross, "one felt in the English version as if Miller were thinking in Yiddish and unconsciously translating . . . and sometimes when his English filters through the density of his background, it succeeds in picking up flavor on the way."[66] Ross's essay has been quoted frequently in the subsequent discourse on the Jewishness or lack thereof in *Death of a Salesman* because it seems to offer an easy answer, a kind of secret decoder ring with which Miller's true intent can be divined.[67] But it is important to note that the degree to which the "Yiddish flavor" of Miller's English dialogue is decodable by an audience is deeply dependent on the way *Salesman* is performed.

Every dialogue, every exchange of words, exists in a context of specific social intonations that give it historical and ideological specificity. Dialogue is never static, even when the words themselves are fixed on a printed page. There is another, less frequently invoked corollary to this idea: nowhere is the specificity of dialogue more evident than in the theater, where every word must be immediately and physically embodied by a specific actor, given a specific tone, and enunciated in a specific location at a specific time. Indeed, it is a misnomer to speak of "dramatic literature," for the playwright's words are not written to be read but to be performed.[68] Just as George Bernard Shaw declared that "it is impossible for an Englishman to open his mouth without making some other Englishman hate or despise him,"[69] it is impossible for an actor to deliver a line without conveying phonological signals about his or her character's (and his or her own) background.

To fully understand the use of language in drama, then, we must consider not only the playwright's language as written but also the ways in which that language is spoken aloud. If listeners decode the performer's accent as Jewish, they are much more likely to read the language and conversation patterns as Jewish specific. For example, Steve Vineberg, comparing the 1949 Broadway production of *Death of a*

Salesman starring Lee J. Cobb to the 1984 production with Dustin Hoffman, writes:

> Whereas Cobb plays Willy without any specific ethnic identification . . . Hoffman is unquestionably Jewish in the role. He recalls sentimental old men, second-generation immigrants . . . who warn listeners of their annoyance at an interruption or contradiction by commenting sarcastically on it, lending their words the lilt of Yiddish folk music.[70]

While Vineberg is an accomplished theater historian and critic, it is important to note that he is not a trained sociolinguist. His "Jewish decoding" of Hoffman's accent is based not on phonetic analysis but on his own prior aural experience of "second-generation [Jewish] immigrants" and "the lilt of Yiddish folk music." The communication of Willy Loman's Jewishness is made possible because both the Jewish actor (Hoffman) and the Jewish listener (Vineberg) share the same culturally specific linguistic code.

The lines written by the playwright (Miller), combined with an actor or director's choices in accent, rhythm, and tone of speech unmistakably indicate a character's Jewish identity to a Jewish audience, while signaling only ethnic or regional difference to audiences unfamiliar with these linguistic codes. Similarly, casting choices, as well as more malleable visual characteristics such as makeup, hair, and posture, can provide a double-coded indicator of Jewish specificity to an otherwise generic character or situation. Casting is especially important, I suggest, because, while a character in a written text may be understood as universal, the body of the actor who brings that character to life on stage or screen is necessarily specific. This is also the case with non-Jewish actors. Novick, for instance, suggests that in a 1999 production of *Death of a Salesman* that starred Brian Dennehy "the Lomans seem as if they might be Irish-Americans, and the play is no less plausible and powerful for that."[71]

That the specificity of the actor's racial, ethnic, or religious background does not conflict with the universality of the character he or she plays may seem counterintuitive. Yet this proposition is at the core of the predominant mode of naturalistic acting that has been taught and practiced in the United States over the last several decades: "The Method." Method acting, as developed by Konstantin Stanislavsky and adapted and refined by influential (Jewish) teachers such as Lee Strasberg, Stella Adler, and Sanford Meisner, depends in large part on the specificity of the actor *precisely in order to generate a universally felt per-*

formance. The actor who plays Willy Loman, for example (and it should be noted that Cobb and Hoffman both trained with Strasberg), is encouraged to draw on his own personality and experience to generate emotions appropriate to the character. Therefore, to the degree that the actor's personality and experience are shaped by factors such as race, religion, and ethnicity, these factors are always embodied in his or her performance of a character. As Steve Vineberg writes in his history of American Method acting:

> Because of Hollywood's Jewish studio heads' obsession with assimilation (their terror of anti-Semitism), [John] Garfield wasn't allowed to play specifically Jewish characters until after the war. But in a sense, he never played anything else, because he was always drawing so closely on himself.[72]

Viewed from this perspective, the importance of casting in the theatrical double coding of Jewishness takes on a new resonance. While I focused earlier on the way that Jewish audiences perceive an actor's underlying Jewishness, here we also see that Jewishness come into play at the level of character development.

Taking the argument a step deeper, I would also contend that the development of the American Method is *inclusively Jewish* to a degree unmatched by previous approaches to acting. First and foremost, Method acting from its inception has been a cultural process for which Jewish American artists can claim a birthright, much as African Americans claim jazz music. Its arrival and subsequent level of acceptance in the United States coincides with their own.

This is partly because so many members of the influential Group Theater (generally credited with the Method through their work in the 1930s) were Jewish. But what is often overlooked is that the Jewish members of the Group, even those who did not speak Yiddish themselves, grew up in homes where Yiddish theater was the primary source of dramatic entertainment. Harold Clurman, for example, writes that "from the age of six, when I had been taken to see Jacob Adler in *Uriel Acosta* at the Grand Street Theatre, I had a passionate inclination toward the theatre."[73]

As Nahma Sandrow notes, Stanislavsky's Moscow Art Theater was the fin de sicle art theater that "most directly influenced Yiddish theater, which was attuned to the intellectual life of its East European environment. . . . In interpreting modern realistic drama, Stanislavsky's group evolved a vividly lifelike method of acting which was to have a widespread effect on modern Western theater, especially in America, where Yiddish immigrants helped to spread it."[74] Thus, while most European (and many American) theater historians attribute the Group's psychologically based and emotionally driven manifestation of the Method to Americans' desire for individual glory, it would be more accurate to say that the American Method differs from "pure Stanislavsky" because (at least in part) the "system" arrived in the United States filtered through the emotionally and politically charged Yiddish theater.[75]

Of course, the Jewish members of the Group were, in part, reacting against the contrived plotlines, star turns, and overly theatrical staginess of the Yiddish theater. Nonetheless, they found the deeply felt emotion and working-class consciousness of the Yiddish theater more appealing than either the bourgeois vapidity of the commercial stage or the aloof and self-consciously artistic style favored by the Theatre Guild and other art theaters.[76]

So while it is fair to say that in the course of its translation from Russian to Yiddish to American the Method became less "authentically" Stanislavskian we should also note that it took on a decidedly political tone. Strasberg's emphasis on the specificity of the actor's emotions is based not on self-aggrandizement but on a liberal assumption of universal humanism. The Method actors believe that their own emotions can be appropriate to the character because people of all races, religions, and nations experience similar emotions in similar ways; otherwise they are limited to playing characters substantially like themselves. Indeed, it was the Group's resistance to typecasting that initially distinguished its repertoire from those of its contemporaries. Clurman, for example, reports the response of Theatre Guild officials to a request by the Group to finance its first production (Paul Green's *The House of Connelly*) in 1931. Theatre Guild Administrative Director Theresa Helburn "conceded that the production succeeded in creating a mood, that it had emotional substance. But the board as a whole was not sure that Carnovsky could pass as a Southern gentleman."[77] The Guild questioned whether the Jewish actor Morris Carnovsky, a veteran of both Yiddish- and English-language theater, could "pass" as a southerner. But the fundamental premise on which the Group operated was that a talented actor could pass as anything, precisely because, at the level of deeply felt emotion, all human beings are essentially the same.

Obviously, the Method actor must likewise believe that the audience shares this common humanity. This is why the actor's interior evocation of emotion in performance can be "read" correctly with a minimum of theatrical mechanics. Yet cultural and psychological specificity is essential to the naturalistic mode of production that dominated the latter two-thirds of the twentieth century. Indeed, the Method virtually equates specificity with truth. Realism demands specificity because a real individual is never generic. Thus, a playwright may argue, as Miller does, that "Where the theme seems to require a Jew to act somehow in terms of his Jewishness, he does so. Where it seems to me irrelevant what the religious character or cultural background of a character may be, it is treated as such."[78] And yet the actor playing the role, in building his or her character, must reconsider the question of "religious character or cultural background"—especially when the playwright consciously omits such information from the written text. As part of this reconsideration, the actor will scrutinize the information provided by the text, with an eye toward an overall "objective" or "motivation" that will shape the performance.

The predominant reading of Willy Loman, whom Leslie Fiedler and others have called a crypto-Jewish character, emphasizes the universalist aspects of the performance narrative because this is the most widely applicable decoding.[79] Michiko Kakutani, for example, writing about the fiftieth anniversary revival of *Death of a Salesman* in the *New York Times*, simply dismisses the Jewish reading of the play.

> 50 years to the day from the play's 1949 world premiere—it is clear that many of the debates that attended the original opening have long since become obsolete. We no longer question whether a play about a little man (a "low-man," as opposed to a king or powerful ruler) can be called a tragedy, just as we no longer question the ethnicity of the play's hero, the Jewishness or non-Jewishness of his locution.[80]

Kakutani may be correct in asserting that the "Jewishness or non-Jewishness" of Miller's dialogue is no longer a widely discussed issue. But what she fails to acknowledge is that no consensus has been reached on the "ethnicity of the play's hero." Moreover, the "we" that "no longer question" Willy Loman's ethnicity represent a text-based reading position that ignores the powerful Method-based performance tradition that propelled *Salesman* into the American dramatic canon in the first place.

When considering the degree to which a play (or film or broadcast) communicates Jewishness, this process of exegesis on the part of the actor (and director) cannot be ignored. As Richard Schechner writes:

> The production doesn't "come out" of the text; it is generated in rehearsal in an effort to "meet" the text. And when you see a play and recognize it as familiar you are referring back to earlier pro-

ductions, not to the playscript. An unproduced play is not a homunculus, but a shard of an as yet unassembled whole.[81]

That the American Method gives the actor greater responsibility for the generation of meaning in performance may be read as another indication of the Jewish influence that shaped its evolution. Just as the modern science of philology was descended from the study of sacred texts, so are the dominant forms of European and early American theater influenced by the models of Christian ritual. Christian theology posits an ideal master interpreter of the scriptures, that is, Jesus Christ; the priests and other ritually empowered readers are presumed to enjoy a superiority of interpretation over the layperson (the individual actor). This hierarchy was mirrored among early Western directors, regardless of their individual religious beliefs. From Saxe-Meiningen to Belasco to Stanislavsky, the director took on the role of the priestly (not to say Christ-like) interlocutor between the sacred text (the script) and the layman (the actor).

But the Group Theater, in adopting the cohesive intensity of the Moscow Art Theater, also adapted this underlying structure. Instead of a master and disciples, the Group organized itself along lines similar to Jewish theological practice. All members (even bit players) had the right to interpret the text. Competing interpretations were debated, improvised, and workshopped until a working consensus was achieved (at least this was the ideal). As in a yeshiva, if the group deferred to a particular interpreter, it was out of respect for the person, not the official sanction.

The Group's collectivist experiment was short-lived, due in part to increasing difficulty in reaching consensus under the time constraints imposed by commercial theater (as well as internal conflicts about how much power a play's director should wield). But its idealistic legacy and the belief that the individual actor must be empowered to make critical interpretive decisions lived on in the Method.

In fact, this empowerment of the actor as interpreter has become the standard in American popular performance, even beyond the ranks of Method-trained actors. This can be seen in the profusion of critical language concerning "acting choices," "motivations," and "interpretation" rather than the delivery of dialogue. We might even see the twentieth-century actor's emphasis on textual exegesis combined with extra-textual collaboration as similar to the Jewish distinction between written law (Torah) and oral law (*halacha*). The interpretation of the written text is shaped and guided by an oral tradition communicated from teacher to student.

The oral tradition of the Method also depends on a deep engagement with the emotions. This explicitly opposes the Anglo-American performance tradition that preceded and continues to exist alongside it. Performance theorist Jos Esteban Muñoz argues that "majoritarian" American performance is distinguished by a "national affect, a mode of being in the world primarily associated with white middle-class subjectivity, [which] reads most ethnic affect as inappropriate."[82] Overt displays of emotion or excitement are configured as incorrect or déclassé. Muñoz further suggests that "the affective performance of normative whiteness is minimalist to the point of emotional impoverishment."[83] In other words, to the degree that an audience perceives a character's behavior as emotionally excessive that character is seen as Other—different from the nonethnic norm.

Muñoz, writing in the year 2000, was concerned primarily with the current state of Latina/Latino identity formation.

> Majoritarian identity has much to do with certain subjects' inability to *act* properly within majoritarian scripts and scenarios. Latinos and Latinas are stigmatized as performers of excess—the hot and spicy, over-the-top subjects who simply do not know when to quit. "Spics" is an epithet intrinsically linked to questions of affect and excess affect. Rather than simply reject this toxic language of shame I wish to reinhabit it and suggest that such stigmatizing speech permits us to arrive at an important mapping of the social. Rather than say that Latina/o affect is too much, I want to suggest that the presence of latino/a affect puts a great deal of pressure on the affective base of whiteness, insofar as it instructs us in a reading of the affect of whiteness as underdeveloped and impoverished.[84]

Though the theoretical language is new, Muñoz's formulation of ethnic otherness as affective excess is eerily familiar to historians of the Jewish American experience. Like *spic*, anti-Jewish epithets such as *kike*, *yid*, and *sheenie* connoted a Jewishness that exceeded the bounds of white middle-class good taste. Consider Miss Wales in *Gentleman's Agreement*, who seeks to distinguish "good Jews" like herself from "the kikey ones" who "ruin it for the rest of us." The "other kind"—a phrase once common among acculturated American Jews—as Miss Wales explains, talk too loud, dress too outlandishly, wear too much makeup, and, worst of all, talk too much about being Jewish.

This rhetoric of ethnicity as excess offers another way to think about the mechanism and function of double coding. Method acting (and, to a lesser degree, all forms of emotive performance) demands emotional affect that the actor provides in excess of the written play text.[85] And to the degree that the actor's emotion exceeds the written text, the performance challenges the emotionally impoverished "national affect" theorized by Muñoz.

Of course, an emotive performance does not by itself constitute a Jewish-specific performance. Rather, when presented in a double-coded fashion that detaches the emotion from its ethnically Other context and presents it in a context of dramatic realism, Method acting validates the emotional response as normal. When Lee J. Cobb as Willy Loman displayed guilt, frustration, and melancholy in *Death of a Salesman*, the performance deracinated such overt displays of emotion, implicitly arguing for their universality.

In contrast to Kakutani, I believe that the question of Willy Loman's Jewishness (or lack thereof) is not so much obsolete as it is improperly formulated. Rather than asking "Is this character Jewish?" we should be asking "Could this character be Jewish?" The ideal of a universal character, a modern-day Everyman, continues to exert a powerful hold on the imaginations of both practitioners and scholars of performance. For the practitioner, this is almost certainly driven by the mythical goal of reaching a universal audience. Plays, films, and television programs that offer "something for everyone" are more likely to garner acclaim, awards, and financial rewards for the artists and producers who generate them. For the scholar, the question is significantly more complicated. Miller frequently asserted his commitment to the liberal humanist ideal that all human beings share certain fundamental emotions or concerns. But he has also invoked a variety of intellectual antecedents, including Jung's theory of archetypes, Carlyle's definition of the mythological hero, and the scientific concept of microcosm, at various times in support of his approach to drama.[86]

In Willy Loman, then, Miller has created a character that is *inclusively* rather than *exclusively* Jewish. As Brenda Murphy notes:

> Although Miller has never accepted the idea that Willy is a "Jewish role," quite rightly pointing out that the play has been interpreted successfully all over the world and in all kinds of ethnic contexts, his three favorite Willys—Lee J. Cobb, Warren Mitchell, and Dustin Hoffman—have all been Jewish.[87]

The idea of a universal character who *could be* Jewish is perhaps one strategy for mobilizing the potential power of the *unmarked*. As the feminist performance theorist Peggy Phelan argues, the unmarked body's resistance to visual identification is a way of calling attention to the failure of the patriarchal "gaze" to circumscribe, identify, and control one's performance.[88] In practical terms, when the Jewish body in performance (Willy Loman) resists identification as a Jew, we may see a way of acting Jewish that is not already inscribed within an anti-Semitic image of the Jew. It is toward this end that the strategy of double coding functions. The limitation, however, is that the ideal of universality restricts the manifestation of the characters' Jewishness to forms that can be encoded so as not to alienate the non-Jewish audience. A character, such as Molly Goldberg, who speaks English with Yiddish-derived sentence construction can be read by a non-Jewish audience as universal, but a character who speaks Yiddish instead of English is Other. Furthermore, as Phelan notes, the unmarked must be understood as "an *active* vanishing, a deliberate and conscious refusal to take the payoff of visibility. For the moment, active disappearance usually requires at least some recognition of what and who is not there to be effective."[89] Willy Loman's lack of ethnicity, then, is meaningful only to the degree that we recognize that the ethnicity he lacks is Jewishness.

Curiously, it is this recognition that Miller himself highlights in his preface to the fiftieth anniversary edition of *Death of a Salesman*, which was published in 1999, just a few weeks after Kakutani's article. There Miller acknowledges for the first time in print that he originally conceived the Lomans as a Jewish family: "As Jews light-years away from religion or community that might have fostered Jewish identity, [the Lomans] exist in a spot that probably most Americans feel they inhabit—on the sidewalk side of the glass, looking in at a well-lighted place."[90] In terms of the play's narrative, then, it is the lack of connection to his Jewish roots that causes Willy Loman's downfall. Having tried too hard to assimilate, to be well liked, to be American, he is left with no core values or beliefs to call his own.

Even here Miller is drawn to the universal import of the Lomans' identity crisis, attributing it to "most Americans." And yet, for an audience that knows the codes, Willy Loman is more than a man who doesn't know how to act; he's a man who doesn't know how to act Jewish.

CHAPTER 3

Fiddling on the Roof, 1964–1971

IN LATE 1962, the playwright Joseph Stein, composer Jerry Bock, and lyricist Sheldon Harnick began shopping their latest musical creation to the usual Broadway producers. Though Bock and Harnick were coming off the successful *Fiorello!* (1959), and their play was based on the work of the well-known fiction writer Sholem Aleichem, they had a hard time finding a producer who would back them. Stein once remarked, "We showed it to one producer, who shall remain anonymous, who said, 'I love it, but what will we do when we run out of Hadassah benefits?'" In the summer of 1964, at an early preview that was in fact a benefit performance for a Jewish organization, several audience members remarked, "Well, we like it, but I don't know if *they* will like it."[1]

The play was *Fiddler on the Roof*, and it went on to become the (then) longest-running show in Broadway history, spanning eight years and 3,242 performances. Apparently, "they" did like it. But did they enjoy *Fiddler* for the same reason "we" did? Consider, for example, that on the marquee of the Imperial Theatre, the name of Zero Mostel (who played Tevye) was featured prominently above the title. Since in 1964 Mostel was one of the most popular actors on Broadway, having won Tony Awards for his roles in *Rhinoceros* (1961) and *A Funny Thing Happened on the Way to the Forum* (1963), it was not in itself remarkable that he received top billing. But to find the name of Sholem Aleichem, perhaps the single most popular Yiddish fiction writer ever, one would have had to look to the poster at the side of the theater's entrance and scan all the way down to the last line, where the following notice appeared in letters less than one-tenth the size of Mostel's name: "Based on Sholem Aleichem's stories." As Norman Nadel noted in the *New York World-Telegram*, "Never has a theater program printed a larger name in smaller type."[2]

While Nadel goes on to state that Sholem Aleichem "is the giant of this proud and tender musical, and the source of its enchantment,"[3] most of the other New York critics focused their attention (and praise) on Mostel, the show's star. Richard Watts Jr. remarked in the *New York Post* that "his most important achievement is what might be dismissed as a negative one—the salutary way in which he evades the temptation to be excessively sentimental by giving the harried Tevye a salty quality of rebelliousness that scorns the weakness of saccharinity."[4] Curiously, for Watts sentimentality seems to be linked to religion. He further lauds Mostel's Tevye for neglecting "pious ostentation" and for his realistic attitude toward "Divine Providence."[5] While it is always dangerous to generalize from a single case, Watts's comments are emblematic of the mainstream response to the 1964 *Fiddler*. Mostel's Tevye is read as Jewish in ethnic terms (Watts makes frequent use of the word *folklore*), but he is not distinguished by denomination; that is, there seem to be no qualms about projecting a nonspecific (and nonthreatening?) "Judeo-Christian" sort of monotheism onto Tevye, which allows him to function as a universal character for an American audience. Or, to use historian Werner Sollors's terms, for most audiences Tevye's Jewishness is strictly a matter of *descent* (an accident of birth) rather than *consent* (a choice to identify as Jewish).[6]

By contrast, another critic, Howard Taubman, writing in the *New York Times*, called Mostel's Tevye "one of the most glowing creations in the history of the musical theatre," but he put a significantly different slant on the performance.

> Mr. Mostel looks as Tevye should. His full beard is a pious aureole for his shining countenance. The stringly ends of his prayer shawl hang from under his vest. . . . He holds long conversations with God. Although his observations never are disrespectful, they call a spade a spade.[7]

It seems that Taubman, the Jewish critic, and Watts, the gentile, are valuing piety differently. Taubman notes Tevye's pious appearance and praises it, whereas Watts credits Tevye not with impiety per se but with resisting the temptation to demonstrate his piety in an ostentatious or self-congratulatory manner. Where Taubman finds Mostel's Tevye "pious enough" (read: Jewish enough, at least in religious terms) to be the ideal manifestation of Sholem Aleichem's fiction, Watts essentially declares that Tevye is "not so pious" (read: not so Jewish) as to be alien or alienating.

The ability of *Fiddler* to walk the fine line between Jewish enough and too Jewish perhaps explains why the Stein-Bock-Harnick musical gained, and continues to command (in revivals and community theaters), a significant audience among both Jews and gentiles. Unlike earlier dramatic incarnations of the Tevye stories—Sholem Aleichem's 1919 Yiddish-language play *Tevye Der Milkhiger* (Tevye the Dairyman); Maurice Schwartz's 1939 film adaptation of the play, also in Yiddish; Arnold Perl's English-language play *Tevye and His Daughters* (1953); and the television play *The World of Sholem Aleichem* (1959)— *Fiddler* was self-consciously constructed to cater to a dual audience. The way in which it negotiates this dual appeal to Jewish and gentile audiences is a prime example of a phenomenon I call the double coding of Jewish American popular performance.

Stuart Hall, in his oft-cited essay "Encoding and Decoding in Television Discourse," invokes a communications model of mass culture in which ideological messages are produced, circulated, consumed, and (subsequently) reproduced.[8] Meaning originates with the producer. In order to be communicated, this meaning is translated, or encoded, into a discursive form: the message. On the receiving end, the consumer must then meaningfully decode this message. The consumer, in turn, reproduces, or enacts, the decoded meaning, completing the communicative event.

Hall recognizes that the meaning encoded by the producer may not (and frequently does not) correspond to the meaning decoded by the consumer.

> The degrees of symmetry, that is, the degrees of "understanding" and "misunderstanding" in the communicative exchange— depend on the degrees of symmetry/asymmetry (relations of equivalence) established between the positions of the "personifications", encoder-producer and decoder-receiver. But this in turn depends on the degrees of identity/non-identity between the codes which perfectly or imperfectly transmit, interrupt or systematically distort what has been transmitted. . . . What are called "distortions'" or "misunderstandings" arise precisely from the *lack of equivalence* between the two sides in the communicative exchange.[9]

Therefore, argues Hall, while most interpretive analyses (especially in theater studies) focus on the message itself (the circulation phase), it is important to note that the processes of encoding and decoding are "determinate moments" in the communication of meaning. A message (and by extension a performance) is polysemic: it can result in multiple meanings, each dependent on the "reading positions" of the decoder-consumer.

Since, for Hall, television (but also theater and film) is presumed to originate from and serve the interests of the corporate structures that constitute the "dominant cultural order," there is a de facto ordering of reading positions. The reading of a performance that corresponds most closely to the producers' intent is considered to be "correct"; Hall calls this the "dominant-hegemonic" reading position. This reading operates inside the dominant cultural codes and serves to reproduce the dominant cultural order. Hall defines the dominant, or hegemonic, code as one that "defines within its terms the mental horizon, the universe, of possible meanings, for a whole sector of relations in a society or culture" and "carries with it the stamp of legitimacy—it appears coterminous with what is 'natural', 'inevitable', 'taken for granted' about the social order."[10]

If, for example, the dominant meaning encoded in *Fiddler on the Roof* is that Jews must adapt their "tradition" to changing times, then an audience reading the performance through the dominant code would fully accept this meaning and act (or continue to act) in a manner consistent with the message. Seth Wolitz suggests something like this when he describes the character of Tevye in *Fiddler* as the "personification of the Jewish immigrant" who "affirms the Jewish-American mythos of *Jewish adaptability and continuity*."[11]

On the other hand, suggests Hall, "it is possible for a viewer to understand both the literal and connotative inflection given by a discourse but to decode the message in a globally contradictory way."[12] That is, a consumer may consciously and oppositionally reject either the claim to truth of a message (that's not the way it really is) or its inevitability (that's not the way it should be). Thus, an audience member may dismiss *Fiddler* as fantasy, as Walter Kerr did when he wrote in the *New York Herald Tribune* that "it might be an altogether charming musical if only the people of Anatevka did not pause every now and then to give their regards to Broadway, with remembrances to Herald Square."[13] Or a viewer may complain that Tevye should emigrate not to America but to Israel, taking issue with the dominant reading, which presents the United States as a natural destination for diasporic Jews.[14]

In practice, however, many (if not most) audiences read the messages of mass culture through what Hall calls a negotiated code or position. They understand clearly the dominant ideology encoded within the message, but they selectively change or discard this ideology in the enactment/reproduction stage of the communication. This happens, Hall suggests, because the dominant code is, by definition, general and "global," while the situation in which the consumer enacts the message is specific and local. So consumers, while acknowledging the privileged status of the dominant reading, nevertheless decode the message in ways that they find practically applicable to their own situations.

In the case of *Fiddler*, an audience member might acknowledge that adaptation to change is necessary but be less willing to accept such change in practice. For example, Tevye's adaptability is signified in the play by his willingness to accept his three daughters' marriages to (in turn) a poor man—and his daughter's choice rather than a traditionally arranged match—a radical, and a gentile. This last example, Chava's interfaith marriage, has been the most contentious issue in the musical, as well as in Sholem Aleichem's stories,[15] and consequently it was delicately finessed by the producers.[16] Indeed, it is arguable that in the stage version of *Fiddler* Tevye does not so much accept the union of Chava and the Russian Fyedka as he endures it, though this scene is played differently in the film version, as I will discuss later in this chapter. The dominant message, that love is more important than strict adherence to tradition, is likely to be understood by all. But how will they react when their own child announces an impending union to a member of a traditionally undesirable group?

Significantly, Hall notes that the "'selective perception'" that characterizes a negotiated reading position "is almost never as selective, random or privatized as the concept suggests. The patterns exhibit, across individual variants, significant clusterings."[17] These clusterings may correspond to what literary critic Stanley Fish has termed "interpretive communities."[18] Fish's idea of a "community of readers" represents an attempt to reposition the power to authenticate a given reading away from the text (or the message in Hall's model) itself. As Marvin Carlson writes, in extending the idea of community of readers to include theater audiences:

> A particularly self-conscious model of such communities may be found in the world of academic criticism in America, where new interpretations are tested against the norms of various reading communities and are given intersubjective validity by these communities. Readings are thus ultimately authenticated not by the text, but by the community.[19]

According to Carlson, the simple act of assembling for the purpose of experiencing a given performance is enough to turn a theater audience into a "'community of readers', socially defined, which shares common values and determines collectively the norms and conventions according to which individual readings will take place."[20] This is a limited case, but it points up the strategic and provisional quality of such community affiliations.

Carlson further suggests that "what the audience brings to the theater in the way of expectations, assumptions and strategies" will influence the "productive activation" of the dramatic text.[21] To the degree that Jews as a group share "expectations, assumptions and strategies" it should therefore be possible to speak of a Jewish reading of a performance or set of performances. This reading, though fraught with analytical and political pitfalls (Who sets the agenda for this reading? What makes it Jewish?), would involve a negotiation with the dominant codes of mass culture. It acknowledges the limits within which the message of the performance has been encoded, but it also employs its own decoding strategies to extract a meaning that has social value within the Jewish community.

But the idea of "strategic reading formations" has much greater potential.[22] The boundaries of the Jewish community in America are hotly contested.[23] Thus, as noted in chapter 1, Jonathan Boyarin calls for a new formulation of Jewish identity, which he calls a critical post-Judaism: "I mean to name an already-existing but unidentified commonality, a way of being Jewish 'otherwise than Being.'"[24] We might also read *critical*, in this context, in the sense of both urgent and important, given the degree to which debates within the Jewish community over the definition of *Jewishness* have escalated in recent years.

Reading Jewish, as the audience-based counterpart to acting Jewish, may provide the answer to Boyarin's call for a critical post-Judaism. By maintaining links to the "expectations, assumptions and strategies" of religious Judaism and/or ethnic Jewish culture, such a Jewish community of readers is neither arbitrary nor necessarily based in victimization. Since membership in this Jewish community is defined by an active choice of reading strategy, it is provisional, contested, and multireal. The same individual can be read as a Jew or a gentile. In fact, if the spectator is so inclined, a character may be read as *both* Jewish and gentile, concurrently or consecutively. Nor is this community exclusively Jewish as much as it is inclusively Jewish. To the extent that this decoding and reproduction of Jewish-specific meanings is itself a performative act, the Jewish community of readers comes to be defined by the negotiated codes it employs to read the performance. So, as was discussed in chapter 1, it is not necessary to be or identify as Jewish in order to be a Jewish reader; it is simply necessary to be literate in the requisite codes. However, because these codes are culturally informed, those readers who have been exposed to Jewish American culture through consent, descent, or simple proximity will have a better chance of recognizing them. Conversely, Jewish audiences whose experience has denied them access to this culture (think of Lenny Bruce's hypothetical Jew in Butte, Montana) will not.

The natural corollary of a Jewish community of readers would seem to be a non-Jewish or gentile community. In fact, the very idea of a gentile community is meaningful only to Jews; it is an imaginary construction: the "they" about whom "we" speculate whether "they" will like or accept a given demonstration of acting Jewish. Except in limited situations in which most participants are assumed to be Jewish unless they identify otherwise (e.g., in a synagogue), no individual refers to himself or herself as "gentile" or "goyish."[25]

Still, one might profitably compare the negotiated codes by which the Jewish community reads a performance with the dominant codes that presumably constitute the hegemonic or "correct" reading strategies. Hall's formulation conflates the use of dominant codes, which simply means a decoding that extracts from a performance the producers' preferred or idealized reading, with the idea of a dominant culture, which seeks to preserve its status at the top of the social hierarchy. This may be sufficient in a society where only members of the dominant culture have access to the means of mass cultural production. But in the case of American Jews, a minority group that is arguably a powerful force within the American entertainment industry, the concepts of dominant reading and dominant culture must be separated.[26]

Specifically, I would argue that, while Jewish American artists are complicit in (and perhaps the driving force behind) the dominant encoding of meaning into a performance, at the decoding end of the communication, the Jewish community of readers is clearly a minority and must adopt a negotiated reading position toward mass culture. Hall argues that a negotiated or oppositional reading of mass culture is necessary when there is asymmetry, a social disjunction, between the producer and the consumer. In the case of Jewish American audiences reading performances by Jewish American artists, however, there is a potential symmetry between producer and consumer.

In Hall's linear model of social status (e.g. a totem pole), this would represent a co-optation of the minority artist by the mass cultural apparatus. Or, in simpler terms, we might say that this apparent disjuncture between Jewish American cultural producers and Jewish American consumers shows that the Jewish artists have "assimilated" or "sold out." Faced with the economic necessity of producing entertainment that will appeal to an idealized "American culture," Jewish American artists internalize the dominant culture, encoding their messages in such a way as to force Jewish American consumers—who share Jewish social conventions and norms with the producers—to adopt a negotiated reading position toward the performance. This is the prevailing narrative delineated in "Jewish cultural studies." Daniel and Jonathan Boyarin, for example, write in their introduction to *Jews and Other Differences: The New Jewish Cultural Studies:*

> Jews, who as a group have clearly achieved enormous economic success in the United States as well as accumulating cultural capital, whether in Hollywood or in Harvard Square, have done so by and large at the cost of deculturation. That deculturation is itself a source of pain and loss, vague and anecdotal at times, overwhelming at others.[27]

While it is certainly true that many successful Jewish artists in theater, film, and television have minimized the importance of Jewish religion and ethnicity in their lives and work, it seems both unfair and simplistic to evaluate this phenomenon purely in terms of pain and loss. The violence implied by such a narrative—deculturation is forced on the Jews or alternatively Jews have allowed themselves to be deculturated through avarice or self-loathing—forecloses any attempt to explore the widely complex and detailed tapestry of Jewish experience on both the production and consumption ends of the American entertainment industry. Moreover, it presupposes and perpetuates an oppositional relationship between authentic and inauthentic Jews that is neither good politics nor good theory.

I would argue, by contrast, that Jewish American cultural producers frequently employ a strategy of *negotiated encoding* when they create their performances. As Carlson points out, when we talk about the reading of a performance, "We are really speaking . . . of two readings, and thus of two simultaneous 'productive activations': that of the performance itself, and that of the audience."[28] In moving from text to performance, the Jewish actor, the Jewish director, and the Jewish writer *must first be Jewish readers.* Before the audience had a chance to employ its various reading strategies to *Fiddler on the Roof,* for example, Stein, Bock, and Harnick applied their reading strategies to Sholem Aleichem's Tevye stories. Moreover, director Jerome Robbins and each of the actors generated their own readings of the *Fiddler* script. The minority, or nondominant, status of the Jewish American artist, combined with the inherently collaborative nature of dramatic performance, means that what Hall calls the encoding stage of the communication is as much a site of negotiation as is the decoding stage.

In my adaptation of Hall's model, there are at least two codes operating at both the encoding and decoding moments of the communicative process. There is a dominant code, which typically naturalizes and legitimates a generic monotheism and the erasure of ethnic specificity, but there is also a Jewish code, which can be decoded by Jewish American audiences—that is, by those who know how to read this code—and goes more or less unremarked by a gentile audience. The term I employ to describe this phenomenon is *double coding*.

In practice, the use of double coding may produce a play like *Fiddler*, which is Jewish enough for a Jewish American audience, but not so Jewish as to challenge the dominant American culture. "We" (Jews) like it, but "they" (gentiles) also like it. Because of the double-coded nature of the performance, however, we may respond positively to very different elements of *Fiddler* than they do. Consider the following two responses to the song, "If I Were a Rich Man," in which the poverty-stricken Tevye, played by Zero Mostel, imagines what his life would be like if he could afford all the things he desires. Walter Kerr writes:

> But he [Tevye] does permit himself one small musical daydream ("If I Were a Rich Man") and when Mr. Mostel dreams he dreams in vocalized snuggles, not in words. For every other line of the lyric he simply substitutes gratified gargles and coos until he has arrived, mystically, at a kind of cabalistic coloratura. The effect is what we all had in mind when we last thought of satisfaction in depth.[29]

Kerr's analysis is an example of a dominant reading. He interprets the nonverbal parts of Tevye's song as *snuggles, gargles,* and *coos,* terms that are ethnically and religiously nonspecific. The phrase "cabalistic coloratura," playfully combining Jewish and operatic designations, is a backhanded compliment, invoking the absurd image of an operatic cabalist. The adverb *mystically* suggests an exoticization of Mostel's performance but also that Tevye's ethnicity is malleable, and (perhaps) not all that important. This is further reinforced when Kerr calls the effect of this vocal performance "what we all had in mind," implicitly universalizing both the form and the content of the song.

Howard Taubman describes the same number this way: "When Mr. Mostel sings "If I Were a Rich Man," interpolating passages of cantillation in the manner of prayer, his Tevye is both devout and pungently realistic."[30]

This passage is an example of a Jewish reading. Taubman decodes the song's nonverbal syllables as *cantillation*, a term specific to liturgical music that strongly connotes Jewish liturgical music. Actually, the song as performed by Mostel contains both nonsense noise (gargles and coos) and quasi-liturgical chanting (cantillation): the latter when Tevye muses on the opportunity to devote himself to scholarship and rabbinic thought, the former when he imitates the barnyard animals he imagines owning.[31] Yet it is significant that Kerr chooses to characterize the song by the sounds of the farm, while Taubman characterizes it by the sounds of the synagogue. Whereas Kerr regards the number as a "day-dream," Taubman hears it "in the manner of prayer." Taubman's read-ing reminds us that to a Jewish community of readers the tradition on which life in Anatevka is based is not some generic "old country" prac-tice, but Judaism. His view of Tevye as "devout and pungently realistic" is a far cry from that of Kerr, who praises but ultimately dismisses "If I Were a Rich Man" as a whimsical fantasy.

Such a Jewish reading of a performance should not be confused with what Henry Jenkins terms "textual poaching." In Jenkins's study of sci-ence fiction fandom, he argues (after Michel de Certeau), that con-sumers of mass culture construct alternate readings of performances in response to a perceived asymmetry between themselves and the pro-ducers. Science fiction fans, writes Jenkins, "operate from a position of cultural marginality and social weakness."[32] Frustrated by a mass cul-tural message that does not conform to the norms and conventions by which they choose to live, and by their own lack of access to the means of cultural production, the fans create an alternative message, which freely and selectively adapts the signs of the performance to meet their own needs for social reenactment. These textual poachers, Jenkins sug-gests, "are selective users of a vast media culture whose treasures, though corrupt, hold wealth that can be mined and refined for alterna-tive uses."[33] The term *poaching* therefore implies an adversarial rela-tionship between the producers and consumers of mass culture. And in the not so subtle moral calculus of Jenkins's argument the poachers are the valiant underdogs working against a sinister and overwhelming cul-ture industry.[34]

By contrast, double coding can be understood as a cooperative proj-ect in which both the producers and the consumers of the performance share access to the same cultural codes. Consider, as an example, the hand gesture made famous by the character of Mr. Spock (Leonard Nimoy) in the television (and film) series *Star Trek*. The series was ini-tially broadcast on NBC from 1966 to 1969, placing it squarely between the stage (1964) and film (1971) versions of *Fiddler*. Nimoy writes:

For what would soon be known as the Vulcan salute, I borrowed a hand symbol from Orthodox Judaism. During the High Holiday services, the *Kohanim* (who are the priests) bless those in attendance. As they do, they extend the palms of both hands over the congregation, with thumbs outstretched and the middle and ring fingers parted so that each hand forms two vees. This gesture symbolizes the Hebrew letter *shin*, the first letter in the word *Shaddai*, "Lord"; in the Jewish *Qabala*, *shin* also represents eternal Spirit.[35]

In Nimoy's performance of this gesture as the character of Spock, there are at least three possible interpretations of this simple sign, each corresponding to a particular reading position.

1. The dominant reader, with no framework in which to put this sign to use, either ignores it or grasps, through context, that it is a gesture of greeting. If the reader is particularly observant (or a regular watcher of *Star Trek*), he or she may note that it is a gesture used primarily by Vulcans, characters that are decidedly Other, since they are not human.

2. The poacher, familiar with the internal codes of *Star Trek*, notes that Spock has performed the Vulcan salute, a fact that may or may not be important to understanding the scene being played. Noting that the gesture is culturally specific within the context of *Star Trek*, the poacher attaches meaning to it as part of a speculation about Vulcan culture.[36] The poacher also repeats the gesture among the members of his or her peer group. They may exchange Vulcan salutes in greeting as a sign of in-group status—the in-group being *Star Trek* fans rather than Vulcans. Jenkins, in fact, notes this exact phenomenon: fans "greet each other with the Vulcan Salute."[37]

3. A Jewish reader, while conscious of the gesture's meaning in the context of *Star Trek*, also understands it to be a gesture used by Jews. He or she may experience a small self-congratulatory pleasure at this recognition and may even feel a brief moment of kinship with the character, Spock, or the actor, Nimoy. The Jewish reader may also associate the contextual meaning of the Vulcan salute with its original meaning (a benediction) and therefore interpret the scene somewhat differently than the non-Jewish reader does. In the extreme case, the character's use of a Jewish-specific gesture in this context might provoke the Jewish reader to infer a parallel between

Spock, the only nonhuman member of the *Enterprise* crew, and his or her own experience as a Jew in a largely gentile milieu. Jeffrey Shandler provides a reading of Spock along these lines in his *While America Watches: Televising the Holocaust*.[38] (It should be noted that an Orthodox Jew, if he or she were watching *Star Trek* at all, would almost certainly be struck by the impropriety of using this very private and sacred ritual gesture in this fashion.)

This third reading illustrates how double coding functions. The Jewish reading of a performance created by a Jewish American artist is in fact based on selective perception, but the signs that the Jewish American audience perceives are based on a correspondingly selective encoding by the producers. And this coded communication is, like the Vulcan salute, based not on a preexisting moment of mutual agreement between sender and receiver but on a shared cultural experience that gives both parties the information necessary to understand the sign in a mutually specific way.

Ultimately, however, it is the presence of the recognizably Jewish code, not the artist's intent, that determines an audience's ability (or inability) to recognize (or imagine) Jewishness in a performance. Moreover, it is quite rare that the artist's intent is a matter of public record, as is Nimoy's. In most cases, *reading Jewish* means employing a largely unconscious complex of codes that cross-check each other. Jeffrey Shandler has playfully theorized this process as "a 'sliding scale' index for the virtual Jewishness of characters, with results as complex and inconsistent as the debate over 'who is a Jew' in the 'real world.'"[39] Mr. Spock, though explicitly not a Jew (nor even human) would seem to score high on the virtual Jewishness scale because "the actor who plays him is Jewish, his Vulcan hand salute is derived from the gesture made by *kohanim* . . . he works for the Federation . . . [and] if Vulcan logic is symbolic of anything, surely it must be Talmudic sophistry!"[40]

Because of the degree to which the American entertainment industry seeks to imitate its own successes, as well as the degree to which other ethnic groups share certain social conventions with American Jews, it is possible (perhaps even likely) for a non-Jewish artist to produce a performance that employs codes that Jewish audiences identify as Jewish. The Vulcan salute has been repeated literally dozens (if not hundreds) of times by Jewish and non-Jewish actors in subsequent episodes of *Star Trek*, as well as its follow-up series *Star Trek: The Next Generation*, the various *Star Trek* films, and so on. It is worth noting, as an example of how textual poaching can recirculate within popular culture, that Robin Williams adapted the Vulcan salute as a gesture of greeting for his character Mork from Ork on the post–*Star Trek* sitcom *Mork and Mindy* (American Broadcasting Companies [ABC], 1979–82). Certainly many of these actors did not know the history of the gesture, nor did they all share the cultural experience that allows a Jewish viewer to decode the sign in such a negotiated fashion. But because (1) the Jewish reading position is negotiated, (2) the performance is polysemic, and (3) the authentication of meaning comes not from the text but from the "community of readers," the latent meaning in the gesture can still be decoded. Or, to put it another way, the Vulcan salute may not be exclusively Jewish, but it is inclusively Jewish.

As Hall points out, *polysemic* should not be confused with *pluralistic;* just because a performance is open to multiple readings does not mean that *any* meaning may be extracted from it. A negotiated or even oppositional reading of a performance can only decode the signs that are present in the message (or circulation) stage of the communicative process. As Hall states, "Unless they are wildly aberrant, encoding will have the effect of constructing some of the limits and parameters in which decoding operates."[41] If Nimoy had chosen some other gesture to use for the Vulcan salute, Spock's Jewishness would not be an issue.

An overwhelming number of Jewish artists and critics, in fact, insist that their work is universal. Norman Nadel's review of *Fiddler on the Roof,* for example, explicitly states, "You don't have to be Jewish to love Tevye."[42] While this may be true, why does Nadel feel compelled to make such a disclaimer? Do we ever see reviews that declare, "You don't have to be Danish to love Hamlet!" or "You don't have to be Anglican to love Henry VIII!"? Yet this kind of denial of cultural specificity is itself an example of double coding, for in the same breath the claim of universality is accompanied by the act of identification. The unspoken coda to "You don't have to be Jewish to love Tevye" is "but it helps."[43]

It helps, because *Fiddler* employs many Jewish codes: elements of performance that are recognizable to Jewish readers because they reflect the actual (or rather *an* actual) Jewish community. American Jews in the Broadway audience of 1964 may have recognized Tevye's speech patterns, for example, as those of their parents or grandparents. They may even have recognized the song "A Sabbath Prayer" as a near-literal translation of the traditional Hebrew blessing said over children on Shabbat. But other aspects of the performance may be read by Jews as Jewish simply because they have recognized enough to understand the characters as Jewish.[44] The musical then becomes a kind of exercise in popular ethnography by the producers, leading to a reification of acting Jewish that starts for the audience with the identifying label rather than the action being identified.[45] The characters are Jews, reasons the audience member. Therefore, their actions are representative of acting Jewish.

In this way, the Jewish community of readers comes to be defined, in a very real sense, by the codes themselves: you are Jewish if and only if you know how to read the proper codes. To put it another way, the codes that are recognizably Jewish come, through the ongoing negotiation between audiences and performances, to define what it means to act Jewish. Thus, the different ways in which acting Jewish is encoded become very important. They are, to use Boyarin's term, "critical" to the formulation of Jewish American identity in the postwar era. The remainder of this chapter will explore two such ways of acting Jewish by comparing the stage and screen incarnations of Tevye in *Fiddler on the Roof*.

The Men Who Would Be Tevye

When *Fiddler on the Roof* opened on Broadway in 1964, helmed by the Jewish director Jerome Robbins, the leading role of Tevye was performed by the veteran character actor Zero Mostel. Mostel, a Jewish American actor, was forty-nine years old. When the gentile director Norman Jewison brought *Fiddler* to the silver screen in 1971, the role of Tevye was played by an Israeli actor, Topol, who was thirty-five years old. The film version became one of the most commercially successful movie musicals of all time and subsequent revivals of the stage version enjoyed moderate success on Broadway in 1976 (with Mostel as Tevye), 1981 (with Herschel Bernardi), and 1990 (with Topol). As of this writing, a 40th anniversary production is currently running on Broadway, featuring Alfred Molina, whose performance as Tevye is discussed later in this chapter. Through the phenomenal success of *Fiddler* on both stage and screen, Sholem Aleichem's Tevye the Dairyman has become one of the most recognizable Jewish characters in American popular culture.

Seth Wolitz, in "The Americanization of Tevye," traces the development of the character of Tevye through his various stage and screen incarnations. According to Wolitz: "Each Tevye recasts Jewish cultural history according to a contemporary ideology in order to absorb the pain-laden past of Tsarist Russia, the Holocaust, and Americanization."[46] Thus, for Sholem Aleichem, Tevye represents a tragic figure clinging to Jewish tradition in a changing Russia, while in *Fiddler* Tevye is a transitional figure, foreshadowing the "Americanization" of the Jews in the post–World War II United States. Wolitz calls the Tevye of *Fiddler* "the personification of the Jewish immigrant and the universal grandfather of Jewish America."[47]

Wolitz's analysis, while insightful in many ways, is limited by his theoretical position as a literary critic. He purports to compare and contrast different Tevyes, but what he really does is compare different iterations of the Tevye stories. Wolitz's analysis is text based, and while he acknowledges certain distinctions between the stage and screen versions of *Fiddler* these distinctions are made on the narrative level; he does not consider the actor who plays the role of Tevye. Why is this a limitation? As a universal Jewish character and a widely popular figure, Tevye is the foremost example of what it means to act Jewish in American popular drama. Yet, although the character of Tevye is universal in many ways, the actor playing the role is necessarily specific. Each actor who plays Tevye infuses the character with his own personality, physicality, and tonality. This is true even if an actor self-consciously tries to imitate another actor's performance. Luther Adler, who replaced Mostel as Tevye on Broadway in 1967, was not the same character as Mostel in 1964 or Topol in 1971 (or, for that matter, Leonard Nimoy, who made his professional stage debut as Tevye in a seven-week summer production of *Fiddler* on Cape Cod in 1971).[48] Differences between the performances of specific actors in the role of Tevye can and do lead to differences in the way acting Jewish is perceived by both Jews and gentiles. Recognizing the importance of the individual actor to the production of meaning within a performance, in the following pages I consider the work of the two "definitive" Tevyes: the stage Tevye of Mostel and the screen Tevye of Topol. Both Mostel and Topol put their own stamp on the role, and both continue to be associated more closely with Tevye than any other role either has played, before or since.

Unlike earlier incarnations of the Tevye stories, *Fiddler* gained, and continues to command, a significant audience among both Jews and gentiles. Hence, the Tevye of *Fiddler* carries a double significance. What the gentile audience likes about Tevye and what the Jewish audience likes about Tevye are somewhat different—and what Tevye signifies for both audiences onscreen is different from what he signifies onstage. It is the explication and analysis of these differences that constitute the remainder of this chapter.

An actor's performance and an audience's reception of it do not exist in a vacuum. When Zero Mostel stepped onto the stage at the Imperial Theatre in 1964, the critics' and audience's perceptions of Tevye were necessarily colored by their knowledge of Mostel's public persona. Born Samuel Joel Mostel in the Brownsville section of Brooklyn in 1915 and raised on the Lower East Side of Manhattan, Zero Mostel began his performing career as a stand-up comic.[49] During the 1940s, he commanded up to two thousand dollars for a single performance, playing New York nightclubs and Catskill resorts. His act was based primarily on physical comedy, especially impressions and pantomime.

His fortunes took a turn for the worse during the McCarthy period. Mostel, who was not a communist but had performed at rallies and benefits for a number of left-wing organizations, including the Communist Party of Boston, was one of sixty-eight actors listed in the book *Red Channels: The Report of Communist Influence in Radio and Television* in 1950. In 1952, a screenwriter named Martin Berkeley claimed to have met Mostel at a Communist Party meeting in Hollywood in 1938. The fact that Mostel had not visited California in 1938 was not enough to prevent him from being blacklisted.

Unable to find acting work for several years, Mostel returned to his first career (as a painter), and between occasional sales of his paintings and what little money his wife (the actress Kate Harkin) was able to bring in from her stage work he managed to survive, barely. Testifying before the House Un-American Activities Committee in 1955, Mostel was asked: "You are also known by 'Zero' as a nickname, are you not?" "Yes sir," he replied, "After my financial standing in the community, sir."[50]

In the late 1950s, Mostel began a comeback, working in the off-Broadway theater, which was not as susceptible to the pressures of the blacklist. He scored a huge critical success in 1958 as Leopold Bloom in an adaptation of James Joyce's *Ulysses*, a role that brought him an Obie award for Best Actor. In 1959, as the blacklist began to lose power, Mostel got back on television by appearing in *The World of Sholem Aleichem*, a screen version of Arnold Perl's play based on the same stories Stein, Bock, and Harnick would use to create *Fiddler*. First broadcast on nonprofit Channel 13 in New York and later shown in large cities around the country, *The World of Sholem Aleichem* helped put Mostel back into the minds of casting agents. But in 1960, while trying out a play called *The Good Soup* in Philadelphia, Mostel was hit by a bus. He refused to allow doctors to amputate his left leg, and spent six months in the hospital, enduring several reconstructive operations that would allow him to walk.

Remarkably, Mostel rebounded and was cast in the American premier of Eugne Ionesco's *Rhinoceros* in 1960—a role for which he won the first of a remarkable three Best Actor Tony awards in five years. In

1962, he opened Stephen Sondheim's *A Funny Thing Happened on the Way to the Forum* and stayed in the show for fifteen months, winning his second Tony along the way. Now at the top of the theater world, Mostel was an easy choice for the producers of *Fiddler*, though they also considered Danny Kaye, Danny Thomas, Alan King, and (according to Harnick) even Frank Sinatra.[51] But they offered the part to Mostel, and after hearing the score and meeting with the writers he decided to accept the challenge. To return to the distinction between the Jewish audience (us) and the gentile audience (them), "we" may have come to *Fiddler* for the subject matter, but "they" came to see Mostel.

The New York critics, who consisted almost exclusively of "them," were occasionally lukewarm about the play itself, but they gushed over Mostel's performance. The *New York Post* review was headlined "The Brilliance of Zero Mostel."[52] The *Journal-American* declared, "Mostel Makes Musical Tick."[53] The *New York Times*, beneath the headline "Theater: Mostel as Tevye in 'Fiddler on the Roof,'" declared "If Sholem Aleichem had known Zero Mostel, he would have chosen him, one is sure, for Tevye" and "They [Mostel and Tevye] were ordained to be one."[54] The *Times* review is especially significant because the author, Howard Taubman, a Jewish critic, refers to Sholem Aleichem to authenticate Mostel's performance. Since the original stories specifically describe Tevye as thin, even gaunt, and Mostel weighed close to three hundred pounds, Taubman is obviously addressing a more fundamental kinship between Mostel and Tevye than simple physical resemblance.

Taking the second point first, Mostel clearly put his own stamp on the character—giving a performance so distinctive and moving that it would be virtually impossible to imagine anyone else playing the role. Indeed, in virtually every subsequent professional production, including the film, and many amateur ones, Tevye has been played by a heavyset (or heavily padded) actor. Mostel put his mark on the role in other ways as well. For example, the song "If I Were a Rich Man" was written only after he was cast in the role and was designed to take advantage of his comic talents. Mostel is credited with the "cantorial" nonsense syllables that make up the bulk of the song and also with preserving its bittersweet ending, where Tevye declares that the best thing about being rich would be more free time "to sit in the synagogue and pray." Lyricist Sheldon Harnick recalled in a 1983 symposium on *Fiddler*:

Along the way, I got scared. The end of it [the song] is very serious, and I wondered if it were too serious. I suggested that we cut it and end on a funnier note. Zero screamed. He said, 'No! These lines—they *are* this man. You must leave them, you must!' He was so forceful about it that we decided to go with his instincts.⁵⁵

In a more recent interview with the *Jewish Journal*, Harnick went so far as to say that he was concerned in 1964 that the show as a whole was "too Jewish," which may also have motivated his desire to cut the verse.⁵⁶ Yet, Harnick added, Mostel "was absolutely right."⁵⁷ Mostel also created his own staging for "If I Were a Rich Man." The distinguishing characteristic of it was that Mostel needed to rest his injured leg, so he performed most of the song seated on his wagon, on a milk can, and so on. Subsequent actors with two good legs have preserved Mostel's choreography.⁵⁸

Mostel's bulk, combined with his injured leg and his desire to respect Tevye's serious side, creates an image of Tevye as a man worn down by life. As Walter Kerr noted in the *New York Herald Tribune*, Mostel's Tevye is "less Mother Courage than Father Complaint."⁵⁹ Yet Mostel was also a gifted comic, and so his weary complaints came across as a sort of good-natured fatalism. What does this mean in terms of acting Jewish?

This question is further complicated by Mostel's well-known background as a nightclub comic, as the star of *A Funny Thing Happened on the Way to the Forum*, and as a blacklisted artist. In *The Haunted Stage*, Carlson suggests that the performance of a given actor in a role is inevitably "haunted" by the "ghosts" of his previous roles because "audience members typically see many of the same actors in many different productions, and they will inevitably carry some memory of those actors from production to production."⁶⁰ For many audience members, then, their decoding of Mostel's performance as Tevye was haunted by their memories of his earlier acting work in *Forum* and *Rhinoceros*, as well as his stand-up comedy. Moreover, given the star billing and celebrity status that Mostel had achieved by 1964, even audiences that had not seen his previous stage work may have brought prior ideas about Mostel to bear on their reading of Tevye. As Carlson notes, in the case of particularly famous actors, "It is quite possible that their [the audience members'] reception has been in fact significantly conditioned by the actor's celebrity, ghosting their reception even in the absence of previous theater experience."⁶¹ Mostel's manner of acting Jewish, then, is colored by his own history of acting. His Tevye carries with him a certain amount of extratextual baggage. In the body of Mostel, Tevye becomes a little more vulgar, a little more liberal, perhaps even a little more subversive than Sholem Aleichem's literary Tevye.

Thus, when Taubman of the *Times* declared that Mostel and Tevye "were ordained to be one," he was not simply praising the actor's skill or the production's verisimilitude; he was (though he may not have been conscious of it) also conferring an aura of traditional authenticity, through the association with Sholem Aleichem, on Mostel's public persona. Wisecracking, New York accented, and world-weary are all apparently authentic components of acting Jewish.

On the other hand, a Tevye haunted by the once blacklisted Mostel occupied a very delicate position, especially for a Jew, in the cold war era. When Mostel's Tevye allowed himself to show fondness (tempered with cynicism) toward the revolutionary character Perchik, an audience familiar with Mostel's career may well have read more into both Tevye's sympathy for the communist cause and his melancholy at the young man's prospects as a member of the family. This is not to say that the presence of Mostel in the role made the character of Tevye a communist but rather that the ghost of Mostel's blacklisting cast a shadow over this portion of the performance and may have helped to reinscribe the stereotype of the Jew as subversive. Wolitz notes this possibility, though he argues that Tevye's leftward leanings are more tenable against the backdrop of the civil rights movement and the Kennedy and Johnson administrations.[62] Certainly a New York audience of the 1960s would have been unlikely to hold such sympathies against either Tevye or *Fiddler;* indeed, if we accept the right-wing stereotype that 1960s New York culture was corrupted in part by Jews and communists, we might go so far as to speculate that *Fiddler* was a hit because, rather than in spite of, its associations with both groups.

In all seriousness, when we consider the degree to which Mostel's past performances affected the *Fiddler* audience's perceptions of Tevye, we see another possible conduit for the process of double coding. For a Jewish audience, Mostel's background fit in well with a preexisting character type—the sharp-tongued schlemiel—which may not have tracked precisely with its preconceptions of Tevye the Dairyman but at least did not overtly contradict them. The Tevye of *Fiddler* in 1964 was Jewish enough to satisfy a Jewish audience in part because Mostel himself was. On the other hand, for a gentile audience the blacklisting of Mostel may have actually sanitized Tevye for their consumption. First, because of the interruption of his career by the blacklist, gentile and conservative audiences were likely to be less aware of (and their decoding process less haunted by) Mostel's earlier, raunchier, nightclub work. Second, the fact that Mostel had been through the gauntlet of HUAC hearings and subsequently returned to Broadway may have indicated to some audience members a kind of ritual purification; he once was lost and now is found. The significant press interest in his near-crippling injury and miraculous recovery lent itself neatly to this kind of redemption narrative: Mostel as recovered sinner. Finally, the comedic and habitually weary nature of Mostel's public persona would not seem to pose much of a threat to the established social order. In a gentile reading, acting Jewish as typified by Mostel means, arguably, accepting the role of court jester: comical, "rebellious" (as Watts declares), but ultimately harmless—which is to say not too Jewish.

The question of how Mostel's persona would haunt Tevye may have been on the mind of Norman Jewison when he chose Topol for the 1971 film version of *Fiddler*. Jewison—who was, as Peter Stone called him, "a gentile in all but his name"—told an interviewer that he felt Mostel was not well suited to the film medium.[63] He was, perhaps, "too big," his facial gestures too emotive for the large screen. As we saw in chapter 2, however, this idea of an excessive performance presence has often been linked to performers that are perceived as "too ethnic." Joseph Stein has suggested that Jewison, concerned about giving a sensitive portrayal of Jews, wanted an actor who was less of a peasant.[64] Did Jewison, with a kind of backhanded cultural sensitivity, intentionally choose a Tevye who would be less stereotypically Jewish than Mostel?

A less conspiratorial reading suggests that Jewison, who is English, may have chosen Topol because he was more familiar with the 1967 London production, in which Topol starred, than with Mostel's version. But it is also worth noting that Topol, who was born Chaim Topol in Israel in 1935, was only thirty-five when shooting began on the film. At the time, he was largely unknown in the United States, having appeared only briefly in a couple of art films. In other words, Topol may have been attractive to Jewison precisely because his performance was unlikely to be received through the filter of the audience's preconceptions. It is certainly not uncommon for directors to prefer working with relatively unknown actors, fearing that the celebrity persona of an established star will disrupt the illusion they seek to create in the performance. In fact, Jewison has often adopted this strategy during his career, eschewing the use of famous actors in films such as *Jesus Christ Superstar* (1973) and *A Soldier's Story* (1984), though he has also directed celebrity vehicles such as *Best Friends* (1982).[65]

Regardless of the reasons for the casting of Topol, the Israeli actor's performance in the film, while powerful, represents a significant departure from Mostel's Tevye.[66] It must also be noted that while Topol's performance may not have been haunted by the audience's memories of his previous roles many audience members (and nearly all the major critics) interpreted the filmic Tevye through implicit or explicit comparison to Mostel's Tevye. As Carlson notes, "Very often the actor who creates a particular role in a popular success . . . will create so strong a bond between himself and that role that for a generation or more all productions are haunted by the memory of that interpretation, and all actors performing the role must contend with the cultural ghost of the great originator."[67] Topol's Tevye, in other words, needs to be understood not only as a statement about acting Jewish, but also as a rebuttal to Mostel's Tevye. Given the significant publicity around the film's casting "controversy"—Mostel was particularly vocal about his offense at not being offered the role—it seems safe to assume that both Jewison and Topol were aware of the degree to which their version of *Fiddler* would be haunted by the stage original. Hence, the encoding of Tevye by Topol was perhaps carefully negotiated. Topol wisely did not directly model his performance on Mostel's, but there are many places in the film where Mostel's presence is felt as an absence, where the younger Israeli actor's performance seems to explicitly rebut the older American's mode of acting Jewish.

Whereas Mostel was a comedian first, an actor second, and a singer last, Topol was primarily a singer, then an actor. In comparison to the original Broadway cast recording, the soundtrack of the *Fiddler* film seems almost to fetishize Tevye's musical virtuosity. The orchestrations are more lavish. Notes at the end of verses and songs are held longer. As a result, the new and improved Tevye is quite literally more operatic, and by extension heroic, than the original. Jewison's camera and editing work reinforces this impression, giving us frequent close-ups of Tevye as he is singing. These close-ups tended to be shot from just below eye level, affording the audience a quasi-erotic view of Topol's powerful vocal cords in action.

Topol's manner of speaking is slower and more ponderous than Mostel's.[68] Where Mostel's Tevye speaks with the rhythms of a nightclub comic, Topol's sounds more like a college professor. While neither Mostel nor Topol has what we might call an authentic Yiddish accent, Mostel's is clearly a product of New York's Lower East Side, while Topol's is just as clearly not New York. Topol's accent in the film is often described as Israeli; this, however, may be colored by critics' a priori knowledge that the actor himself is Israeli—one way in which the actor's biography does haunt the reception of his performance. To the theatrically trained ear, Topol's speech is closest to what overseas drama schools teach as "standard American";[69] since almost nobody in America actually speaks that way, Vincent Canby of the *New York Times* interpreted it as "a British accent that one might accept in a highly stylized stage production but that doesn't jibe with the realistic circumstances of the film."⁷⁰ Compared to Mostel's Lower East Side tones, Topol's classically articulated English suggests an upward mobility that reflects (generally speaking) the fortunes of later generation Jewish Americans.

Canby goes on to write of Topol that "although I feel he's miscast, [he] displays such willingness to please, it's almost rude not to respond to him." Why does Canby feel Topol is miscast? First, he is clearly younger and healthier than Mostel's Tevye; this can be seen in the close-ups. On a technical level, Topol is not only stronger vocally than Mostel, but he is also stronger physically. He leaps about the movie sets in ways Mostel, with his injured leg, could never have done. During "If I Were a Rich Man," for example, we see him bound up a ladder in his barn and violently pitch hay from the loft in time with the music. As a result, he generates more admiration but less sympathy. Canby concedes that Topol does shoulder the movie. "However," he writes, "he shoulders it as if he were a youngish Moses instead of a rueful Job, which amounts to a kind of theatrical blasphemy." In other words, where Mostel's Tevye was inescapably human, Topol's Tevye, especially in the close-ups, which accentuate his youth and also make him seem larger than life, seems at once more and less than human.

As with Mostel, understanding Topol's performance becomes particularly complicated when we consider the differing perceptions of Jewish and gentile audiences. For a Jewish audience, Topol, who first began his performing career while serving in the Israeli army, is almost a comic book hero. He is a strong, vital, masculine figure; Canby calls him "a vigorous young actor who, with no great effort, could probably flatten half of the Czar's troops." The film version of *Fiddler* was released in 1971, with the memory of the Six-Day War still fresh in the minds of American Jews; Topol's Tevye as dairyman-cum-sabra must have carried a particular appeal. Yet haunting this performance is the memory of Mostel's more vulnerable and perhaps more sympathetic Tevye. In a sense, the film asks the audience to choose between two archetypes of Jewish masculinity: first, the vigorous Topol, who, despite his beard and *tsitsis*, conforms to the classic Western "leading man" stereotype; and, second, the "Father Complaint" of Mostel, an imposing physical presence but older and clearly damaged.

The stakes of such a choice are evidenced by an example of a gentile reading: Canby's unease with Topol's portrayal of Tevye. On one level, Canby's critique of Topol is simple: he feels the performance is unrealistic. Ironically, the stage version of *Fiddler* was never done in a realist style, but for the film Jewison shot on location in a remote Yugoslavian village in an attempt to re-create the feel of the shtetl where the play takes place. Still, I believe Canby has a point: Topol's Tevye is *not* as well rounded a character as Mostel's. Jewish and gentile critics alike agree that Mostel's Tevye is a real, three-dimensional person, going beyond a stereotype even as he is redefining one. He has both good and bad sides to his character—in fact, many took Mostel and the play's authors to task for Tevye's refusal to accept his daughter Chava's marriage to a gentile. He is a character whom audiences might want to claim as their relation but not necessarily emulate. Topol's Tevye is unequivocally positive; he even appears more sympathetic to Chava, aided by Jewison's use of the film medium. Onstage Tevye's blessing, "God be with you," at the play's close is uttered to the air. He does not turn to look at Chava as she departs. In the film, Tevye does not look at Chava, but he speaks the blessing directly to the camera—and by extension to the audience. This device, combined with Topol's good-natured expression and self-mockery as he derides his wife Golde for telling Chava where they are going in America, creates the strong impression that Tevye has come around—that he accepts (if not approves) Chava's mixed marriage.

So Canby feels Topol's Tevye lacks a certain dimension, and his claim has some merit. It is a bit disturbing, however, that Canby critiques Topol as unrealistic but calls Leonard Frey, who plays Motel the Tailor, "the best thing in the film." Frey's Motel is as stereotypical and two dimensional as Topol's Tevye. However, Canby asserts that the "timid tailor do[es] succeed in capturing the sensibility of Yiddish expression." By mentioning Frey's timidity and his Yiddish sensibility in the same sentence, Canby implies an equation of timidity with Jewishness that is most revealing. If the mousy Motel is Canby's epitome of Jewish masculinity, little wonder that he has trouble accepting Topol's high-testosterone Tevye.

In a feature article published three and a half weeks after his initial review, Canby offers a backhanded compliment to the stereotype of the weak, passive Jew. In this later piece, entitled "Is 'Fiddler' More DeMille than Sholem Aleichem?" Canby suggests that Job is a more heroic figure (or archetype) than Moses, because "Moses has a hot-line to God, whereas Job (and Tevye) seem often to be talking into receivers that someone has left off the hook"[71] For Canby, Job's indomitability of spirit is what Sholem Aleichem is all about. He goes on to declare: "There are hints of Aleichem throughout the film, but don't be fooled. Deep within it there beats the mechanical heart of Cecil B. DeMille's 1956 'The Ten Commandments.'"[72] For Canby, the comparison to DeMille is not a compliment. Moreover, what Canby considers to be the overblown epic quality of the film is traceable to two things: first, the director makes, in Canby's words, "a big ethnic thing out of it"; and, second, the casting of Topol is the movie's "boldest step, and one that is most distorting."[73] This is somewhat ironic, for he seems to feel that the movie is too Jewish yet Topol is not Jewish enough.

If Wolitz is correct in the assertion that each Tevye represents a recasting of Jewish cultural history, it is clear that Canby is not ready to accept this casting of the Jews. He much prefers Frey's Motel, or Mostel's downtrodden Tevye; this gentile critic is discomfited and perhaps a little threatened by Topol's Jewish machismo. While it is dangerous to generalize from Canby to gentile audiences as a whole, it is worth noting that there have been few, if any, explicitly Jewish characters in the three decades since the film *Fiddler* who have commanded the screen in the way Topol's Tevye does. Ironically, with more than four decades having passed since the stage premier of *Fiddler* and more than a quarter century since Mostel last essayed the role in a 1978 Broadway revival, it is Topol's performance that is rapidly becoming the standard against which all other Tevye's are judged. The wide availability of the film on videotape and DVD means that audiences around the world have access to Topol's performance, while the ranks of those who have seen Mostel perform the role continue to dwindle.

Among those who have seen both Mostel and Topol, and many more Tevyes besides, are the original *Fiddler* creators, who seem, oddly enough, to agree with Canby. Stein complains of Topol's performance that "He didn't play a peasant."[74] As a result, Stein says, much of the humor of the stage version was lost. Peter Stone attributes this to the fact that the director, Jewison, was not Jewish and was overly concerned about offending the Jewish audience.[75] This raises yet another question: does the Jewish audience actually find the wisecracking, world-weariness of Mostel's Tevye a more recognizable mode of acting Jewish than the vigorous, heroic stereotype of Topol's Tevye? Perhaps Mostel's Tevye is more readily accepted as an example of acting Jewish than Topol's because it is less universal. As Michael Feingold suggested in another context, "In art the things you assert are your identity; the questions you raise are your way of transcending it. Pretending that you have no ethnic identity is no use for the purposes of transcendence."[76]

Postscript: "Goyim on the Roof"

If you don't have to be Jewish to love Tevye, do you have to be Jewish to play him on the Broadway stage? Or is a goyish Tevye unkosher? To whom? These are some of the questions posed by the most recent revival of *Fiddler*, starring Alfred Molina as Tevye, which opened on 26 February 2004 and is still running (and still featuring Molina) as of this writing, despite being shut out of the 2004 Tony awards. The controversy around the casting of the forty-nine-year-old Molina, the first non-Jew to play the role on Broadway, began almost immediately after the choice (made by non-Jewish director David Leveaux) was announced. By the time the show began previews in late January of 2004, reports *New York Times* critic Ben Brantley, "a nickname for the revival had already begun circulating among theater insiders: 'Goyim on the Roof.' "[77] In a widely quoted editorial in the *Los Angeles Times*, Jewish novelist Thane Rosenbaum complained, "The sensation is as if you're sampling something that tastes great and looks Jewish but isn't entirely kosher."[78] Similar criticisms flourished in the Jewish press. Caleb Ben-David, for example, wrote in the *Jerusalem Post:*

> I'm old enough to have seen the original 1960s Broadway production, with Yiddish theater veteran Herschel Bernardi having replaced the legendary Zero Mostel as Tevye. Both men, along with Topol in the film version, were more than able to bring to the role the authentic ethnic flavor needed to play Sholem Aleichem's best-known character. That's not quite the case with the star of the new *Fiddler*, the non-Jewish British-Spanish actor Alfred Molina.[79]

In response, Anglo-Jewish critic John Heilpern declaims:

> Yet the criticism that Tevye is played by a non-Jew, Alfred Molina, leaves me incredulous. I don't remember any fuss when Antonio Banderas, a Spaniard, played Guido, an Italian, in *Nine*. Actors act, and Mr. Molina is a very fine actor. He isn't Zero Mostel or Topol; nor is he trying to be. But where is it written that only a Jew can play a Jew? If that were the case, Laurence Olivier, the son of a priest, wouldn't have given us his memorable Shylock, and Nathan Lane, a Catholic, wouldn't have been able to play Max Bialystock.[80]

Molina himself echoes this statement, as noted by Mark Kennedy for the Associated Press:

> One thing Molina didn't worry about was that he isn't Jewish. "In a way, that's irrelevant. It's not about nationality—it transcends it.

Does that mean I have to be Danish to play Hamlet?" he asks. "I'm sure that on some personal or maybe familial level, a Jewish actor might have a connection or might strike a resonant chord in a very private or personal way. But ultimately that's not really what it's about," he says. "What it's about is finding a way to tell a story as authentically and as clearly as possible. I don't have to be Jewish to play a Jew. I don't have to have that experience. My job is to give the audience that experience."[81]

But Molina's response, however sincere, seems somewhat uninformed (or maybe un-Jewish), given the significant role *Fiddler* has played in Jewish American culture over the last four decades. As Jeffrey Shandler notes, in the mid-1960s "it was *Fiddler* that was the source of public Jewish American pride." Alisa Solomon writes, "In the popular American imagination, *Fiddler* defines the mythic Jewish past."[82] And Elysa Gardner, in a positive review of Molina's performance for *USA Today*, points out that *Fiddler*'s "songs and images have become as ingrained in Jewish American culture as bagels and bar mitzvah bashes."[83] Even today, it seems, what is at stake in the portrayal of Tevye is no less than Jewish Americans' collective self-image.[84]

Molina's performance, of course, is inevitably judged against both earlier Tevyes, and that performance, while garnering generally positive reviews (and a Tony nomination), has left many critics uninspired. Jeremy McCarter, for example, writes, "Mr. Molina has a clear and strong (if limited) voice, and he moves passably well, though I do not envision him in 'Movin' Out' anytime soon. But there's something missing. He smooths out Tevye's folds and sands down his edges, making him neither gruff nor disputatious. He makes Tevye, above all, an amiable man, in a way that sitcom dads are often amiable."[85] In my own experience of Molina's performance, I noted that his accent is closer to Topol's standard American, but his phrasing is more naturalistic and less showy. His emotions are expressed in an understated way; he does not yell nearly as much, nor laugh nearly as loud as his predecessors. Perhaps most important for consideration here, he lacks the sense of melancholic irony that characterizes the original production (and to a lesser degree the film). When Mostel and Topol tell God, "I know we are the chosen people, but once in a while couldn't you choose somebody else?" the line speaks to a kind of pride in powerlessness that is often associated with the humor of *Yiddishkeit*. When Molina delivers the same line, it is merely a punch line. Jewish critic John Lahr makes the point more directly: "The production's panache reverses the English joke "Look British, think Yiddish"; in this "Fiddler," it's indubitably a case of "Think British, look Yiddish."[86]

Still, in spite of all the "goyim on the roof" cracks, the current production has done well critically and commercially. Audiences and critics, Jews and non-Jews, have found much to enjoy in Molina's performance. Does this suggest that audience tastes have changed since 1964? Since 1971? I think not. Rather, I believe that this revival, like many revivals of "classic" shows, serves as a kind of screen on which audiences can project their nostalgic feelings about the original. If some spectators feel that Molina's Tevye suffers by comparison to Mostel's or Topol's, it nonetheless evokes the memories of those performances in a context that is heightened and revitalized by a live Broadway production. As McCarter suggests, "Though [*Fiddler*] is only 40 years old, it's Broadway's version of roots music."[87] In other words, the performance of the revival is something akin to a communal celebration. For Jewish audiences, this is a celebration of the glory days of the 1960s, when Jewish American writers and artists stood at the center of the New York scene and ethnic became fashionable. For general audiences, what is being celebrated is the Broadway musical itself, as exemplified by one of the all-time surefire hits. The musical about tradition has itself become one. And you don't have to be Jewish to love it.

Through the example of *Fiddler on the Roof*, it becomes clear that representations of Jews in the theater do more than simply reflect the playwright's vision of the Jewish experience. They provide a gentile audience with popular images of Jews, and they teach a Jewish audience, by example, what it means to act Jewish. To the extent that these functions are often in conflict, is it too facile to say that every Jewish American artist is a fiddler on the roof, trying to scratch out a tune without losing his balance?

Double coding offers both producers and consumers of American popular culture a strategy with which to meet this challenge. While such codes and strategies were in circulation prior to 1964, *Fiddler*, as the first explicitly Jewish work of American popular culture since *The Jazz Singer* to achieve massive "crossover" appeal, marks a watershed in their evolution. In the decades since *Fiddler*, cultural producers and consumers, both Jewish and gentile, have become increasingly sophisticated. These more complex examples of double coding are explored in subsequent chapters.

CHAPTER 4

How Jews Became Sexy,
1968–1983

"What's a nice Jewish girl like me doing on the cover of Playboy?"

*T*HIS CAPTION APPEARS, self-referentially enough, on the cover of *Playboy*'s October 1977 issue,[1] which features a photograph of Barbra Streisand, wearing white shorts and a T-shirt emblazoned with the *Playboy* logo, reclining across the bottom half of a large white circle; Streisand's extended left leg forms a line that transforms the circle into a *Q*, which presumably refers to the questions she will answer in what the leading headline bills as: "THE FIRST IN-DEPTH INTERVIEW WITH BARBRA STREISAND." The caption ("What's a nice Jewish girl . . .") appears suspended above and to the right of Streisand's head, evoking a cartoon-style thought bubble. The location of the caption and the use of the first person ("like me") suggests that this is a question that Streisand is asking herself. Yet perhaps there is a more interesting question: why has *Playboy*, the self-appointed arbiter of feminine sexual attractiveness, chosen to feature "a nice Jewish girl" on its cover? How did Streisand become, in fact, "the first female celebrity in 24 years" to pose for the magazine's cover?[2]

In March of 1962, fifteen years prior to her *Playboy* appearance, Streisand made her Broadway debut as Miss Marmelstein in Jerome Weidman and Harold Rome's *I Can Get It for You Wholesale*. Critics praised the nineteen-year-old actress for her comedic skill but described her variously as a "homely frump," "a sloe-eyed creature with folding ankles," and "a girl with an oafish expression, a loud irascible voice and an arpeggiated laugh."[3] John McClain, writing in the *New York Journal-American*, wrote of Streisand that she "plays a secretary and resembles an amiable anteater."[4] The story of Streisand's transition from "anteater" to (Playboy) "bunny" is not a saga of personal transformation; in fact, photos of Miss Marmelstein from 1962 reveal a physiognomy and physicality remarkably similar to those of Streisand in 1977.[5] Her *Playboy* cover represents the apotheosis of an evolution in the way the Jewish body is perceived by an American audience. That is, the very characteristics of Streisand's stage and screen persona that marked her as a "homely frump" in 1962 mark her as a cover girl in 1977. Hence, the presence of the label "Jewish" on the magazine's cover carries a dual significance: on one hand, it suggests that Streisand has become a sex symbol *in spite* of her Jewishness; on the other hand, it suggests that Streisand's Jewishness somehow contributes to her sex appeal.

This chapter examines how Jewishness came to be perceived (at least in part) as sexually appealing in American popular entertainment during the period from 1968 to 1983. Because of Streisand's central role in this evolution, particular attention is paid to her body of work, beginning with her appearance in the film *Funny Girl* (1968) and culminating in her title role (and directing turn) in *Yentl* (1983). I also explore corresponding changes in the perception of the male Jewish body, with special attention to the stage and screen work of Woody Allen. Like Streisand, Allen established a critically and commercially successful film career built largely around a screen persona that varies little from film to film. And, like Streisand, Allen's screen persona is identifiably Jewish, whether as Allan Felix in *Play It Again, Sam* (1969, Broadway; 1972, film), Alvy Singer in *Annie Hall* (1977), or Isaac Davis in *Manhattan* (1979). In fact, because Allen played a string of explicitly Jewish characters throughout the 1970s critics have repeatedly interpreted his 1983 film *Zelig* as a metaphor for Jewish assimilation.[6]

While Streisand's and Allen's Jewish personae—their modes of acting Jewish—changed little between 1968 and 1983, the ways in which those personae were perceived changed significantly. As Robert Leslie Liebman observed in a 1984 article about the schlemiel in the work of Woody Allen, "Traits which are shameful in one context (or era) can be adorable in another."[7] The gawky singer and geeky comedian of the mid-1960s became the sexy superstars of the early 1980s; in so doing, Streisand and Allen both benefited from and helped to drive a shift in the way Jewishness was perceived as an element of sexual desirability. I will further argue that Streisand's and Allen's performances especially emphasize the sexual attractiveness of Jews as perceived by gentiles (and vice versa), and therefore present a complex and provocative example of the double-coding phenomenon described in chapter 3.

Funny Girl

Columbia Pictures' 1968 film *Funny Girl*, directed by William Wyler, is based on the 1964 Broadway musical of the same name with music by Jule Styne, lyrics by Bob Merrill, and book by Isobel Lennart. The show is ostensibly a biography of the Jewish American entertainer Fanny Brice, the top female box office draw of the 1920s and 1930s, star of vaudeville, Broadway, radio, and the Ziegfeld Follies. However, as Katheryn Bernheimer writes, "*Funny Girl* just so happens to be an equally accurate portrait of Barbra Streisand, the unconventional actress who made her screen debut in the hit musical."[8] Like Brice, Streisand was born and raised in New York City. Both women began their performing careers while still in their teens and neither was classically attractive, but both used musical talent, determination, and a healthy dose of humor to achieve fame and fortune. As a result, *Funny Girl* is often perceived as being as much, if not more, a thinly veiled biography of Streisand as of Brice.[9] It is important to note, however, that this characterization of *Funny Girl* is retrospective. When the stage musical first opened, Streisand was widely praised for her performance, but reviews focused primarily on the degree to which the show accurately captured the story of Brice. Similar responses greeted the film release.

Furthermore, as Felicia Herman notes, the description of *Funny Girl* as "a watershed in Jewish film history" is similarly inflected with a kind of nostalgia for "the countercultural movements of the 1960s and 1970s, which sanctioned overt ethnicity as a form of revolt against the white, male, Anglo-Saxon Protestant ruling elite."[10] This is not to say that *Funny Girl* was a minor film in the evolving public perception of Jewish women but rather to argue that it was just the first step in a series of works by Streisand and others that helped to redefine appropriate female behavior.

Streisand turned to the real-life example of Fanny Brice as a foundation for the behavioral model that Letty Cottin Pogrebin would later define as the archetypal "Jewish Big Mouth."

> [T]he character of the clever, outspoken, Jewish girl has become a film convention that empowers every woman. Most important, films portraying the Ugly Duckling who rises above her appearance have assured girls with big noses and frizzy hair that they too can invent their own kind of terrific and leave Miss America in the dust.[11]

Ironically, *Funny Girl* takes the first step toward this validation of Jewish womanhood by deemphasizing the real-life Jewishness of the other characters in the film. For the role of Nicky Arnstein, Brice's first husband, the Jewish director William Wyler cast Omar Sharif: tall, dark, handsome, and Egyptian.[12] More importantly, the only explicitly Jewish behavior Nicky exhibits in the film is marrying Fanny.[13] Similarly, the character of Florenz Ziegfeld (Walter Pidgeon) demonstrates no recognition of the real-life producer's (admittedly conflicted) history with Jewishness.[14]

Fanny's Jewishness, then, is established primarily by contrast. As she explains early in the film, "I'm a bagel on a plate of onion rolls." This declaration is a small but significant example of double coding. As Norman Nadel commented, "Only those who have known the magic of a bagel can appreciate how right that is."[15] In 1968 (and even more so in the 1920s, when the scene is set), the bagel was "ethnic food," unfamiliar to the majority of the viewing audience. Thus, a dominant reading of the line emphasizes Fanny's exotic Otherness. But for the Jewish audience ("those who have known the magic of a bagel"), Fanny's self-characterization carries a wealth of sensory and cultural associations—associations that are familiar rather than exotic.

And just as the bagel is distinguished by its unique appearance, so does the question of Brice's (and by extension Streisand's) appearance dominate the encounter between the Jewish American performer and the mainstream entertainment industry. From the posing of the musical question, "Is a nose with a deviation / a crime against the nation?" to the selective retelling of Fanny's biography (Brice ultimately capitulated to the necessity of rhinoplasty, but Streisand's character does not), *Funny Girl* represents Fanny's appearance as the primary manifestation of her Jewish identity, as well as the primary obstacle she must overcome on her way to stardom. For Herman, this preoccupation with the Jewish nose undermines the film's insight into the Jewish American dilemma.

> The reduction of Jewishness to mostly physical qualities reduces the struggle for acceptance by Jews to the almost banal question of whether society can accept a woman who "looks Jewish" as beautiful. Though both Fanny's success in the film and the popularity of the film itself have been taken by some as a symbol of Jewish acceptance in America, the film so oversimplifies the meaning of Jewish "difference" that the real complexities of Jewish integration remain ignored.[16]

While Herman correctly points out that Jewish "difference" is far more than physical, the importance of physical difference as an element of Jewish identity formation cannot be so easily brushed aside. "Dealing with the idea of the difference of the Jewish body" writes Sander Gilman, "becomes part of the search for identity."[17] Joshua Halberstam reports, based on his investigation into "the private conversations of American Jews," that:

> Most American Jews aren't aware of [the] genetic studies and evo-
> lutionary theories, but they have no problem with the notion of
> "looking Jewish." Barbra Streisand looks Jewish; Sharon Stone
> does not. If you are casting for a "typical"-looking Jew, you search
> for someone with curly hair, large nose, dark complexions, and
> dark eyes, not the fellow with the straight blond hair and tiny
> bobbed nose.[18]

That Halberstam uses the example of two Hollywood actresses, as well as the metaphor of theatrical casting, to get his point across, is note-worthy for two reasons. First, casting is one of the few areas in con-temporary American social life where judging a person based on phys-ical appearance is practiced openly; an actor is that rare worker who can be legally discriminated against based on race, gender, or disability. Second, Halberstam's explanation of "looking Jewish" recognizes the inherent link between theatrical performance and the presentation of one's body in everyday life.

In her oft-quoted essay on the performative nature of gender, Judith Butler writes:

> The body is not a self-identical or merely factic materiality; it is a
> materiality that bears meaning, if nothing else, and the manner of
> this bearing is fundamentally dramatic. By dramatic I mean only
> that the body is not merely matter, but a continual and incessant
> *materializing* of possibilities. One is not simply a body, but, in
> some very key sense, one does one's body and, indeed, one does
> one's body differently from one's contemporaries and from one's
> embodied predecessors and successors as well.[19]

For Butler, a philosopher and gender theorist, the physical body is sim-ply a starting point. Her intent is to show that most behaviors that are conventionally regarded as masculine or feminine are not biologically determined but socially constructed. Moreover, the mechanism by which society comes to perceive these behaviors as gendered, and by which these perceptions are enforced and perpetuated, is "fundamen-tally dramatic." When we meet someone, we don't determine their gender by means of a chromosome test or by inspecting their genitals; we evaluate their behavior, the way in which they "do" their body, the way in which their body performs. We are in a sense the audience for their performance, and in interpreting that performance we bring to bear a host of decoding strategies. Some of these strategies are conscious and some unconscious, but nearly all are learned rather than innate. Similarly, an individual may "stage" his or her gender (or other aspects of identity) in conscious ways (clothing, cosmetics, hairstyle) or unconscious ways (speech patterns, mannerisms). To suggest that gender is a performance is not to disavow its reality but to argue that this reality is neither fixed nor stable, dependent as it is on the web of performer-spectator interactions that characterize everyday life.[20]

So, too, with looking Jewish. What it means to look Jewish has varied significantly from time to time and place to place. The stereotypes cited by Halberstam ("curly hair, large nose, dark complexion, and dark eyes"), bear a tenuous connection (at best) to the historical origins of Judaism in the Mediterranean region and no connection at all to the real variety of appearances among Jews in America and around the world, something Halberstam is quick to point out.[21] In other words, there is little or no link between the biology of a Jewish body and the ways in which that body is recognized as Jewish, whether on the movie screen or the street corner.

As Butler notes, however, even if the way one "does one's body" is individually determined, it is also constrained by historical and social norms. Or, as Harley Erdman (citing Butler as an influence) writes in *Staging the Jew*, "Ethnicity, as shaped by history, as lived in the moment, is all too real most of the time. The power of culture, as expressed in both the beauty of difference and the injustice of oppression, asserts itself continually."[22] Sociological studies of perception further confirm that the ways in which viewers interpret each individual's performance of his or her body do coalesce around culturally specific types. As Schneider writes:

> One way in which we simplify the complex world of other people is to organize them into groups. We talk of Germans, Jews, and Italians; of college students, policemen; even of little old ladies in tennis shoes; and we attribute certain characteristics to all members of each group. On reflection, we are all perfectly willing to grant that college students come in all different shapes and sizes and that they have very different orientations toward the world; yet we still find ourselves classifying people into groups and then imputing certain characteristics to the members of the groups.[23]

Or, as Halberstam argues, "Caricature? Of course, but caricatures always define type, and ethnic stereotyping is precisely the nub around which group self-image rotates."[24] We therefore need to understand looking Jewish as one element of acting Jewish on the stage, the screen, or the street. By positing Fanny Brice's body—not her religion or behavior—as the obstacle she must overcome in order to succeed, *Funny Girl* demonstrates that the woman who looks Jewish can gain acceptance not by erasing, hiding, or avoiding her Jewish looks but by acting Jewish.

Play It Again, Sam

Buoyed by three Oscar nominations, *Funny Girl* was still in theaters on 12 February 1969, when *Play It Again, Sam* opened on Broadway at the Broadhurst Theatre. This three-act comedy, written by and starring Woody Allen, marked the writer/comedian's Broadway debut. Allen plays Allan Felix, "a slight, bespectacled young man of about twenty-eight or twenty-nine who looks as if he just stepped out of a Jules Feiffer cartoon."[25] As the play begins, Allan's wife Nancy (Sheila Sullivan) has just left him. Despondent, he turns to his cinematic idol, Humphrey Bogart, for advice. Bogart (Jerry Lacy)—who appears at various moments throughout the play in dream sequences visible only to Allan (and the audience)—both represents and satirizes the film noir model of tough, autonomous masculinity against which Allan measures himself. When Allan asks him, "Why can't I be cool? What's the secret?" Bogart responds, "There's no secret, kid. Dames are simple. I never met one who didn't understand a slap in the mouth or a slug from a forty-five."[26] Allan, by contrast, is a mass of insecurities: neurotic, hypochondriacal, and self-pitying. "I managed to fool one girl into loving me," he says, "and now she's gone."[27] Yet at the same time he dreams of being tough, desirable, and sexually aggressive. The disparity between Allan's idealized image of masculinity (Bogart) and his real-life behavior is the main source of comedy in the play.

Allan is as an example of what David Biale calls "the Jew as Sexual Schlemiel . . . the little man with the big libido and the even bigger sexual neurosis, a character comically unable to consummate his desire."[28] While citing Allen as the foremost interpreter of the Sexual Schlemiel, Biale traces its roots back through Philip Roth's Portnoy, borscht belt comedians, the American Yiddish theater, and "fin-de-siecle Hebrew and Yiddish literature."[29] By the 1960s, Biale argues, the Jew as Sexual Schlemiel is a firmly established archetype. Referring to Roth's *Portnoy's Complaint* (1969), a novel published the same month that *Play It Again, Sam* opened, he writes, "Roth's self-conscious exploration of the myth of Jewish erotic neurosis only works because Roth's readers *already know the codes.*[30] Similarly, for the audience that is familiar with this archetype Allan Felix does not need to explicitly label himself as Jewish; in fact, he is never explicitly labeled at all. His persona is already recognizable as a mode of acting Jewish.

But if *Play It Again, Sam* depends on the stereotype of Jewish sexual insecurity for its humor, Allen also uses humor to reposition that insecurity as somehow sexually attractive. After a series of ill-fated blind dates, Allan succeeds in winning the affection of Linda (Diane Keaton), the wife of his best friend Dick (Tony Roberts). Allan doesn't accomplish this by acting suave, sophisticated, or tough. Rather, it is when he stops trying to emulate Bogart and starts to be himself that he achieves romantic success. As Allan tells Bogart in the final scene, "The secret's not being you, it's being me. True, you're not too tall and kinda ugly. But I'm short enough and ugly enough to succeed by myself."[31] "And," writes Robert Leslie Liebman, "since much of his [Allan's] appeal arises from his being a schlemiel, she loves him, not in spite of that fact, but in part at least, because of it."[32]

For a general audience, one that does not recognize Allan as a Jewish character, *Play It Again, Sam* is simply a variation on "to thine own self be true." But for an audience that knows the codes Allan carries the banner for a Jewish masculinity that is explicitly contrasted with both Bogart and the only other male character in the play, Dick. While Bogart represents the dashing, macho image of masculinity offered by Hollywood, Dick represents a kind of Jewish inside joke on the stereotype of the repressed Christian male. Even his name, "Dick Christie," is a dirty joke: the goyish phallus.[33] Dick is ambitious, glib, and incapable of expressing emotion. He responds to Allan's divorce in financial terms: "Why do you feel like crying? A man makes an investment—it doesn't pay off."[34] For both Bogart and Dick, sentiment and emotional expression are forms of weakness, a weakness from which Allan suffers. But it is precisely this weakness that wins Linda's heart. And only when Allan emulates Bogart's toughness, in a playful reprise of the closing scene in *Casablanca*, does Linda surrender him and return to Dick (just as Ingrid Bergman returns to Paul Henreid).

As with Streisand's Fanny Brice, the Jewishness of Allen's Allan Felix is shown to be appealing by contrast. This pattern repeats itself in Allen's subsequent films, in which, as Biale writes, "Jews have the libidinal energy to win over gentile women from their desiccated WASP culture."[35] But because *Play It Again, Sam* does not explicitly identify its protagonist as Jewish, this aspect of the play (and the 1971 film, which featured the same cast) went largely unnoticed by gentile critics.[36] For

example, Richard Watts Jr., writing in the *New York Post*, called the
play "a handsome and deserved tribute to Humphrey Bogart," while
Judith Crist of NBC-TV predicted it would "warm the hearts of movie
nuts and Bogey fans."[37] The Jewish reader must wonder if Watts and
Crist left the theater during the intermission. Yet a dominant reading
position often allows viewers to ignore even the explicit Jewishness of a
character when acknowledgment of the character's Jewish identity
might be a barrier to the universalist reading. As Schneider notes, "We
neglect both situational pressures and disconfirming evidence in our
push to categorize a person according to group membership."[38] So
audiences for whom Allan's ethnicity is a source of neither anxiety nor
pride focus instead on the play's romanticization of Bogart, who, like
Allan, overcame being "not too tall and kinda ugly" to succeed as a
ladies man.

The Way We Were

In *The Way We Were* (1973), Streisand reprises the role of the Jewish
Big Mouth, this time as Katie Morosky, a left-leaning activist who falls
in love with Hubbell Gardiner (Robert Redford) during the period
immediately before and after World War II. The film begins in 1944,
when Katie and Hubbell meet in a New York nightclub, where
Hubbell (then a naval officer) is on leave. But this meeting is immediately followed by an extended flashback (lasting about twenty-five minutes or a quarter of the film) to their shared college years. In college,
Katie is shown as an outspoken Jewish radical, making anti-Franco
speeches on behalf of the Young Communists League (YCL). Hubbell
is the campus golden boy, a handsome, blond decathlete to whom Katie
refers disparagingly as "America the Beautiful."[39] As in *Funny Girl*,
Streisand's character is initially framed as physically unattractive. But
by 1973, with Streisand established as a movie star, convincing the
audience that she is an ugly duckling requires more effort. Director
Sydney Pollack takes multiple opportunities to comment on Katie's
alleged homeliness. When she makes an antiwar speech on the campus
quad, Hubbell's fraternity brothers wave placards reading, "Any Peace
but Katie's Piece." In several other scenes, her frizzy hair and Jewish
nose are presented alongside the impeccably coiffed, blonde beauty
queen who is Hubbell's steady girlfriend. At the senior prom, Katie is
serving refreshments (a convention borrowed from the teen films of the
1950s and 1960s that signifies her inability to get a date). When her fellow communist Frankie (James Woods) finally asks her to dance, she

tells him, "You know, I've never been to a dance before, except the one the YCL gave for Spain."

Katie initially sees Hubbell the way the Young Communists see America: beautiful and empty. She is not attracted by his physical beauty, and only when he writes a brilliant short story for their senior English class does she become interested in him. Still, another scene is required, one in which Hubbell demonstrates his sense of humor and disavows the elitism of his fraternity brothers, before Katie allows herself to be smitten.

When the film's action returns to 1944, Katie and Hubbell consummate the romance that was interrupted by graduation and the war. Katie's appearance has changed significantly: her hair is straight ("I have it ironed" she tells Hubbell), and her wardrobe is stylish and more flattering. Pollack's direction aids her transformation: the camera sees Katie in soft focus, the cinematic gaze lingering at length on her proudly Semitic profile. Clearly, her Jewishness is intrinsic to her sexual appeal to Hubbell. Here, however, the way Katie *acts Jewish* is even more important than the way she *looks Jewish*. It is her passion for politics and compassion for humanity that captivate Hubbell and lead to their eventual marriage. Exasperated during an argument, Hubbell complains that Katie is "sure about everything"; in the next breath, he asks, "Do you know you're beautiful?" Moreover, Katie's politics and Jewishness are explicitly conflated. For example, when she becomes pregnant she tells Hubbell that her father has given his approval to three potential boy's names: "Solomon David Gardiner, Thomas Jefferson Gardiner, or Eugene V. Debs Gardiner."

Herman notes that some critics regard the ultimate failure of Katie and Hubbell's marriage as a critique of Jewish-gentile intermarriage. Yet,

> Katie and Hubbell's relationship fails not because Katie is a Jew and Hubbell is not but rather because Katie represses her idealism in order to stay with him; and when she finally decides to stand up for what she believes in, Hubbell cannot accept her autonomy. The divorce occurs more for reasons of gender than of religion or ethnicity.[40]

Perhaps this is why the Jewishness of Streisand's character, while much more explicit than in *Funny Girl*, was unremarked by critics invested in the universal appeal of the romantic plot. Vincent Canby, for example, managed to review *The Way We Were* for the *New York Times* without once using the word *Jew* or *Jewish*, though he does call Hubbell "a

WASP of the sort that can only be true in romantic movies."[41] As a further demonstration that not everyone recognizes the double-coded
indicators of Jewishness, Canby attributes Katie's frizzy hair to "the era
of the electric curling iron."[42] Lawrence Grobel, on the other hand,
acknowledges the intermarriage aspect of the film but deemphasizes its
importance, writing, "In the film, Streisand lives out the fantasy of
thousands of women whose features aren't perfect, as she captures the
all-American blond-haired, blue-eyed gentile by the sheer force of her
personality and wit".[43] While Grobel's description clearly identifies
Redford's Hubbell as a "gentile," he seems to suggest that Streisand has
"passed" by appealing to a vast audience and demonstrating a sex appeal
not normally associated with Jews.

Film critic David Desser offers other perspective.

> In the melting-pot myth, as seen especially in popular culture, it
> is a white male prerogative to have relations with the dark female,
> who may be fearsome or villainous but who is nevertheless in
> many instances a potential object of desire so long as she marries
> the white male and lives in his white society. . . . [But] attraction
> to the dark woman, and the eventual marriage to her or the rejec-
> tion of such a marriage in favor of one's own race, is problema-
> tized because of the questions of race and gender. A kind of inter-
> mediary is therefore needed, a gender and racial ambiguity needs
> arise—one found in that conflated, mythic Other known as the
> Jews.[44]

Desser is commenting on the portrayal of intermarriage in early cinema, but his comments suggest another factor at work in the Jewish sex
appeal Streisand demonstrates in *The Way We Were*. Jewish-gentile
intermarriage was certainly a concern among Jews in the early 1970s, as
evidenced by the incredibly hostile response of Jewish organizations to
the short-lived 1972 television comedy *Bridget Loves Bernie*.[45] Yet
white-black miscegenation was probably a larger source of anxiety to
the population at large. As Michael Rogin and Karen Brodkin have
noted, American Jews in the middle of the twentieth century were commonly thought to occupy a kind of anomalous position on the racial
ladder, somewhere between white and black.[46] With the rise of the sexual revolution and the "Black Is Beautiful" movement, perhaps
Streisand and other Jewish performers became the unlikely beneficia-
ries of the white gentile audience's anxiety about interracial romance.
As a "white" woman and a Jew, Katie Morosky offers the white gentile
audience a "safe" way of exploring the sexual appeal of the Other. At

the same time, the resolution of *The Way We Were* shows Jewish women that they can act Jewish and still attract a goyish hunk like Robert Redford, though once they get him they might not want to keep him.

Annie Hall

Regarded by many as Woody Allen's best film,[47] *Annie Hall* (1977) earned Allen Oscars for Best Director, Best Picture, and Best Screenplay (Allen with Marshall Brickman), as well as a Best Actress award for Diane Keaton in the title role. As the character Alvy Singer, Allen once again reprises his role as "sexual schlemiel"; but what distinguishes *Annie Hall* from Allen's earlier films, such as *Bananas* (1971), *Sleeper* (1973), and *Love and Death* (1975), is that for the first time this schlemiel is explicitly identified as Jewish. Indeed, the film presents the romance between Alvy and Annie (Keaton) as an intercultural encounter. As Bernheimer writes:

> The relationship between neurotic *nebbish* Alvy and all-American *shiksa* Annie provided Allen with the perfect opportunity to mine his favorite themes, chief among them the difference between Jews and gentiles. Although religion is never an issue between Alvy and Annie, much of the tension in their romance can be attributed to ethnic conflicts.[48]

Some of these ethnic conflicts are portrayed quite explicitly. In the most commonly cited scene in the film, Annie takes Alvy home to meet her WASP family.[49] As Annie and her parents (Colleen Dewhurst and Donald Symington) exchange flat, suburban banalities over flat, suburban cuisine, Alvy imagines himself as he must appear to them: as a black-clad Hassidic Jew, unable and unfit to participate in polite society. This is contrasted, via split screen, with a scene of dinner at the Singer household: a conversational and gastronomic free-for-all. Although the humor depends on exaggeration of both cultural stereotypes, Allen clearly stacks the deck in favor of his own Jewish background: the Singers (including Mordechai Lawner and Joan Newman as Alvy's father and mother) are loud and vulgar, but they are alive in a way that the Halls are not; or, to put it in comedic terms, this juxtaposition of scenes positions the Jew as comedian and the gentile as straight man.

This is also the model for Alvy and Annie's relationship. As in *Play It*

Again, Sam, Keaton ably sets up Allen's punch lines. So, in addition to the more explicit contrasts the film draws between Jewish and gentile culture, *Annie Hall* also suggests that Allen's hip but self-deprecating sense of humor is intrinsic to Alvy's Jewishness. And because this film (unlike Allen's other works) is so explicitly framed as an intercultural encounter, Alvy's mode of acting Jewish—as the humorous sexual schlemiel—stakes a claim as an archetype of Jewish masculinity. As a result, even the characteristics of Alvy's behavior that are not explicitly marked as Jewish become part of the film's representation of Jews.[50] Bernheimer writes: "Although Allen is an intensely private person, he has revealed more about himself to the audience than almost any other contemporary film artist. Because he is so thoroughly Jewish, Allen can thus be credited with providing audiences with a detailed profile of a specific Jewish personality."[51] However, the significance that viewers attach to Alvy's "specific Jewish personality" is conditioned in large part by the cultural knowledge and expectations they bring to the film. Members of the Jewish audience, those who already recognized the schlemiel as such in Allen's earlier work, respond to the familiarity of the character. For them, Allen's appeal lies in his ability to observe the humor in everyday situations. But audiences not familiar with Jewish performance codes see the intercultural encounter from the point of view of Annie; like her, they learn what it means to act Jewish as the film progresses. Early in the film, for example, Annie orders a pastrami sandwich on white bread with mayonnaise. Alvy's rolling eyes and horrified expression are an in-joke to some of his viewers and a "teachable moment" for the rest.

Biale, though he does not use the term *double coding,* nevertheless sees this educational function of Allen's films as "a hidden agenda . . . to identify America with Jewish culture by generalising Jewish sexuality and creating a safe, unthreatening space for the schlemiel as American anti-hero."[52] The comic fumbling of the schlemiel, Biale argues, deeroticizes the Jewish body, undermining the "Jew as hypersexual" stereotype that is a staple of racial anti-Semitism.[53] In this reading, Alvy does seduce the Christian woman, Annie, but his seduction is so ludicrously inept that it represents no threat to Christian culture. Biale continues, suggesting that a

> deep insecurity about the Jew's position in American culture
> seems to underlie this instinctive turn to comedy. Perhaps the dis-
> tancing afforded by comedy can at once relieve anxiety and win
> over a potentially hostile gentile audience. If Jewish sexual neuro-
> sis is as funny as Allen would have it, if America can laugh at the

Jew and see its own neuroses in his, then perhaps the Jew will be accepted as an organic part of the cultural landscape.[54]

The phenomenal critical and commercial success of *Annie Hall* suggests that by 1977 this kind of acceptance was not far away. Indeed, the anti-Semitism that Alvy experiences in the film is largely of his own paranoid imagining, such as when he insists that a coworker's slurred inquiry "Did you eat?" is actually a taunt: "Jew eat?" Of course, this makes Alvy the perfect reflection of a certain portion of his audience: those prepared to hear a Jewish-specific (and often anti-Semitic) discourse when there is none intended. We might read this "Jew eat?" moment as Allen's own kind of resistance to the external stereotyping of his films as Jewish. Alternatively, it may be a joke at the expense of Jewish critics, who complained that Allen's public persona perpetuated anti-Semitic stereotypes: they, like Alvy, get overexcited about nothing at all. Perhaps, in fact, "Jew eat?" carries both meanings. The degree to which Allen's manner of acting Jewish represents a response to this kind of perception of the self as Other is addressed later in this chapter.

"The First In-Depth Interview with Barbra Streisand"

Playboy magazine's October 1977 issue hit newsstands almost simultaneously with the theatrical release of *Annie Hall*. While Allen was promoting the appeal of the schlemiel, Streisand was carrying the banner of Jewish women into the lion's den: *Playboy*, the symbol of white male heterosexuality in America. Given *Playboy*'s obsession with the female body, Streisand's interview must be considered with regard to the complex history of the "Jew's body," a history fraught with both ambiguity and anxiety. This history has its roots in a discourse of race that dates back to the nineteenth century.[55] Nineteenth-century science, in the service of burgeoning European and American nationalism, postulated genealogical difference as the underpinnings of cultural difference. These genealogical differences were organized in a strict hierarchy, which purported to explain "scientifically" why the white European was the epitome of the civilized modern man, why the Negro was biologically incapable of attaining the lofty moral and intellectual perch of the Englishman, and why the Jew, though cunningly intelligent, would always remain physically and morally defective.

In this model, the Jews were not only inferior but also a mongrel race. Many of the physical defects of the Jew were attributed to prolonged interbreeding with blacks. This theory served two functions: first, miscegenation served as an illustration of the Jews' moral inferiority; and, second, it provided a mechanism of "degeneration" that explained away the politically inexpedient fact that early Christianity (and Christ himself) was descended from Jewish blood. This model of Jewish racial impurity reached its apotheosis, of course, with Adolph Hitler, and the shadow of the Holocaust forms the backdrop of any attempt to decode Jewishness through the physical traits of performers.

As Gilman notes, the Jew's nose often serves as the focal point of this conversation:

> The Jew's nose makes the Jewish face visible in the Western Diaspora. That nose is "seen" as an African nose, relating the image of the Jew to the image of the Black. It was not always because of any overt similarity in the stereotypical representation of the two idealized types of noses, but because each nose is considered a racial sign and as such reflects the internal life ascribed to the Jew and African no less than it does physiognomy.[56]

As a result, the Jewish audience regards Streisand's refusal to "fix" her Jewish nose as a key element of her personal legend.[57] Rather than downplaying or ignoring the importance of her nose as an element of her public persona, Streisand tells *Playboy* (only partly in jest) that her nose is, like Samson's hair, the secret of her success.

> *Playboy:* What is it, do you think, that makes your voice so special?
> *Streisand:* My deviated septum. If I ever had my nose fixed, it would ruin my career.[58]

When Lawrence Grobel, the interviewer, follows up by asking if she ever considered rhinoplasty, Streisand elaborates.

> In my earlier periods, when I would have liked to look like Catherine Deneuve, I considered having my nose fixed. But I didn't trust anyone enough to fix it. If I could do it myself with a mirror, I would straighten my nose and take off that little piece of cartilage from the tip. . . . See, I wouldn't do it conventionally. When I was young . . . it was like a fad, all the Jewish girls having their noses done every week at Erasmus Hall High School, taking perfectly good noses and whittling them down to nothing. The first thing someone would have done would be to cut off my bump. But I love my bump, I wouldn't cut my bump off.[59]

Streisand's response is telling in both what she says and what she does not say. She freely acknowledges that her nose differs from the classically beautiful ideal (represented by Catherine Deneuve). She similarly locates the desire to change one's nose in the Jewish American community in Brooklyn, where she grew up. At the same time, she suggests that the desire to look like someone else is an adolescent phase; one that she herself has outgrown. Yet she does not condemn her high school classmates for their assimilative desires. On the contrary, she is critical of "Jewish girls having their noses done" not because the procedure (or the desire for it) is inauthentically Jewish but because it is unnecessary.

Streisand makes it equally clear that her nose is her own, not to be trusted to others' ideas of beauty, be they Jewish or gentile. In a separate portion of the interview, when she has been asked about her professional reputation as a stickler for detail, she explains:

> Once, after I'd OK'd the photograph for an album cover, I noticed something about it looked funny—only to find out it was my nose. It had been retouched, the bump was removed. Somebody at the lab probably thought, This will please her. I told the lab people that if I'd wanted my nose fixed, I would have gone to a doctor.[60]

In this context, Streisand seems to indicate that her decision to "keep" her nose is an individual choice, albeit one made in the face of both external and internal anti-Semitism.[61] Streisand is not claiming that the Jewish nose or the Jewish body is particularly attractive. She implies instead that beauty and sexual attractiveness are, like ethnicity, based in performance. She is beautiful and sexy because she chooses to act beautiful and sexy. A Jewish reader might turn to her performance of her public persona as a valorization—"nice Jewish girls" can be just as sexy as the "playmates" who occupy the pages surrounding the Streisand interview.

But on another level Streisand's exegesis of her own face to the readers of *Playboy* is a way of asserting that Jewish women do not necessarily look "different," nor are women who look different necessarily Jews. As Vivian Sobchack writes in "Postmodern Modes of Ethnicity":

> We live in what seems to be the advanced stages of an age of representation, and thus we are perhaps more aware of the inauthenticity and theatricality of "being American." . . . In this context, nearly all those visible markers that once separated the cultures of "ethnic" descent from the "American" culture of consent, that

signaled the boundaries of otherness and gave it ethnic identity, integrity, and authenticity, are detached from their original historical roots and have become "floating signifiers" available for purchase by anyone. Ethnicity, too, seems based on consent.[62]

As anti-Semitic physical typing diminishes, more overtly Jewish faces can be screened without calling attention to themselves. The codes remain but only to the degree that they are internalized in cultural memory. With each reappearance, the nose with the bump becomes less the "Jewish nose" and more "Barbra Streisand's nose." The tortured history of the former is replaced with the star power of the latter.

In 1968, *Funny Girl* asked whether society could accept a woman who looks Jewish as beautiful. In 1973, *The Way We Were* answered with a resounding yes. Speaking to *Playboy* in 1977, Streisand implicitly declared the question no longer relevant. This not only opened the door for stereotypically Jewish-looking women to play romantic leading roles, but it also set the stage for the more complex interrogation of Jewish female sexuality that Streisand would undertake in the film *Yentl* (1983), to be discussed later in this chapter.

Manhattan

Released in 1979, *Manhattan* was Woody Allen's follow-up to *Annie Hall.*[63] Once again, Allen plays a variation on the schlemiel, Isaac Davis, a forty-two-year-old, twice-divorced television writer. When we first meet Isaac, he is dating Tracy (Mariel Hemingway), a seventeen-year-old blonde knockout. Isaac alternates between astonishment at his good fortune ("Can you believe I'm dating a girl who does homework?") and taking Tracy's attraction to him for granted. "You can't be in love with me" he tells her, while praising himself for "my wry sense of humor and astonishing sexual technique." Later, when explaining that the difference between their ages is too great to be overcome, he tells her that when she is thirty-eight he'll be sixty-three: "You'll be at the height of your sexual powers . . . of course, I will, too, probably." During the course of the film, Isaac leaves Tracy to pursue a relationship with Mary Wilke (Diane Keaton). Mary is the mistress of Isaac's best friend (Michael Murphy), and this forms the central comic premise of the film. But in *Manhattan* Keaton's character is not simply a comic foil for Allen, as she was in *Annie Hall.* Instead, she becomes a more traditional romantic object, allowing Allen as Isaac to transcend the schlemiel and become, if only for a while, a more conventional leading man.

This is consistent with the overall tone of *Manhattan*, which is much more self-consciously concerned with definitions of male sexuality. The film is framed as Isaac's story, told in retrospect. It opens with Allen's voice-over: "Chapter One. He adored New York City. He idolized it all out of proportion. No, make that: He romanticized it all out of proportion." As the voice-over continues, Allen continues to revise his self-description, finally settling on: "Chapter One: He was as tough and romantic as the city he loved. Behind his black-rimmed glasses was the coiled sexual power of a jungle cat. New York was his town and always would be." The joke here is intertextual; since Allen has not yet appeared on the screen, this description of a Raymond Chandler–style hero is funny only in contrast to Allen's established schlemiel persona. But Isaac's rewriting of his own introduction is also a signal that this persona is about to undergo a revision.

Isaac is as neurotic, hypochondriacal, and hypersexual as any of Allen's earlier characters, but he is also demonstrably emotional and protective. In his earlier works, Allen played a man who sought relationships with women as a means of overcoming his own insecurities. But in *Manhattan* first Tracy and then Mary are drawn to Isaac because he is more stable than they. Tracy turns to Isaac as a father figure, and Mary sees him as a superior alternative to the married man with whom she was previously involved. To further emphasize Isaac's desirability as a stable mate, when Isaac first walks alone with Mary the film's soundtrack supplies an instrumental version of Gershwin's "Someone to Watch over Me." When the lovers consummate their relationship, Mary tells Isaac that he is "wonderful" in bed but also (or perhaps because) "You're someone I could imagine having children with."

Isaac's suitability as a father is showcased elsewhere in the film, as we see him expressing his love for his son Willy. This is played against a more conventional view of masculinity in the scene where Isaac goes to pick up Willy from the home of his ex-wife Jill (Meryl Streep) and her lesbian lover Connie (Karen Ludwig). Isaac plays the entire scene dressed in a tight black T-shirt, evoking Marlon Brando's Stanley Kowalski in *A Streetcar Named Desire*.[64] Isaac's comic inability to match this conventional standard of masculinity is juxtaposed with his display of paternal affection and commitment, as he and Willy leave the apartment and are next seen playing playground basketball with the "Father and Son All-Stars." So, while Isaac still has elements of the schlemiel in his character, he also has some more traditional masculine virtues.

In fact, by the end of the film, when Isaac has seen the error of his romantic ways and made a commitment to Tracy, he has transcended the schlemiel almost entirely and become, in Yiddish terms, a mensch—a person, one of the good guys. The mensch stereotype is as recognizable to a Jewish audience as the schlemiel and is perhaps even more easily identified with. But rather than presenting one view of masculinity as superior to another *Manhattan* spoofs all such constructions. Throughout the film, Mary refers to her ex-husband Jeremiah as "sexually masterful."[65] She repeatedly cites his sex appeal as the reason she married him and why she had trouble divorcing him. Isaac feels intimidated by this memory, but when the audience finally meets Jeremiah we get the real punch line: Mary's ex-husband is played by Wallace Shawn, an actor who is physically very similar to Allen. Shawn's Jeremiah is short, nonathletic, balding, and nasal voiced. Shawn is also Jewish, though this is much less a part of his public persona than it is for Allen. After meeting Jeremiah, Isaac comments on how the man failed to live up to his expectations, adding, "It's amazing how subjective all that stuff is."

Yentl *and* Zelig

Having spent the 1970s demonstrating the appeal of characters who proudly assert both their Jewishness and their sexuality, Streisand and Allen each directed and starred in films released in 1983 that addressed the question of "passing." In *Yentl*, Streisand plays a young Jewish girl who masquerades as a boy in order to gain access to the yeshiva education that women were denied in late-nineteenth-century Russia.[66] In *Zelig*, a faux documentary, Allen plays Leonard Zelig, the 1920s "human chameleon" whose desire to be liked is so strong that he changes his personality and physical features to match whatever group he is with.[67]

These two films represent the culmination of the historical trajectory I have laid out in this chapter vis-à-vis the perception of the Jewish body in performance. In their earlier works, Streisand and Allen adopted and adapted stereotypical Jewish traits, helping to reposition Jewishness as consistent (if not synonymous) with sexual attractiveness. In so doing, they implicitly challenged conventional ideas of beauty, sex appeal, and what it means to act Jewish. In *Yentl* and *Zelig*, this challenge is made explicit. Elaine K. Ginsberg notes that "both the process and discourse of passing challenge the essentialism that is often the foundation of identity politics, a challenge that may be seen as either threatening or liberating but in either instance discloses the truth that identities are not singularly true or false but multiple and contingent."[68] Thus Gilman sees *Zelig* as Allen's attempt "to lay to rest the polar definition of self-hatred espoused by writers such as Bettelheim," Whitfield calls the film a "cinematic exploration of the radical instability of identity."[69] In a similar vein, Allison Fernley and Paula Maloof write that *Yentl* "provides us with a very powerful and potentially disruptive situation that calls into question and threatens to destroy conventional sexual configurations."[70]

In both films, the disruption of conventional identities is mirrored and enhanced by a corresponding disruption of conventional film genres. *Yentl* is no ordinary musical; all eleven songs are sung solo by Streisand and are used as a means of revealing Yentl's interior monologue. *Zelig* carries the frame of the documentary to the extreme, blurring fiction and reality by including commentary from such real-life figures as Susan Sontag and Saul Bellow, alongside those of fictional characters such as Eudora Fletcher (Mia Farrow) and Paul Deghuere (John Rothman); groundbreaking computer technology was used to insert Allen's character into 1920s newsreel footage.

That said, the passing that is performed in *Yentl* and *Zelig* is not as simple as it may first appear. Yentl successfully passes as a boy in the eyes of her study partner Avigdor (Mandy Patinkin), and Zelig passes as a host of disparate characters, but the audience is in on the joke, so to speak. In fact, in each case the dramaturgy of the film *requires* that the audience be aware of the protagonist's "true" identity. The dramatic tension of *Yentl* depends on the audience's awareness of Yentl's masquerade. Much of the humor in *Zelig* depends on the viewer's ability to recognize the real historical figures improbably juxtaposed with Allen's smiling countenance.

As a result, though both films play (in the best sense of the word) with the *idea* of passing, they ultimately reject the *practice* of passing in favor of a grounded and fixed identity. Allen explains, regarding *Zelig*: "I wanted to make a comment with the film of the specific danger of abandoning one's own true self, in an effort to be liked, not to make trouble, to fit in, and where that leads one in life in every aspect and where that leads on a political level."[71] Similarly, in *Yentl*, Streisand's character is clearly portrayed as the exception that defines the rule of Jewish femininity. When Yentl is forced to abandon her masquerade, she does not stand and fight for a reconsideration of gender roles in Russian Jewish culture but instead emigrates to America at film's end.

And yet this exploration of the idea of passing is not without importance, especially when it is set against the backdrop of Streisand and

Allen's prior work. Because the two actor-directors have established themselves as arguably the most recognizably Jewish performers in American entertainment, the desire to pass that is evidenced in the films' takes on a double-coded significance. For Jewish audiences in 1983, *Yentl* and *Zelig* asserted both the possibility of passing and the undesirability of doing so. But for the dominant reader who is able to mark Streisand and Allen as Jews the films reconfirm a belief in the desirability of passing and the impossibility of doing so.

Perhaps the most telling indicator of the way audience perceptions of Jewishness changed between 1968 and 1983 is that Rex Reed, reviewing *Yentl* for the *New York Post* in 1983, unwittingly echoed Norman Nadel's comment about *Fiddler on the Roof* two decades earlier, declaring: "The movie [*Yentl*] is like rye bread; you don't have to be Jewish to love it."[72] In 1964, Nadel, a Jewish critic, used this one-liner as a way of staking claim to *Fiddler* on behalf of the Jewish audience, while reassuring the gentile audience that the musical was not too Jewish to be enjoyed by all. When Reed, a gentile critic, repeats the quip, it has a converse meaning: he acknowledges the Jewishness of *Yentl* while claiming the right to enjoy it for a general audience. To paraphrase another popular advertising slogan of the day: you've come a long way, *bubbe*.

CHAPTER 5

The Desire to Remember, 1989–1997

BY THE LATE 1980s, Jews had achieved an unprecedented level of social acceptance in the United States.[1] In theater, film, and television, thanks in part to the strides made by Barbra Streisand and Woody Allen (among many others), the question of whether the mainstream American audience would accept explicitly Jewish characters and themes was largely settled in the affirmative. This is evidenced in part by articles in the popular press that trumpeted a new wave of Jewish-themed entertainment. *Newsweek*, for example, declared in 1992 that "A new breed of leading man has swum into the television mainstream. He's funny, he's highly verbal and he's slightly neurotic. Oh, and Jewish."[2] The scholarly community also took note. In 1993, for example, both *Television Quarterly* and *Studies in Popular Culture* published articles on the emergence of Jewish characters on television.[3] In 1994, the *Jewish Folklore and Ethnology Review* dedicated an entire issue to "Jews and the Media."[4] Even more significant, perhaps, is the number of articles that were *not* written, as the explicit Jewishness of several major films—*Driving Miss Daisy* (1989), *Bugsy* (1991)—and Broadway plays—*Lost in Yonkers* (1991), *Broken Glass* (1994)—passed without similar fanfare.

Where an earlier generation of performances had used the strategies of double coding and acting Jewish as a means of negotiating their position as social Other, many Jewish theater artists in the 1990s turned their attention inward. This was especially true of those generations born after the Holocaust. For many of their parents, Judaism was a constrictive and outdated tradition associated with a history that had produced more pain than pleasure, more suffering than salvation. Their link to that history was tenuous and made more so by the cultural trauma of the Holocaust. As a result, children of the post-Holocaust era tend to approach the question of acting Jewish from a different direction than the artists discussed earlier in this book. Playwright David Mamet, born in 1947 (the year *Gentleman's Agreement* was released), recalls: "In my childhood home, and in the homes of my friends of like extraction, there was a feeling of tenuousness. . . . We do not know how a Jewish home (finally, we do not know how a *Jew*) is supposed to look."[5] Mamet first addressed this topic publicly in two essays—"The Decoration of Jewish Houses" and "A Plain Brown Wrapper"—which open his 1989 collection *Some Freaks*.[6] His 1991 film *Homicide* explores the issue further, through the story of an acculturated Jewish detective whose investigation into the murder of an elderly Jewish shopkeeper leads him into an ordeal of self-examination with regard to his own ethnic identity. Mamet's most recent and ambitious attempt to examine his generation's crisis of Jewish identity was a trio of autobiographical short plays produced on Broadway under the collective title *The Old Neighborhood* (1997).

The playwright Wendy Wasserstein, born in 1950, approaches the question of acting Jewish from the point of view of an upper-middle-class woman educated at Mt. Holyoke and Yale in the 1960s and 1970s. In works such as *Isn't It Romantic?* (1984) and *The Heidi Chronicles* (1989), which won a Pulitzer prize, Wasserstein questions the relationship between Jewishness and feminism, between the desire for the homely comforts represented by *The Goldbergs* and the arguably unfulfilled promise of liberation represented by *The Way We Were*. Writing a satirical piece for the *New Yorker* titled "Shiksa Goddess," which pokes fun at Hillary Clinton's discovery (conveniently during her campaign to become a U.S. senator from New York) of possible Jewish ancestry, Wasserstein offers a wry summation of her relationship to her ethnicity:

> I've had a happy life thinking of myself as a Jewish writer. I came to accept that when my work was described as being "too New York" it was really a euphemism for something else. I belonged to a temple, and on my opening nights, my mother told friends she'd be much happier if it was my wedding. In other words, I had a solid sense of self.[7]

Though written in jest, "Shiksa Goddess" playfully asserts Wasserstein's belief in both the immutability of Jewish as an identifying designation and the often problematic interpretation of what that identifier means, especially for women of her generation. In *The Sisters Rosensweig* (1992, Lincoln Center; 1993, Broadway), Wasserstein confronts the question of Jewish female identity head on, exploring the sense of dislocation that comes from losing the connection to one's roots. As she writes in the introduction to the trade edition of *Sisters*, "Despite their maturity, most of the characters in the play are struggling with who they are. There's a reason why these three sisters are from Brooklyn, and the play takes place in Queen Anne's Gate, London" (xi).[8]

As Mamet's successor to the title of "arguably America's leading playwright," Tony Kushner weaves his own interrogation of acting Jewish throughout his epic *Angels in America: A Gay Fantasia on National Themes* (1992, Los Angeles; 1993, Broadway), another recipient of the Pulitzer prize. Shortly after the premier of *Angels*, Kushner began working on a new adaptation of S. Anski's classic Yiddish play *A Dybbuk, or Between Two Worlds*; after years of workshops and regional presentations, Kushner's *Dybbuk* made its New York premier at The Public Theater in late 1997. Asked by Rabbi Norman J. Cohen to explain the importance of Jewish identity in his work, Kushner (born in 1956) replied:

> We didn't know Yiddish [in my family], we didn't know Hebrew, we didn't know prayers. We went to a very Reform—I mean sort of reformed out of existence—Jewish congregation. Still it's all in there somehow, so that when I read translated Talmud . . . you can sort of smell it out. The Jewish essence or some essence of the culture is still in there, and waiting to flower.[9]

This desire to reconnect with a lost "Jewish essence" should not be confused with the essentialist view of Jewish identity that earlier Jewish artists had rebelled against. On the contrary, Kushner's attempt to "smell out . . . some essence of the culture" evokes Jonathan Boyarin's call for "a *critical post-Judaism* . . . an already-existing but unidentified commonality."[10]

Writing in 1990, the Jewish sociologist Shmuel Eisenstadt declared:

> Although there are many indications of problems, those among the Jews who are concerned seem able to combine historical communality with full participation in American society. . . . Thus, instead of the "classical" problem of physical and cultural survival in the modern world, the crucial question for Jews becomes one of how to find new ways of authenticating their Jewishness in this new setting.[11]

This chapter focuses on three plays that use acting Jewish as a means of addressing the "crucial question" of their own era: Kushner's *Angels In America*, Wasserstein's *The Sisters Rosensweig*, and Mamet's *The Old Neighborhood*. In one sense, these plays demonstrate the possibility of

articulating explicitly themes of Jewish identity that previously could be
presented only in an implicit, double-coded fashion. But it is not simply that these plays discuss Jewishness explicitly because they *can;* it is
also that they *must* if they are to remain relevant to the concerns of a
Jewish audience in a "postethnic" America, where tenuous, consent-
based "affiliation" trumps fixed, descent-based "identity."[12]

These plays, I argue, look to the past for clues about how to act Jewish. Even more importantly, they portray the desire to remember as
itself a key element of acting Jewish. It is this desire to remember that
distinguishes such works from earlier "Jewish revivals" such as *Fiddler
on the Roof* and *Funny Girl*. The artists discussed earlier in this book—
Arthur Miller, Gertrude Berg, Joseph Stein, Barbra Streisand, and
Woody Allen—were of an earlier generation. They could react against
an essentialist view of Jewishness precisely because they had direct
experience with it. They could freely adapt, abandon, and "play" with
elements of their Jewishness because they and their Jewish audiences
brought enough extratextual experience to the performance to supply
the culturally specific context. As Barbara Kirshenblatt-Gimblett
explains about *Fiddler on the Roof*, "a Jewish audience could fill in the
blanks with all that it already knew about the virtual Jewish world of
Anatevka."[13] For the post-Holocaust generation of American Jews,
filling in the blanks is not as simple a task.

Mamet, Wasserstein, and Kushner grew up with these performances, but because their generation lacked the necessary cultural context they found them unsatisfying as guides to acting Jewish. In
response, their work attempts to reconstruct the heritage that was
denied them by their parents' desire to assimilate. Rather than viewing
the transmigration of Jews from Europe to America, from poverty to
middle-class respectability, as a narrative of inevitable progress, the
Kushner, Wasserstein, and Mamet performances of the 1990s took a
less than charitable view of the melting pot ideal. What earlier generations regarded as reasonable accommodations to life in the New
World, the current generation of Jewish American playwrights sees as
a compromise that has robbed them of their cultural birthright.
Although these playwrights do expect their Jewish audiences to bring a
common cultural context to the reading of their work, the experience
that this generation of American Jews shares is not the densely packed
memory of their parents and grandparents; instead they share the anxiety that comes from an unfulfilled, and perhaps unfulfillable, desire to
remember.

In this sense, acting Jewish, as it is discussed in this chapter, is more
concerned with the moral, ethical, and historical aspects of Jewishness

than the examples discussed earlier and less concerned with the external performative signs of Jewish difference. This should be understood, though, as a shift in emphasis rather than a complete change. Underlying the question of how Jewishness is or is not recognized by audiences in the early examples is the belief that the recognition of Jewishness is meaningful in terms of moral and ethical behavior. Even in the explicit portrayals of Jewishness discussed in this chapter, the question of what performative codes indicate Jewishness is never very far from the question of acting Jewish in religious or ethical terms. Furthermore, the phenomenon of selectively invisible, double-coded portrayals of Jewishness did continue throughout the 1990s. My focus here, however, is on the new interrogations of acting Jewish that are made possible in this era by a greater acceptance of Jewish characters in mainstream American entertainment.

Angels in America

Millennium Approaches, part 1 of Kushner's eight-hour epic *Angels in America*, had its world premier at San Francisco's Eureka Theatre in May 1991, at which time part 2, *Perestroika*, was presented only as a staged reading. The first production of both parts opened 1 November 1992 at the Mark Taper Forum in Los Angeles. On the strength of the Los Angeles production, *Angels* arrived on Broadway in 1993 already anointed as a don't-miss cultural event. "Not within memory," writes David Savran, "has a new American play been canonized by the press as rapidly as *Angels in America*."[14] In addition to the 1993 Pulitzer prize for Drama, *Millennium Approaches* and *Perestroika* earned a total of seven Tony awards, including unprecedented back-to-back designations for Best Play in 1993 and 1994.[15]

Performance scholars, too, have lavished considerable attention and praise on Kushner's complex drama. In the introduction to their 1997 anthology *Approaching the Millennium: Essays on Angels in America*, editors Deborah Geis and Steven Kruger write:

Bringing together an impressive array of characters (female and male; gay, straight, and bisexual; black and white; Jewish, Mormon, and WASP; angelic and human; historical and fictional)— complicated by their portrayal by only eight actors—Kushner's epic vision places itself explicitly in the current American conflict over identity politics yet also situates that debate in a broader historical context.[16]

To fully explore all the ramifications of *Angels* would require much more space than can be devoted to them here. My present focus is on the way that Kushner's play explores the question of acting Jewish, with special attention to the way he uses the ideas of history and memory to inform this issue.

From the point of view of acting Jewish, it is significant that *Angels* begins with a Jewish funeral. Alone onstage, Rabbi Isidore Chemelwitz (Kathleen Chalfant) of the Bronx Home for Aged Hebrews is eulogizing Sarah Ironson, grandmother of the yet-to-be-introduced character Louis (Joe Mantello), whom Kushner calls "the closest character to myself that I've ever written."[17] Sarah, the rabbi tells us, was

> not a person, but a whole kind of person, the ones who crossed the ocean, who brought with us to America the villages of Russia and Lithuania—and how we struggled, and how we fought, for the family, for the Jewish home, so that you would not grow up *here*, in this strange place, in the melting pot where nothing melted. Descendants of this immigrant woman, you do not grow up in America, you and your children and their children with the goyische names. You do not live in America. No such place exists. Your clay is the clay of some Litvak shtetl, your air the air of the steppes—because she carried the old world on her back across the ocean, in a boat, and she put it down on Grand Concourse Avenue, or in Flatbush, and she worked that earth into your bones, and you pass it to your children, this ancient, ancient culture and home.
> (Little pause)
> You can never make that crossing that she made, for such Great Voyages do not anymore exist. But every day of your lives the miles that voyage between that place and this one you cross. Every day. You understand me? In you that journey is.
> So . . .
> She was the last of the Mohicans, this one was. Pretty soon . . . all the old will be dead. (I,10; ellipses and italics in original)[18]

Thus, from the very outset of the play Kushner stresses the importance of an essential Jewishness, something that is worked "into your bones." This Jewish essence is clearly linked to a particular Jewish history, a history of eastern European culture ("some Litvak shtetl") but also a history of migration ("In you that journey is"). But even as the Rabbi's speech emphasizes the importance of remembering and remaining connected to that history, his conclusion ("Great Voyages do not anymore exist" and "Pretty soon . . . all the old will be dead") acknowledges the tenuousness of that connection.

Despite what would seem to be a particularly Jewish opening—the Rabbi alone onstage speaking outward in the second person—critical responses to *Angels* varied widely in the importance they attached to the play's portrayal of acting Jewish. John Simon, for example, reviewing the show for *New York* magazine, saw the Rabbi's reference to Sarah as "the last of the Mohicans" as evidence of "Kushner's thirst for ecumenism."[19] John Lahr used the metaphor of the Great Voyage to describe the play itself.[20] Perhaps speaking to a perceived demographic difference between New York audiences and national ones, the reviews in the *Christian Science Monitor* and *USA Today*, both national dailies, never once use the words *Jew* or *Jewish*, focusing exclusively on the play's treatment of "homosexual themes."[21]

Clive Barnes, on the other hand, suggested in the *New York Post* that George C. Wolfe's direction gave "that gay-corpse humor a proper Harvey Fierstein Jewish twist, making it in sensibility very much a Gay Fantasia on New York, rather than American, Themes."[22] And Michael Feingold pointed out that the Rabbi was "played by a younger and distinctly Gentile actress," suggesting that the "blasphemy and gender subversion . . . stave off pomposity."[23] Alisa Solomon went so far as to suggest that Kushner's construction of the scene, with the Rabbi alone onstage speaking outward in the second person, directly implicated "an American theater audience—itself largely Jewish and liberal" in his admonition.[24]

We might also note in passing that the casualness of Solomon's assertion that the American theater audience is "largely Jewish" suggests that this claim reflects conventional wisdom among theater critics, which may also explain why Barnes extrapolates so easily from "Jewish" to "New York." Since New York represents a cultural center for both Jews and theater in the United States, it is perhaps not surprising that *New York*, when used as an adjective, frequently serves as a code word for *Jewish*. Consider, for example, Wasserstein's acknowledgment, cited earlier, that "'too New York' . . . was really a euphemism for something else."[25]

In *Angels*, when we finally meet Louis in the fourth scene, he is outside the funeral home immediately after the service. "My grandmother," he tells his lover Prior (Stephen Spinella) with his first line of the play, "actually saw Emma Goldman speak. In Yiddish" (I, 19). The reference to Emma Goldman adds a layer of leftist politics to Kushner's construction of Jewish history, prefiguring what will be one of the play's central themes and one that will be taken up later in this chapter:

the dialectic opposition of two historical Jewish American figures: Roy Cohn (Ron Liebman) and Ethel Rosenberg (Kathleen Chalfant again). At the same time, Louis's reminiscence is indicative of the unreliability of memory: "But all Grandma could remember," he adds, "was that she spoke well and wore a hat" (I, 19).

As *Angels* progresses, Louis is established as a man who identifies himself openly as Jewish, gay, and liberal. Yet these labels by themselves give him little guidance about how to *act*. As a result, Prior's declining health due to AIDS sends Louis into a crisis of self-examination that continues throughout both parts of *Angels in America*. As Solomon writes, "In failing as a gay man, Louis fails as a Jew."[26] He abandons Prior in his hour of greatest need because neither his Jewishness nor his homosexuality provide firmly rooted models of behavior on which he can draw to overcome his fear of suffering.

Eve Kosofsky Sedgwick, in her pioneering study of gay identity, *Epistemology of the Closet*, has argued that gay and Jewish identity formation, while similar in form, "in that the stigmatized individual has at least notionally some discretion . . . over other people's knowledge of her or his membership in the group," are nevertheless distinguished from one another.

> A (for instance) Jewish or Gypsy identity, and hence a Jewish or Gypsy secrecy or closet, would nonetheless differ again from the distinctive gay versions of these things in its clear ancestral linearity and answerability, in the roots (however tortuous and ambivalent) of cultural identification through each individual's originary culture of (at a minimum) the family.[27]

Sedgwick's point is that Jewish identity can be validated by family and community history in a way that gay identity cannot. Yet Louis's inability to act Jewish is occasioned precisely by the fact that his Jewish identity lacks a "clear ancestral linearity and answerability." As a result, his search for self-definition plays itself out in the negative. Jewish, gay, and liberal become conflated in the experience of being Other. This mirrors, to some degree, Kushner's own experience. As the playwright told the Jewish newspaper the *Forward* in 1995, "The model I used in the process of coming out [as a gay man] was everything I knew about the Jewish experience in the twentieth century."[28]

But for Louis, even the position of Other is unstable because of American society's own lack of history. "[T]here are no angels in America," he tells Belize (Jeffrey Wright), "no spiritual past, no racial past, there's only the political" (I, 92). In his desire for a history to guide his action, Louis seems almost nostalgic for a time and place of overt oppression.

> And it's just weird, you know, I mean I'm not all that Jewish-looking, or . . . well, maybe I am but, you know, in New York, everyone is . . . well, not everyone, but so many are but in England, in London I walk into bars and I feel like Sid the Yid, you know I mean like Woody Allen in *Annie Hall*, with the payess and the gabardine coat, like never, never anywhere so much . . . (I, 91).

Louis's reference to *Annie Hall* carries a double significance. It evokes a desire for a dominant culture against which he, as the Jewish Other, can define himself. But he wants that definition to remain within his control; as was demonstrated in chapter 4, Allen's film, especially the scene Louis describes, represents the Jewish desire to be different from, *and superior to*, a vacuous WASP culture. At the same time, in referring to *Annie Hall*, Louis is acknowledging Woody Allen's status as a relevant figure in his impoverished history of American Jewish culture. Louis can't connect with his grandmother's Great Voyage, but he can identify with Alvy Singer in *Annie Hall*. As played by Joe Mantello, Louis comes across as a gay version of the modern schlemiel; Frank Rich writes, "Mr. Mantello . . . is a combustible amalgam of puppyish Jewish guilt and self-serving intellectual piety."[29] Yet, though he may grasp at the double-coded stereotypes of an earlier generation, Louis also resists and ultimately rejects them in his search for a more meaningful way to act Jewish.

While Louis may be the character in *Angels* who most resembles its author, the most dominant Jewish character in the play is arguably Roy Cohn. This is especially true in performance, as evidenced by the fact that Tony voters named Ron Liebman, who played Cohn the Best Actor of the 1992–93 season, while Joe Mantello was nominated (and did not win) in the Best Featured (i.e., supporting) Actor category. That Roy Cohn is such an important figure in *Angels* highlights Kushner's desire to remember Jewish history in a way that goes beyond the simple nostalgia of, for example, *Fiddler on the Roof*. As Kushner explains, though he did not consciously set out to write a play about being Jewish, "I think by bringing Roy in in the first place I guaranteed that a certain amount of energy was going to be going into the Jewish question, because Roy was Jewish in a very interesting way."[30]

The real Roy Cohn, a Jewish lawyer educated at Columbia University, first came to national attention as the Assistant U.S. Attorney in the 1951 prosecution of Julius and Ethel Rosenberg on charges of espionage. Due in part to Cohn's machinations, the Rosenbergs were convicted and sentenced to death. At the time, many American Jews believed the Rosenbergs were unjustly persecuted because of their ethnicity.[31] Cohn was subsequently appointed chief counsel to Senator Joseph McCarthy's Government Committee on Operations of the Senate, and played a significant and controversial role in the Army-McCarthy Hearings of 1954 before outcry over his political tactics and revelations about his homosexual activities led to his resignation. After leaving government service, Cohn established himself in private practice as a high profile attorney in New York City. Disbarred on ethics charges in 1980, Cohn died of AIDS in 1986 at the age of 59.[32]

As portrayed by Ron Liebman, Roy is the kind of Jewish character that most American Jewish theater artists have refused to portray—at least explicitly. He is a comic villain, powerful and power hungry, vain and vindictive. As John Lahr declared in *The New Yorker*, "Ron Liebman has become almost Jacobean in the snarling, vigorous excesses of his performance."[33] John Simon echoed this sentiment, suggesting that Liebman is "more Roy Cohn tha[n] Cohn himself ever was."[34] As a closeted homosexual, he evidences both the deceitfulness and the degeneracy of the Jew as represented in anti-Semitic theoretical stereotypes that date back to medieval Europe, where the Jew's inner spiritual perversity was thought to be manifested outwardly through sexual perversity.[35]

"As a liberal Jewish audience," writes Solomon, "Roy is the villain we, like Louis, love to hate."[36] Michael Feingold calls Liebman's Cohn "a horror cartoon."[37] But the Jewish audience does not hate Roy simply because he is an embarrassment. Nor do "we" hate him just because he sees no conflict between his Jewishness and his vicious behavior. The Jewish audience also hates Roy Cohn because he has what they desire, a self-assured autonomous identity that depends on neither a ruptured history nor a projection of the self as Other but simply on his own will to power. In one scene, Roy explains to his doctor, Henry, why he is not a "homosexual."

> Like all labels they tell you one thing and one thing only: where does an individual so identified fit into the food chain, in the pecking order? Not ideology or sexual taste, but something much simpler: clout. Not who I fuck or who fucks me, but who will pick up the phone when I call, who owes me favors. . . . Because *what* I am is defined entirely by *who* I am. Roy Cohn is not a homosexual. Roy Cohn is a heterosexual man, Henry, who fucks around with guys (I, 45–6, italics in original).

For members of the Jewish audience, who, like Louis, are grasping for identity, Roy's absolutist proclamation that who he is defines what he is can be dangerously seductive. It might, in fact, be more appropriate to say that Roy is the character we hate to love.

The Jewish audience, I suggest, cannot help but be drawn to Roy's exuberant mode of acting Jewish. His speech, though politically and personally hateful, is peppered with Yiddish expressions. It is also important to note that Roy is *funny*, especially in Liebman's virtuosic portrayal, and his humor draws on the borscht belt tradition of insulting Jewish comedians such as Sid Caesar and Don Rickles.[38] As one critic remarked, there are times in the show when Liebman is "so over-the-top he'll turn into Jerry Lewis."[39] Another remarked that Liebman's face is "almost a plastic mask of nastiness."[40] In this sense, *Angels* continues the practice seen in chapter 4 of positioning the Jew as comic versus the gentile as straight man (double meaning intended).

It should be noted that the comic quality of Roy has much to do with Liebman's portrayal. Accounts of other actors who have played Roy, for example, David Schofield in the 1993 London production, address their violent and vituperative qualities but not their humor.[41] Even more significantly, several London critics who were impressed with Schofield's performance nonetheless identified Louis as the central character in the play, suggesting that Liebman's humorous portrayal was responsible, at least in part, for the centrality of Roy to the New York production.

Alternatively, perhaps the "liberal and Jewish" American audience postulated by Solomon is responsible for Roy being placed at the center of the American conversation about *Angels*. Although Roy has shown no special loyalty to other Jews—in fact, he has shown a willingness to sacrifice Jewish victims (the Rosenbergs) to protect his own position—he is, like it or not, a Jew who has achieved a position of power in the gentile world and therefore a kind of iconic cultural hero. As Linda Winer wrote in *Newsday*, "Ron Liebman's justly acclaimed Roy Cohn is still staggering proof of the seductive appeal of nonstop evil."[42] Perhaps this is why Frank Rich declared that Cohn's "dark view of life is not immediately dismissed by Mr. Kushner."[43]

Ultimately, of course, Kushner shows the pushy and ruthless Roy to be an unsatisfactory model for acting Jewish. Louis calls him "the polestar of human evil" and "the worst human being who ever lived" (II, 95). For Louis, as for the liberal Jewish audience, Roy's self-serving conservatism and lack of ethics ultimately define him as a villain in the story of Jewish American culture. And, as Stephen J. Bottoms notes, "The presence of Kushner's other–very different—Jewish characters defuses any danger of this depiction being read as an affirmation of the 'truth' of this stereotype."[44] But as a villain Roy represents an important touchstone for Kushner in his desire to connect with the past. Roy's villainy is most obvious vis-à-vis his role in the conviction and execution of Ethel and Julius Rosenberg, the Jewish American couple accused of delivering nuclear secrets to the Soviet Union during World War II.

Kushner's decision to include the ghost of Ethel Rosenberg, who was executed with her husband on 18 June 1953, as a character in *Angels* shows the importance of his leftist politics in his desire to reconnect with Jewish history. Ethel, who was played by the same actor who played the Rabbi (Chalfant), returns to haunt Roy. Although this premise is predicated on the idea that she was unjustly executed, Kushner does not bring Ethel back from the dead in order to retry the espionage case. "What matters," writes Solomon, "is Ethel's power to recall, in strong, testy terms, a Jewish American politics that looked beyond Roy's rabid individualism and Louis's vapid liberalism."[45] In this sense, Ethel is not so much Roy's personal specter as she is a representative of Louis's grandmother, who was buried at the beginning of the play. Ethel, too, has made a Great Voyage—from New York to the electric chair to Heaven . . . and back; she, too, represents the Jewish refusal, or inability, to melt into the melting pot.

These themes, which run throughout *Angels in America*, coalesce in the final act of part 2, *Perestroika*. Roy lies dead in his hospital bed. Belize has summoned Louis to say Kaddish (the Jewish prayer of mourning) over him. At first Louis balks, objecting: "My New Deal Pinko Parents in Schenectady would never forgive me, they're already so disappointed, 'He's a fag. He's an office temp. And *now look*, he's saying Kaddish for Roy Cohn'"(II, 124). Belize convinces Louis that even Roy deserves forgiveness, or at least peace, yet Louis runs into another problem: he cannot remember how to say the prayer. He begins; he falters. And then Ethel appears, prompting him. Together, in counterpoint, the two characters say the entire Kaddish over Roy's body, and the slow roll of the ancient Aramaic prayer gives the scene a primal, ancient feel that bespeaks a desire to remember the past, to remember the dead. In the end, Kushner seems to tell us, Roy, Louis, and Ethel are united by something essentially Jewish. But this unifying Jewish essence is not just linked to religion; it is also defined by attitude. Louis and Ethel punctuate the Kaddish with the epithet "You sonofabitch" (II,126), a moment Frank Rich describes as evocative of "the gallows humor of Lenny Bruce."[46]

As if to reinforce this idea that Louis has finally managed to forge a

link with his Jewish past, two scenes later Sarah Ironson, the grandmother whose burial began the play, appears onstage for the first time.
Sarah is played by the actor playing Louis, metaphorically enhancing
the connection between the generations. Speaking in Yiddish (translated by Rabbi Chemelwitz), she gives Prior a message for her grandson.

> *Sarah Ironson:* Tell him: az er darf ringen mit zain Libm Nomen.
> Yah?!
> *Rabbi Isidor Chemelwitz:* You should struggle with the Almighty!
> *Sarah Ironson:* Azoi toot a Yid.
> *Rabbi Isidor Chemelwitz:* It's the Jewish way. (II, 138)

But Kushner does not rest on this reductive definition of acting Jewish.
In the final moments of *Angels*, the Epilogue, Louis is once again beset
by anxiety about how to reconcile his Jewishness and his liberal politics.
He and Belize banter over the rights of Palestinians to the West Bank
and the Gaza Strip (II, 148).

Neither the Rabbi nor Roy nor Ethel nor his grandmother can give
Louis the stable Jewish identity he desires. Why not? Because, Kushner
tells us, Jewish identity is not meant to be stable. It is Louis's anxiety,
his unfulfilled and perhaps unfulfillable desire to reconcile five thousand years of history, ethics, and ritual with the demands of an ever-
changing and uncertain future, that for Kushner is the quintessence of
acting Jewish.

The Sisters Rosensweig

In October of 1992, as *Angels in America* prepared to open in Los Angeles, Wendy Wasserstein's *The Sisters Rosensweig* opened at New York's
Lincoln Center Theater, under the direction of Daniel Sullivan.[47] Following a successful run there, the play moved to Broadway, opening at
the Barrymore Theatre in March 1993, where it ran an additional 556
performances, remarkably long for a nonmusical play in the 1990s. *Sisters* earned the Tony award and Outer Critics Circle award as the Best
Play of the 1992–93 Broadway season, as well as a Best Actress Tony
for Madeline Kahn and a Best Director nomination for Sullivan. Set in
a sitting room in Queen Anne's Gate, London, in 1991, the play chronicles a tumultuous weekend in the lives of three middle-aged sisters.[48]
Pfeni Rosensweig (Frances McDormand at Linclon Center, Christine
Estabrook on Broadway), an itinerant journalist, and Gorgeous Teitelbaum (Madeline Kahn), a radio talk show host in Newton, Massachu-

setts, have come to the home of their older sister, expatriate banker
Sara Goode (Jane Alexander), to celebrate her fifty-fourth birthday.
Also present at the celebration are Sara's eighteen-year-old daughter
Tess (Julie Dretzin); Tess's Anglo-Lithuanian boyfriend Tom Vali-
unus (Patrick Fitzgerald); Pfeni's boyfriend Geoffrey Duncan (John
Vickery), a bisexual English theater director; Sara's notoriously anti-
Semitic boyfriend Nicholas Pym (Rex Robbins); and a newcomer
named Mervyn ("Merv") Kant (Robert Klein).

"The play," wrote Robert Brustein in the *New Republic*, "is primarily
about Jewish identity," a sentiment echoed by Doug Watt in the New
York *Daily News*, who called *Sisters* a comedy "about middle-class Jewish manners."[49] Mel Gussow, reviewing it for the *New York Times*,
noted that "The play is steeped in Jewish culture and humor," adding
"but the emotional subtext is broader."[50] William Henry III summed
things up, explaining that for these three sisters the problem "is not
getting to Moscow but failing to stay, spiritually, in their ancestral Jewish Brooklyn"[51] Howard Kissell, reviewing the Broadway production,
suggested that the Jewish identity question pervades every part of the
play, even those subplots that do not explicitly address it.

> Believe me, I feel deep (Jewish) guilt suggesting that Wasser-
> stein's play, which has moved to Broadway with all its hilarity
> intact, has serious undercurrents. But, if anything, it now seems
> more focused and so the issues seem unmistakable.
>
> Even the bisexual director seems more integral to the play,
> which is, in part, an homage to the cozy America of the '50s, in
> which Jews felt more at home than they had anywhere for cen-
> turies.[52]

Brustein notes that "the main action concerns Sara's reluctant attraction to a shamelessly Jewish furrier named Mervyn from Roslyn
(Robert Klein) who prefers to call her Sadie."[53] Brustein's use of the
phrase "shamelessly Jewish" implies, correctly, that for Sara Jewishness
is somehow shameful. When we first meet Sara at the rise of the play,
she is being interviewed by her daughter Tess for a school project.
Asked to narrate her early years, Sara has gravitated not to her childhood in Brooklyn but to her entrée into the Anglophilic upper class as
a member of an a cappella singing group at Radcliffe College. We subsequently learn that Sara embraced highbrow English culture, making
London her permanent residence, naming her daughter after Tess of
the D'Urbervilles, and dating a member of the peerage. Twice
divorced, most recently from an English banker whose only contribu-

tion to her life seems to have been the Anglo-Saxon last name Goode, Sara works as an executive with the Hong Kong/Shanghai Bank. Ironically, banking, a profession stereotypically associated with Jews, has proved to be Sara's avenue of upward mobility, delivering her out of the middle-class Jewish American environment in which she was raised. She is, however, too smart and self-aware not to recognize the implications of her life choices. As she declares to Merv late in the play:

> Look, Merv, if you're thinking, "I know this woman who is sitting next me. I grew up with her, with women like her, only sometime in her life she decided to run away. She moved to England, she dyed her hair, she named her daughter Tess and sent her to Westminster. She assimilated beyond her wildest dreams, and now she's lonely and wants to come home," you're being too obvious. Yes, I'm lonely, but I don't want to come home. (57)

Yet by the play's conclusion, it is all too clear that Sara does, indeed, want to come home, or at least to return to a time when she had a clearer sense of self.

Sara insists on decorum in her household, gently but firmly chastising her sisters and her daughter for emotional, overly dramatic and/or vulgar behavior. When Pfeni interjects the phrase "pish-pish" into conversation, Sara remarks critically, "there's something very New York about your tone today," further noting, "New York in a way that has very little to do with us" (8, 9). In her critique of New York behavior, Sara echoes a litany of stereotypical binaries that posit Jews as loud, emotive, vulgar and déclassé, as opposed to the more restrained, rational, high-class WASP culture. As we have seen, this binary was often used to represent the anti-Semitic viewpoint: in *Gentleman's Agreement*, for example, when Kathy characterizes Green's "Jewish" behavior as "hotheadism, shouting and nerves."[54] We see it also in the critique of American Method actors by Anglophile critics and in Vincent Canby's backhanded compliment in declaring Zero Mostel more appropriate than Topol for the role of Tevye.[55] We have also seen this stereotype revalued by Jewish artists, most notably in the work of Woody Allen and Barbra Streisand, where an emotionally and affectively rich Jewish culture is juxtaposed with a repressed and overly restrictive WASP culture.[56] Wasserstein's approach bears the hallmark of the latter, as Sara's arc through the play consists largely of the barriers to expressing her "true" emotions being eroded by the loud, humorous, and even vulgar emotional displays of Merv, Pfeni, and Gorgeous. In the penultimate scene of *Sisters*, the title characters assemble alone in the parlor in self-conscious imitation of Chekhov's *Three Sisters*. But, whereas Chekhov's scene is bleak, cheerless, and repressed, Wasserstein's scene quickly degenerates—or, more appropriately, regenerates—into a warm, emotional, comic moment, as Sara and Pfeni tease and tickle Gorgeous and mockingly fight over a shoe (97–98).

The primary vehicle for Sara's growing acceptance of her Jewishness is her romance with Merv Kant. Merv's last name carries a triple implication: it refers not only to the German philosopher but also ("can't") puns on Sara's inability for most of the play to open up to him and the kind of acting Jewish that he represents; third, as Merv tells Sara without provocation and a bit aggressively, "It used to be Kantlowitz" (22). When Merv first arrives at Sara's home to deliver something to Geoffrey her first impulse is to push him away. He represents precisely the kind of stereotypical Jewishness that she has moved to England to escape: he is a furrier, a trade perceived as Jewish dominated; he lives in Roslyn, Long Island, a locality that signifies, at least to a New York Jewish audience, his Jewish identity; and worst of all (from Sara's point of view) he has come to London as part of a delegation from the American Jewish Congress to meet with British and European Jewish leaders.

Sara and Merv's first scene together is a study in dueling declarations of identity. In the space of about five minutes, Merv mentions his work with the American Jewish Congress, his meeting with the rabbi of Dublin, his abbreviation of his last name, his daughter who lives in Israel (three times), his liberal politics, and the degree to which he finds English culture (particularly the food) foreign and exotic. He also uses the words *Jew* and *Jewish* often, attempting three times to apply the label Jewish to Sara. In addition to rebuffing or ignoring Merv's attempts to label her as Jewish, Sara makes a point of accenting her Englishness each time Merv accents his Jewishness. For example, when Merv notes that his daughter is a forest ranger in Haifa, Sara responds primly that she intends for *her* daughter to go to Oxford; when Merv says, "So you and your sister are from New York," Sara responds, "My sister is a traveler, and I live right here in Queen Anne's Gate" (23); and when Merv expresses his fondness for London's Simpson's in the Strand restaurant, Sara responds dismissively, "Only Americans eat there" (25). Merv also takes pointed notice of the number of books on Benjamin Disraeli in Sara's sitting room. As if to reproach her for admiring the English statesman who converted from Judaism to the Anglican Church to allow him to hold public office, Merv counters, "Personally, I prefer Adlai Stevenson" (27), the liberal politician widely popular among Jewish college students of Merv and Sara's generation.

The time of the play's setting, August 1991, is meant to coincide with the dissolution of the Soviet Union. The more obvious purpose of this chronology is to set up a subplot in which Tess and her boyfriend Tom plan to go to Vilnius to help the Lithuanian people achieve democratic liberation. However, the time period also allows Wasserstein to use the fall of the iron curtain as a metaphor for Sara's liberation from her own repression of her identity. In the play's most carnivalesque moment, Geoffrey contrives a skit "[i]n honor of our kindest innkeeper Sara Goode's birthday, and the collapse this very day of the Soviet Union" (44). Pfeni plays the role of "the Grand Duchess Anastasia Rosensweig Romanov" and declares her relief at finally being able to come out of hiding. The scene concludes with the entire cast singing a chorus from the Broadway musical that Geoffrey is directing, an adaptation of the novel *The Scarlet Pimpernel*, a celebration of one of the classic secret identities in Western literature.⁵⁷ Although Sara participates reluctantly and stiffly in this carnival of revelation, the celebration—which concludes with Merv's scene-ending line "Sara, you really know how to throw a good Shabbes!"(48)—prefigures the liberation Sara will experience when she finally allows herself to accept that she is Sara Rosensweig rather than Sara Goode.

As the play progresses, Merv and Sara play out a stilted but sincere courtship, with the question of Merv's Jewishness and Sara's lack thereof always foremost in the conversation. As Michael Feingold writes, "[U]nderlying the whole evening is a scattered debate about how Jewish these Jewish sisters should be—an uncomfortable bedfellow for the love intrigue, since the banker [Sara] is actively antireligious and the man in the case insistently Zionist."⁵⁸ But Merv and Sara do find common ground eventually, and their coming together is effected by a shared memory of 1950s Jewish American culture. Merv, it turns out, once had a tryst with Sara's high school classmate Sonia Kirschenblatt, and it is this memory of a simpler time, before Sara left her childhood home in Brooklyn, that both softens her heart and excites her sexually. "I could never love you, Merv," says Sara, "But Merv, just for one night I could be Sonia Kirschenblatt at the Brighton Beach Baths and you a Columbia sophomore" (58). For both Sara and Merv, the desire to remember incites a remembrance of desire. Their sexual encounter, which closes the first act, seems to be an important step in Sara's reconnection to acting Jewish.

The casting of the original production highlights the degree to which Merv's appeal to Sara is rooted in his frank and proud assumption of his Jewish identity. Robert Klein, playing Merv, brings with him the echoes of his early career as a stand-up comedian, as well as a man-

ner of speech and presence that reads as Jewish to an audience familiar
with the requisite cultural codes. So obviously does Klein display his
Jewishness that several observers in the mainstream press found it necessary to draw on the Yiddish lexicon to adequately describe his performance. Jeremy Gerard, for example, wrote in *Variety* that "Klein, never
better, gracefully captures Merv's menschy sweetness."[59] David Patrick
Stearns in *USA Today* called Klein's Merv "a dumpy but amiable
nudge."[60] While Brustein, using a more oblique—but nonetheless
decipherable—code, suggested that "Klein's Mervyn, on the other
hand, was a congenial loud mouth, a good-natured version of Alan
King."[61] On the other hand, Jane Alexander's Sara, as Clive Barnes
declared in the New York *Post*, "is as peerlessly English as only a New
York Jew can be." Brustein wrote, "I found Alexander's Sara, though
womanly, a trifle too coiffed, but so is the role." Gussow noted, "Ms.
Alexander assumes an artful Englishness."[62] How much of this
response can be attributed to the fact that Alexander is neither Jewish
(though she has played other Jewish roles) nor easily readable as Jewish? Michael Feingold suggested as much, writing in the *Village Voice*
that "watching Jane Alexander act is always a pleasure; watching her
deny her Jewishness is like watching Joyce Chen cook *latkas*."[63] As in
the films of Woody Allen, Jewish sexuality is figured as sensuous and
enjoyable, in contrast to a more repressive and joyless WASP sexuality.

Because her romantic encounter with Merv is the primary vehicle of
Sara's "coming out" as a Jew—Howard Kissell in the *Daily News* called
Sara's transformation a "conversion."[64] *Sisters* seems to imply that sexuality and Jewish identity are somehow linked: to repress one is to
repress the other; to free one is to free the other. As Sara tells Merv at
the beginning of the second act, "I'm a cold, bitter woman who's
turned her back on her family, her religion, and her country! And I held
so much in. I harbored so much guilt that it all made me ill and capsized
in my ovaries. Isn't that the way the old assimilated story goes?" (81).
Though Sara's intent seems to be sarcastic, it is at the end of this scene,
after Merv has left the room, that Sara breaks down and weeps as she
remembers and mourns her lost Jewishness, singing a parody of her a
cappella group's old standard, "MacNamara's Band."

> Oh my name is Moishe Pupick
> And I come from Palestine,
> I live on bread and honey
> And on Manishewitz wine.
> Oh my mother makes the best
> Gefilte fish in all the land . . .

And I'm the only Yiddish girl
In MacNamara's band. (83)

As the scene ends, Sara regards a lackluster gift from Nick Pym with distaste, breaking her Anglophile facade as she says through tears, "It's brilliant, Nick. Absolutely fucking brilliant" (83). Accepting the label of "Yiddish girl" also apparently breaks down her insistence on proper behavior, as well as her attraction to the anti-Semitic Nick.

Sara's relationship to acting Jewish is also played out in her relationship with Tess. Linda Winer, writing in *Newsday*, suggested that "Wasserstein has written a traditional play about the need for tradition, a throwback play about continuity, a rebelliously unstylish play against rebellion."[65] Nowhere is this more apparent than in Sara's relationship with her own daughter. Tess's attraction to social activism represents her response to a perceived absence of history and feeling in her upbringing. As she tells Nick, "I feel completely irrelevant coming of age as a white European female" (40). When Sara belittles Tess's ambition to support Lithuanian independence, asking, "[D]on't you think it's just slightly irregular for a nice Jewish girl from Connecticut to find her calling in the Lithuanian resistance?" Tess responds, "But I'm not a nice Jewish girl from Connecticut. I'm an expatriate American who's lived in London for five years and the daughter of an atheist" (10). Tess's sense of longing points to the perceived crisis of third-generation Jewish Americans. Raised by assimilationist parents, Tess has no relevant model for what it means to act Jewish.

As with Louis in *Angels*, however, Wasserstein seems to configure this absence of Jewishness as itself a form of acting Jewish. In a world without the guiding "tradition" of *Fiddler on the Roof*, the very lack of tradition becomes its own kind of cultural inheritance. Tess asks Pfeni, after explaining that she feels alienated from the Lithuanian freedom movement, "Are we people who will always be watching and never belong?" Pfeni seems to nod in the affirmative: "How did you get to be so young and so intelligent?" (100). Whether the "we" in Tess's question refers to Jews or Rosensweigs is left open, but both meanings seem to operate within the play. Sara and her daughter's lack of connection to Jewish tradition is made painfully evident, but it is in fact this precise lack of connection that unites them with the other Rosensweig sisters, Pfeni and Gorgeous, each of whom presents a variation on the role of memory as a guide to acting Jewish.

Like Sara, Pfeni has "changed her name for business purposes," but in her case the change—from Penny to Pfeni–has been to move away from the assimilated and toward the exotic. Once a serious journalist, by the time of the play Pfeni has become a travel writer, having grown disillusioned with the leftist social agenda that once inspired her. When Tess informs her of her plans to travel to Lithuania to aid the resistance, Pfeni responds by recommending a restaurant in Vilnius. While Pfeni seems more closely connected to the family's Jewish origins—she also tells Tess that "Vilnius was once the Jerusalem of Lithuania" (10)—she, too, struggles to define her identity.

Pfeni's identity crisis is played out through her on again, off again relationship with Geoffrey, a bisexual English theater director. Her attraction to Geoffrey frustrates her, partly because of his inability to commit to their relationship. More importantly, she regards her unhappiness with his inability to commit, her jealousy of his ex-boyfriend, and her desire for children, specifically Jewish children, as a betrayal of her feminist values. For Pfeni, acting Jewish is closely linked to feminism through the idea of independence and rebellion. When, for example, Tess asks her why she doesn't carry suitcases on her travels, she responds, "Because your grandmother Rita told me that only crazy people travel with shopping bags. So I've made it my personal signature ever since" (7). Her mother, Rita Rosensweig, provides a model of Jewish behavior that, though she cannot imitate it, she can at least find some comfort in rebelling against. The promise (continually deferred) of a sedate middle-class family life akin to her mother's is a threat to her sense of herself as both a woman and a Jew. Hence, when Geoffrey is particularly charming, she mockingly asks, "Are you sure you're not part of some antifeminist, anti-Semitic plot?" (68).

For Geoffrey, on the other hand, Pfeni's Jewishness, along with her status as an American and an independent woman, is the source of her appeal. He makes it clear that he finds her a refreshing and exotic departure from traditional English culture. Indeed, his affinity for 1950s American pop music and his love of the musical theater seem to suggest that his desires are drawn to precisely the milieu from which Pfeni has retreated: the upwardly mobile middle-class experience shared by millions of American Jews, especially in the entertainment industry, in the 1950s. Pfeni finds that experience vapid and limiting, preferring instead to focus her memories of home on the older, Yiddish-accented friends of her father. This is the New York that Sara insists "has very little to do with us." But as Geoffrey's enthusiasm for "nice American Jewish girls" shows us, even the largely deracinated Jewish bourgeoisie of the 1950s and 1960s is apparently a more colorful and vibrant context than the English upper crust can provide.

Ultimately, Pfeni undergoes her own rebirth and restoration of faith, occasioned by Geoffrey's decision to go back to dating men. She resolves to return to serious journalism and a long-abandoned book project on the oppression of women in Afghanistan. Pfeni, like Tess, is drawn to the plight of the oppressed. This suggests a liberal politics often associated with Jews of Wasserstein's generation. Yet it also suggests that the desire to remember what it means to act Jewish is linked in *Sisters* to an idea of oppression. Indeed, how else to explain the presence of Sara's anti-Semitic suitor Nick Pym than to bring the Rosensweig sisters' Jewishness into stark relief? Yet this is not exactly the "romance of the yellow star" that Finkielkraut delineates.[66] Rather, it seems to be a recognition that the value of one's identity increases in proportion to the difficulty of maintaining it. Pfeni's heartbreak at her split with Geoffrey is reconfigured, by the end of the play, as a healthy challenge that has reminded her of the liberal feminist values she holds dear.

At the opposite end of the spectrum (in terms of both class and gender politics) is the third Rosensweig sister, Gorgeous Teitelbaum. Like her sisters, Gorgeous has reinvented herself, adopting the fictitious title of "Dr. Gorgeous" to host a local radio advice show in the suburbs of Boston. Yet, while Sara and Pfeni have redefined themselves away from their Jewish American origins, Gorgeous has created a persona more stereotypically Jewish than even their mother Rita's. She has become a modern-day yenta, dispensing folksy advice and wisdom from her mentor, Rabbi Pearlstein of Newton. Her presence in London is occasioned by a junket she is leading for members of the Temple Beth-El Sisterhood. True to the archetype of the "Jewish American princess," Gorgeous is preoccupied with fashion, appearance, and material wealth. Yet she is also the only one of the Rosensweig sisters who is religiously observant, insisting on lighting *shabbes* candles over Sara's objections.

Though Gorgeous is, in the words of Gussow, "the one clear Jew of the trio," her strong sense of Jewishness does not seem to make her significantly happier than her sisters.[67] The perfect "funsy" facade she demonstrates in her opening scene is gradually picked apart over the course of the play. Rabbi Pearlstein, we learn, was indicted for tax fraud, which provided the occasion for Gorgeous to take over his radio show. Her designer clothes are all gray-market knockoffs. Her apparently idyllic marriage to a Harvard lawyer is struggling under the pressure of his recent unemployment. Moreover, as the youngest of the Rosensweig sisters, Gorgeous feels compelled to measure her achievements against those of her sisters, who have taken more obviously independent and feminist paths. Confronting Sara, who she feels patronizes her, she exclaims:

Well, you can speak with your lad-di-dah British accent, and
Pfeni can send my children postcards from every ca-ca-mamie
capital in the world, but I know that deep inside both of you wish
you were me! Dr. Gorgeous Teitelbaum, a middle-aged West
Newton housewife who wears imitation Ferragamo shoes and is
very soon to have her own cable call-in talk show! (75).

Here Wasserstein makes explicit the choices faced by a Jewish American woman who came of age in the 1960s. While Sara and Pfeni have
rebelled against their mother's mode of acting Jewish, Gorgeous has
embraced it, with all its accompanying promises and perils.

The appeal of Gorgeous's character was enhanced by Madeline
Kahn's performance. As with Ron Liebman's portrayal of Roy Cohn in
Angels, Kahn's use of humor and emotion moved a supporting character closer to the center of the play. "Despite Sara's pivotal role and Jane
Alexander's forceful interpretation," wrote Jan Stuart in *Newsday*, "it is
Gorgeous who really holds us." Howard Kissel concurred: "Her irritat-
ing but commanding high-pitched voice, the air of self-deprecation
that masks a ferocious self-importance, her look of perpetual dizziness
make the status-conscious suburban Jewish matron, a stock character,
believable, even poignant. As well, of course, as absolutely hilarious."
John Simon, writing in *New York* magazine, declared, "Madeline Kahn,
as Gorgeous, is once again her special blend of philosopher and fool,
shrewd observer and egocentric, outrageous jokester and wistful waif
. . . whom none could improve upon."[68]

Like Liebman, Kahn was awarded a Tony for Best Actress, indicating that her role made a greater impression on the audience than one
might guess based on her number of lines. Arguably, this level of performance in the character of Gorgeous changed the balance of the play.
A Jewish audience, while wincing, perhaps, at the larger than life
stereotype she represents, may relate to Gorgeous more easily because
she is so recognizable. Further, the highly emotional and comic performance of Kahn may have read, in double-coded fashion, as more
authentically Jewish than Alexander's Sara or Frances McDormand's
Pfeni. Gorgeous, especially as she was embodied by Kahn, celebrates
the joyous contradictions of the upwardly mobile Jewish American
milieu that much of the audience is likely to share.

Ultimately, the *Sisters Rosensweig* seems to validate, at least to some
degree, each sister's version of acting Jewish. Wasserstein accomplishes
this by emphasizing their shared past, their literal and metaphorical sisterhood. Yet, though reference is made to their grandmother's youth in

Poland and the history of European anti-Semitism, the point of origin around which they orient themselves is their Jewish American mother, Rita. In the penultimate scene of the play, Sara, Pfeni, and Gorgeous toast Rita's memory, and in the warm glow of remembrance their conversation is peppered with Yiddish phrases and laughter, mimicking an accent they themselves never possessed. Even Sara uses the phrase "pish-pish" (94). Here Wasserstein parallels Kushner, Mamet, and other Jewish playwrights of her generation in showing the desire to remember as a viable mode of acting Jewish, but she locates the authentic Jewish past to be remembered not in eastern Europe or Israel but in the United States. Due in part to the increasing opportunities for acculturation in the United States and in part to the historical rupture of the Holocaust, it seems that the "old country" has given way to the "old neighborhood" as the source of Jewish ethnic identification.

The Old Neighborhood

David Mamet speaks directly to the anxiety caused by a ruptured Jewish history in *The Old Neighborhood*, which opened 19 November 1997 at New York's Booth Theatre under the direction of Scott Zigler. *The Old Neighborhood* is actually an umbrella title for three closely connected short plays: *The Disappearance of the Jews*, *Jolly*, and *Deeny*. *The Disappearance of the Jews* was actually written fifteen years earlier and published in 1987 as part of a collection called *Three Jewish Plays*.[69] In 1989, inspired by a growing interest in questions of Jewish identity, Mamet revisited the play and revised it.[70] He also wrote *Jolly* and *Deeny* in 1989. The 1997 production, however, marks the first time that the three plays were performed together as *The Old Neighborhood*. The constant in the three plays is the character of Bobby Gould, a semiautobiographical figure who appears in a number of Mamet's plays. Wrestling with a midlife crisis occasioned by the dissolution of his marriage, Bobby has returned to his "old neighborhood" in Chicago.

The Disappearance of the Jews consists of an extended conversation between Bobby (Peter Reigert) and his childhood friend, Joey (Vincent Guastaferro). The desire to remember is at the center of the play from the first line: "What I remember . . ." says Joey, "what I remember was that time we were at Ka-Ga-Wak we took Howie Greenberg outside" (3).[71] From these childhood reminiscences the conversation ranges far and wide, covering not only events that Bobby and Joey experienced themselves but also events that they would have liked to experience.

"I'll tell you something else," says Joey, "I would have been a great man in Europe" (18). Joey looks to the history of Jews in Europe as an antidote to what he sees as the spiritual emptiness of contemporary culture.

> [T]his shit is dilute, this is schveck this shit, I swear to god, the doctors, teachers, everybody, in the law, the writers all the time geschraiying, all those assholes, how they're lost . . . of course they're lost. They should be studying talmud . . . we should be able to come to them and to say, "What is the truth . . . ?" And they should tell us. What the talmud says, what this one said, what Hillel said. (19)

For Joey, Europe represents a time and place where the question "What is truth?" could be answered. In this imaginary Europe, that answer would come from a Jewish tradition (the Talmud and Hillel) that has been lost in Joey and Bobby's (and Mamet's) generation.

The European Jewish culture of Joey's imagination is not simply defined by a more immediate connection to Judaic theology but also by the threat of anti-Semitic persecution. When Bobby interrupts Joey's fantasy by reminding him that the Holocaust would be on the horizon, he responds, "Fuck the Nazis, Bob. I'm saying, give a guy a chance to stand up. . . . Give 'im something to stand for" (20). For Joey, a Jewishness one has to fight for is worth more than one that comes easily. In this, he echoes what the French philosopher Alain Finkielkraut has called "the romance of the yellow star."[72] Finkielkraut, who was born in 1949 (two years after Mamet), describes his own romance this way.

> [T]he Judaism I had received was the most beautiful present a post-genocidal child could imagine. I inherited a suffering to which I had not been subjected, for without having to endure oppression, the identity of the victim was mine. I could savor an exceptional destiny while remaining completely at ease. Without exposure to real danger, I had heroic stature: to be Jewish was enough to escape the anonymity of an identity indistinguishable from others and the dullness of an eventful life.[73]

But for Mamet, as for Finkielkraut, this romanticization of suffering is both unearned and unsatisfying. Hence, Bobby rejects Joey's attempt to imagine himself as a heroic Holocaust survivor: "You don't know what the fuck you would have done, what you would have felt. None of us know" (22).

So Joey spins another fantasy: "I'll tell you where I would of loved it:

in the shtetl. (*Pause*) I would of loved it there. You, too. You would have been Reb Gould. You would of told them what Rabbi Akiba said" (22). This time, however, the conversation quickly turns comic when Bobby asks, "You think they fooled around?" (22). After some discussion of the sexual habits of shtetl dwellers, during which Joey's repetition of the word *shtetl* becomes a kind of punch line, Joey's desire to remember shtetl culture degenerates from "what Rabbi Akiba said" to a personal fantasy of sexual license: "But on the other hand who's to say what could go on. At night. In Europe" (24). The pauses between each sentence are heavily suggestive of illicit sexuality, though Leslie Kane—in *Weasels and Wisemen: Ethics and Ethnicity in the Work of David Mamet*—points out that the punctuation of the line also allows the audience time to be struck by a second meaning: "For the veiled reference to nighttime raids connotes night terrors far removed from a night of pleasure, given the recollection that pogroms took place under cover of night to plunder, pillage, and prey upon unsuspecting Jews."[74] Bobby is clearly more troubled than Joey about the possible anti-Semitic persecution in their mutually imagined Europe, yet he also recognizes that such persecution can be a means, if an unsatisfactory one, of establishing Jewish identity. In the following exchange, Bobby speaks of his son by his non-Jewish wife.

> *Bobby:* What is there to tell? The kid is a Jew.
> *Joey:* (Pause) Well, Bob, the law says he's a Jew, his, you know what the law says, he's a Jew his mother is a Jew.
> *Bobby:* Fuck the law.
> *Joey:* Well, all I'm saying, that's what the law says . . .
> *Bobby:* Joey, Joey, what are you saying, a kid of mine isn't going to be a Jew? What is he going to be? Look at him . . .
> *Joey:* I'm, I'm only talking about . . .
> *Bobby:* I know what you're talking about. What I'm saying, common sense? They start knocking heads in the schoolyard looking for Jews, you fuckin' think they aren't going to take my kid because of . . . are they going to take him, or they're going to pass him up 'cause he's so . . .
> *Joey:* I'm talking about the law.
> *Bobby:* 'Cause he's so blond and all, "Let's go beat up some kikes . . . Oh, not *that* kid . . ." (13–14)

Bobby explains that while the religious determination of Judaism may be ritually based on maternal descent, the social reality of Jewish identity is genealogical, inheritable from either parent ("a kid of mine isn't going to be a Jew? What is he going to be?"). Moreover, the decision of who is a Jew is not made by Jews themselves ("Fuck the law") but dictated by the visual strategies of anti-Semites ("'Cause he's so blond and all"). Mamet flirts with the strategy employed by Allen and Streisand in the 1970s: to accept the social reality of Jewish physical stereotypes but to revalue them, to establish Jewish physicality as superior. Joey illustrates this idea a few lines later, referring to the "goyim" derogatorily as "those Nordic types, all right, these football players, these cocksuckers in a fuckin', wrapped in hides" (16). But Joey's commentary is undercut by his flattened and distorted vision of European Jewish history, in which anti-Jewish persecution apparently begins with the Visigoths and ends with the Chicago Bears.

While Joey seeks to reconstruct his Jewish heritage in an idealized Europe (perhaps suggested by *Fiddler on the Roof*), Bobby looks to the Hollywood of the 1920s as a golden age for acting Jewish.

Bobby: Jesus, I know they had a good time there. Here you got, I mean, five smart Jew boys from Russia, this whole industry.
Joey: Who?
Bobby: Who. Mayer. Warners. Fox.
Joey: Fox? Fox is Jewish?
Bobby: Sure.
Joey: Who knew that?
Bobby: Everyone.
Joey: Huh. (*Pause*) I always saw their thing, it looked goyish to me.
Bobby: What thing?
Joey: Their castle, that thing on their movies . . .
Bobby: No
Joey: I thought it was a goyish name.
Bobby: "Fox"?
Joey: Twentieth Century-Fox. (*Pause*) Century Fox. (*Pause*) Charlie Chaplin was Jewish.
Bobby: I know that, Joe.
Joey: Yeah? People fool you. You know who else is Jewish? (25–26)

The Jewish audience of *The Old Neighborhood* will recognize a desire to "claim" a well-known artist (Warner, Chaplin) as a member of the "tribe," even if that artist has made little or no public acknowledgment of his or her Jewish background. Indeed, as discussed earlier, the audience's knowledge of "who's Jewish" can be an important element in the double coding of a performance. As Jeffrey Shandler writes in "Is There a Jewish Way to Watch Television?"

> The Jewish search for Jews on TV is, it seems to me, particularly important as part of the larger search that Jews make for other Jews in "real life." . . . This is in part a product of living in a diaspora culture, in which alternative notions of place that are independent of physical turf flourish.[75]

Bobby and Joey, faced with the spiritual and ethnic emptiness of their old neighborhood, attempt to recover the film industry as what we might call a Jewish space. The communal acknowledgment of the powerful role Jews have played in the entertainment industry ("Five smart Jew boys . . . this whole industry") serves a similar purpose. As Joey's surprised reaction to finding out Fox is a Jewish name indicates, this claiming of Jewish American artists has more to do with labeling than with decoding. Still, Joey's excuse for not knowing Fox was Jewish ("I always saw their thing, it looked goyish to me") indicates a rudimentary awareness of the kind of decoding strategies Jewish American audiences employ toward mass culture. Joey's desire to reaffirm his competence at decoding Jewishness ("You know who else is Jewish?") also indicates the degree to which knowing the codes becomes an indicator of in-group status.

At the same time, this exchange represents Mamet's attempt to poke a hole in double coding, to reveal the "open secret." As he told *Playboy* in 1995:

> Earlier you asked about things you cannot say—well, here are two: You cannot say you are a Jew first and then an American. And you cannot say that the movie business is a Jewish business. If there is anything wrong with that, I don't know what it is. Except that the Jewish moguls kept the Jews out of the movies. Where are the Jewish characters?[76]

For Mamet, while double coding can provide a sense of community, it is an inauthentic basis for acting Jewish because it lacks the explicit assertion of Jewish specificity. Like Louis in *Angels* and the Rosensweig family in *Sisters*, Bobby and Joey want more from their Jewish identity than an *idea* of difference.

In "The Decoration of Jewish Houses" Mamet writes:

In Mel Brooks's film *The History of the World, Part I*, Chloris
Leachman, as Mme. Defarge, harangues the canaille in a wonder-
fully dreadful French accent. She says, "We have no home, we
have no bread, we don't even have a *language*—all we have is zis
lousy *accent*."

Similarly, our second generation had no language. Our parents
eschewed Yiddish as the slave language of poverty, and Hebrew as
the dead language of meaningless ritual.[77]

What Mamet does not say, though he implies it, is that Brooks, a Jewish American filmmaker, is explicitly dramatizing the situation of
American Jews. Nor does Mamet extend the possibility that an accent,
however, impoverished, can serve as a vehicle for cultural continuity.
Rather, he bemoans the fact that American Jews seem to take no pride
in their heritage.

Still, if all they have is a lousy accent, Jewish American theater artists
make the most of it. Mamet seems to suggest as much, explicitly stating
the superiority of Jewish-style conversation over gentiles' gentle speech.
Joey disparages gentiles, saying, "what have they got, you talk about
community, six droll cocksuckers at a *lawn* party somewhere: 'How is
your *boat*'" (12). The implication is clear: the richness, even the vulgar-
ity of Jewish speech is a clear contributor to a sense of community—and,
further, this sense of community is something uniquely Jewish.

In *Jolly*, the second play of *The Old Neighborhood*, the distinctiveness
of the Jewish conversational style is essential to establishing a sense of
community. Here Bobby conducts an extended conversation with his
sister Julia, nicknamed Jolly (Patti LuPone). The subject is their mutual
sense of lost identity caused by their parents' divorce and their mother's
remarriage to a gentile. Their conversation is conducted with what
Kane calls "a language of affection," in which:

Jolly not only deciphers the coded phrases that intimate with few
words the depth of her brother's pain, she communicates her pro-
found love for him. Repeatedly using that wonderful Yiddish
phrase (of varying spellings) "Bubeleh"—or the shorthand,
"Buub" for which there is no apt English equivalent.[78]

Jolly and Bobby's desire to reconstruct their lost history, their need to
connect with one another as siblings and Jews, is expressed through an
insistence on the importance of shared experience. As they catalog the
various traumas inflicted on them by their mother and stepfather, they
seek to reassure each other that they are not alone. Their speech pat-

tern, as often seen in Mamet's work, is one of mutual reinforcement.[79] They frequently complete each other's sentences as a way of indicating that they are thinking along common lines. As Jolly says to her husband Carl (Jack Willis) at the play's end, "Bobby will be here a while, you see. And he's the only one who knows. (*Pause*) 'Cause he was *there*" (85, emphasis in original).

The final play in *The Old Neighborhood*, *Deeny*, puts Bobby in conversation with an ex-girlfriend (Rebecca Pidgeon). This is the most obscure of the three plays in the trilogy. The language is poetic and abstract, the cues to the characters' relationships with each other few and far between. Unlike *The Disappearance of the Jews* and *Jolly*, there is no explicit reference to Jewishness. In fact, there is no implicit reference to Jewishness. But coming at the end of Mamet's exploration of the desire to remember and balanced by the impossibility of imagining the Jewish past in a satisfactory way, I would argue that Jewish identity is felt in *Deeny* as that which is not there. It is a palpable absence, an active vanishing, not Jewish but not not-Jewish.

At least, the absence of Jewishness is palpable for a Jewish audience, which has been primed by the first two plays to think about what it means to act Jewish. As Mamet explained to the *New Yorker*, "As Bettelheim says in *The Uses of Enchantment*, the more you leave out, the more we see ourselves in the picture, the more we project our own thoughts onto it."[80] What we project onto *Deeny* is the completion of the disappearance of the Jews begun in the first play.

A gentile audience, though it might not project a cultural identity crisis onto the play, can hardly fail to notice that Mamet is depending on his audience to bring a shared cultural context to bear on his work. Ben Brantley, reviewing *The Old Neighborhood* for the *New York Times*, began his review with the provocative phrase, "They speak in code, of course, the characters in 'The Old Neighborhood.'"[81] Brantley identified this code not as specifically Jewish, however, but as decipherable by "anyone (and presumably that is everyone) who has ever yearned for a sense of safety, order and human connection that the world as it is can never really provide."[82] John Heilpern, in his review of the play for the *New York Observer*, used his own sort of code to indicate that Mamet's play might be more appealing to a Jewish audience than he himself found it: "The laughter comes easily from many in the audience, as if attending a ritual. 'I never should have married a shiksa,' Bobby confesses, and the word 'shiksa' brings smug laughter, too. What's going on?"[83] Heilpern's comments are particularly fascinating because he himself identifies as Jewish and knows very well what *shiksa* means. It is not the word that he does not understand; it is the audience's response to it. Heilpern is English, though, not American, and perhaps this explains why he clearly feels excluded from the imagination of Jewish American community occasioned by *The Old Neighborhood*. His choice of words makes clear that he feels the play is too obscure, and perhaps "too Jewish" for him. Though he himself finds the play boring and vacuous, "many in the audience" laugh, "as if attending a ritual." Since laughter is not a response typically associated with ritual, we may understand Heilpern's reference to ritual as an indication of the religious specificity of the play. Similarly, he cites the audience's response to a Yiddish word, "shiksa," as "smug." Why smug? Because, presumably, those who are familiar with this particular code word feel a sense of superiority from their ability to recognize the phrase. When I saw this production in 1997, I also noted that a significant portion of the audience laughed in recognition at the Yiddish phrases sprinkled throughout the play. But I would argue that this laughter is "smug" only to those who are not laughing. For the in-group audience, the laughter is the very opposite of smug; it is the creation (yes, perhaps the "ritual" creation) of a kind of *communitas*, a sense of belonging that binds a group together through shared experience.[84] Thus, even though the text of *The Old Neighborhood* argues strongly that depending on double coding to maintain a sense of Jewish identity is a losing proposition, the experience of the play in performance depends on the very strategies it decries.

Angels in America, The Sisters Rosensweig, and *The Old Neighborhood* dramatize the desire to remember the Jewish past as a guide to acting Jewish in the present. That all three plays do so with explicit reference to the history of anti-Semitic persecution suggests that Kushner, Wasserstein, and Mamet have taken to heart the dual injunction of the post-Holocaust era: never forget, never again. But of course it is the historical rupture of the Holocaust, and earlier of the vast transmigration of Jews from Eastern Europe to the United States, that make meaningful remembrance difficult, if not impossible, as symbolized by the frequent nostalgic references to prewar Vilnius in *Sisters*. *Angels in America* accomplishes the feat, but only through supernatural assistance, which is perhaps Kushner's way of calling for a return to a more spiritual understanding of Jewishness. *The Sisters Rosensweig* appeals to the power of the maternal and familial to serve as a locus of identity formation. *The Old Neighborhood*, on the other hand, presents a prospect that is more bleak but not utterly without hope. In the end, perhaps, what the search for a lost Jewish essence reveals is that the desire to remember is itself the defining element of acting Jewish at the millennium and beyond.

CHAPTER 6

You Know Who Else Is Jewish?

Reading & Writing Jewish
in the Twenty-first Century

Today's New York Times *Arts and Leisure Guide lists sixteen plays written by Jews, but, as the joke goes, who's counting?*
—Ellen Schiff, *Awake & Singing*

*I*N FEBRUARY 2003, The Jewish Museum in New York City
unveiled a major exhibition entitled *Entertaining America: Jews, Movies,
and Broadcasting.* The exhibition, curated by J. Hoberman and Jeffrey
Shandler, attracted local and national media attention and was accompanied by the publication of a catalog that "examines the ways in which
the subject of Jews and the entertainment media has been presented
from the beginning of the twentieth century to the start of the current
millennium."[1] This impressively researched, sumptuously illustrated
volume was soon joined on bookstore and library shelves by three new
scholarly texts: Vincent Brook's *Something Ain't Kosher Here: The Rise of
the "Jewish" Sitcom,* Eliot Gertel's *Over the Top Judaism: Precedents and
Trends in the Depiction of Jewish Beliefs and Observances in Film And Television,* and David Zurawik's *The Jews of Prime Time.*[2] In the space of one
year, the number of books catalogued by the Library of Congress under
the subject heading "Jews on Television" had doubled from three to
six. In 2004, a similar wave of scholarly interest in Jewish American
popular culture broke, with the publication of Andrea Most's *Making
Americans: Jews and the Broadway Musical,* Paul Buhle's *From the Lower
East Side to Hollywood: Jews in American Popular Culture,* and Jack Gottlieb's *Funny, It Doesn't Sound Jewish: How Yiddish Songs and Synagogue
Melodies Influenced Tin Pan Alley, Broadway, and Hollywood,* among others.[3] To what can we attribute the recent rise in scholarly attention paid
to Molly Goldberg, Tevye, and Jerry Seinfeld?

As I stated at the outset, it is not the purpose of this book to discover
a lost or hidden Jewishness in the performances under consideration.
Nor is it my desire to "out" particular artists and performers as Jews. I
am, however, deeply interested in the desire of Jewish critics and audi-

ences to do exactly this. To what purpose are books such as those just mentioned (and this book as well) published? And why now?

As we have seen throughout the preceding chapters, acting Jewish can hardly be separated from reading Jewish. Each reformulation of acting Jewish has been accompanied by a concomitant, often responsive attempt by the audience to renegotiate the terms of its interaction with the performance. At no time has this been more true than today. In "an era of ethnic identification," the Jewish audience asks, as does Joey in *The Old Neighborhood*, "You know who else is Jewish?"[4] Yet, as Hoberman and Shandler note, "Collecting the names of Jewish celebrities, especially those prominent in popular entertainment, is not a recent phenomenon."[5] So why, at the dawn of a new century, has this practice gained a new currency in both scholarly and popular discourse? To answer this question, we must further explore the meaning of *reading Jewish*.

Reading Jewish describes the attempt to apply a Jewish-specific reading strategy to a performance text. As with the Lenny Bruce routine described in chapter 1, reading Jewish is in part a way of dividing the world into the binary categories of Jewish and goyish. But, like that routine, this reading is itself a kind of performance, which, like all performances, is as provisional and contested as the question of Jewish identity itself. For example, in a 1999 Arts feature in the Sunday *New York Times*, writer Joseph Hanania identified—unequivocally and without explanation—several contemporary television characters as Jewish or not-Jewish. In Hanania's view, the character of Rachel (Jennifer Aniston), on the popular NBC comedy *Friends* (1994–2001) is a classic example of the Jewish American princess, while NBC's *Mad about You* (1992–99) is essentially a comedy about the intermarriage between the Jewish Paul (Paul Reiser) and the gentile Jamie (Helen Hunt).[6]

Two weeks later the *Times* published—under the headline "How Can You Tell?"—a letter from reader Matt Mendres of Elmwood Park, New Jersey, which asked: "As a long-time viewer of both programs, I cannot recall any references to Jennifer Aniston's character on 'Friends' being Jewish, or to Helen Hunt's character on 'Mad About You' being non-Jewish . . . [so] how did [Hanania] make these deductions?"[7] Mendres is correct in his assertion that there have been no explicit references to these characters' religion or ethnicity. But the double-coded indicators of Jewishness as embodied by the performances in question are visible to anyone who knows how to decode them. That Hanania, the author of the article, did not feel a need to explain his decoding process suggests that he, like most media-savvy American Jews, performs this Jewish reading intuitively. Indeed, the very fact that the process is largely unconscious accounts for its communicative force. Because the reader has not consciously considered the codes used to identify Jewishness, he or she is more likely to perceive them as natural and inevitable rather than arbitrary and constructed. Moreover, because the process is not intellectualized, it is not subject to critique. Jewishness is perceived as a gestalt that resists analysis.

Still, as Jon Stratton points out, to simply ask *whether* characters and performers in American theater, film, and television are Jews "is both foolish and instructive. It is foolish because it appeals to a reductionist and simplistic understanding of who is a Jew, but it is instructive because it enables us to appreciate just how blurred the category has become."[8] Consider the following entry from "Jewhoo" (www.Jewhoo.com), "a [Web] site that celebrates the Jewish contribution to civilization and is well on its way to being a Jewish biographical encyclopedia."

ACTOR

Steve Guttenberg—His first memorable role was in Barry Levinson's "Diner", 1982, which also launched the careers of Paul Reiser, Daniel Stern, and Ellen Barkin (all Jewish), as well as Mickey Rourke, Kevin Bacon, and Tim Daly (who are not).[. . .] Guttenberg gives out little in the way of personal information and we were reluctant to list him until a magazine journalist, who interviewed him, told us that Guttenberg mentioned he was Jewish before the formal interview began. Guttenberg was born in New York in 1958 and is divorced. We have often thought he would be perfect to play Adam Sandler's father if the right project could be found. They both somehow have an [sic] "persona" of frat boy/class clown—but a "nice Jewish boy" underneath thing going. Hard to explain. Trust us on this. Guttenberg, by the way, was the subject of a profile in the "Jewish Exponent" newspaper earlier this year. (Yes, he is Jewish. Our source was correct.) Updated with link, August 2003.[9]

Jewhoo—a pun on the popular search engine Yahoo—contains hundreds of such entries, each presented as an answer to the question of whether a particular celebrity is Jewish. Hence, the point made in passing about which of Guttenberg's *Diner* costars are Jewish is very much in keeping with the site's ethos. But in addition to the "Is he or isn't he" question, the entry reflects the underlying problems inherent in such identification. The actor's Jewishness is something that has been discovered, detective fashion, through an unnamed informant ("a magazine journalist"), whose story is later confirmed by a more reliable print source ("the 'Jewish Exponent'"). This information, however, is presented in the context of something already suspected ("We have often thought"), due to his onscreen persona, but "Hard to explain. Trust us on this." The site's editors nonetheless stake a claim to objectivity by noting that because of Guttenberg's previous public silence on the subject of his identity "We were reluctant to list him." All of this attention to verification, ironically, obscures the fact that the label Jewish as applied to this performer is devoid of any religious or ethnic specificity. While the implication is that Jewishness is a fixed identity that can be proved or disproved, the nature and significance of that identity are not discussed. This does not mean that the editors of Jewhoo consider Jewish identity meaningless; if they did, why would the site exist? Rather, they have chosen to leave this part of their biographical entry as an open text, allowing the reader to project his or her own definition of Jewishness onto the subject. As the editors state in their responses to "Frequently Asked Questions," "We did not want to become a party to the debates as to, 'Who Is a Jew?' . . . We have decided to leave it to the Jewhoo visitor to decide as to the Jewishness of the person. . . . We realize this is a sensitive matter. Think of us as an informational service." By opting out of defining Jewishness, the editors demonstrate a notion of acting Jewish remarkably similar to that which marks *Gentleman's Agreement*; Jewishness is implied to be a matter of choice, not only by the person self-identifying as Jewish but by the audience that receives this identification. Yet Jewhoo also refuses to list celebrities who do not have significant Jewish ancestry (at least one Jewish parent) and do not "practice Judaism" (another term left open) unless the editors receive so many queries about a particular person that it is more practical to list them (with caveats) than to explain why they won't. The category of Jewish in this context has become blurry, indeed.

In contrast to the popular and self-consciously humorous guessing game exemplified by Jewhoo, the recent publications by Hoberman and Shandler, Brook, and Zurawik are hardly "reductionist and simplistic." These scholarly analyses recognize that reading Jewish is not simply a case of cataloging, of separating the Jews, the almost Jews, and the righteous gentiles from the herd of popular entertainers. Nor are they simply measuring performances against an existing standard of religious or ethnic authenticity. Rather, these books represent an attempt to imagine a meaningful Jewish culture, Kushner's "Jewish essence," in a postethnic America. This reading process must therefore be understood as both *heuristic*—adopted as a provisional model for the purpose of learning—and *performative*, defining acting Jewish in the moment of describing it. Furthermore, like the formulation "You don't have to be Jewish . . ." the act of decoding Jewishness is both playful and political. It playfully destabilizes the boundaries of ethnic and religious essentialism, yet it also declares a belief in Jewish as a meaningful designation, a desire to imagine oneself as part of a Jewish community of readers.

What distinguishes this latest wave of scholarship in Jewish American popular entertainment from an earlier generation of research on "representations of the Jew" is the willingness to suspend, though not discard, the conventional binaries of insider and outsider, dominant and oppressed, American and Other. Rather than shoehorn Jewishness into existing theories and conversations about ethnic, racial, and religious identity in the United States, Jewish critics are striving to locate themselves and their work in what one such critic, Davida Bloom, has called "the Gray Zone between Other and Not."[10]

One characteristic that virtually all the recent studies in Jewish popular culture share with popular projects such as Jewhoo is the listing or cataloging of artists, characters, and performances as Jewish. In the case of *Entertaining America*, itself the catalog of a museum exhibition, this seems only natural. One particularly interesting element of the exhibition and the catalog is the "Star Gallery," a "by no means comprehensive" list of twenty-two stars, including two converts (Sammy Davis Jr. and Marilyn Monroe) and two cartoon characters (Betty Boop and Superman), along with several of the "usual suspects" in the Jewish celebrity conversation (Barbra Streisand, John Garfield, Paul Muni).[11] Brook's introduction to *Something Ain't Kosher Here* includes two illustrative tables, a "Timeline of 'Jewish' Sitcoms" stretching from 1948 to 2002, and "Phases of 'Jewish'-Trend Sitcoms" covering the period 1989 to 2002. Both tables serve to list and quantify Brook's object of inquiry, as well as to justify his identification of "the rise of the 'Jewish' sitcom" as a definable and analyzable trend in American entertainment.[12] Zurawik's *Jews of Prime Time* presents a less schematic and more anecdotal collection of characters and performances, yet his organization of chapters and subheadings, especially the prominence of three chapters (out of a total of eight) devoted to the theme of intermarriage, reveals a similar desire by the author to delineate the boundaries of Jewishness.

Lists and categories are important means of structuring knowledge. We could hardly function without them. Traditional Judaism seems to have a particular fondness for such structures, from the 613 *mitzvot* (laws or commandments) to the *Mishnah* (Oral Law), which is further subdivided into six *sedarim* (orders), each encompassing several *maskey-hot* (tractates), and on and on. Yet, as the French philosopher and historian Michel Foucault has shown, the ordering of things within an epistemological system often tells us more about the desires and ideologies of those making the classification than about the things themselves.[13] What property of an object, idea, or person is most important in distinguishing it from (or declaring it similar to) others? Brook and Zurawik's books, for example, are classified by the Library of Congress under the subject "Jews in Television" (PN 1992.8.J48), a subset of Television (PN 1992). Hoberman and Shandler's book is shelved several aisles over, under "Jews in the Performing Arts," a subset of PN 159, Performing Arts. All three fall under the classification PN—Theater, Speech, and Communications—itself a subset of P (Literature) as opposed to, say, D (History), G (Anthropology), or H (Sociology). This reflects the attitudes of the creators of the Library of Congress classification system about how ideas and scholarship are, or should be, organized. Specifically, it appears that the genre of performance under consideration is a more relevant datum than either the scholar's methodology or the ethnic, racial, religious, or geographical identification of that performance. The point here is not to dismiss the Library of Congress or any other classification system, nor to abandon classification entirely. It should be clear, however, that the choice to order one's perception in terms of Jewish and not-Jewish is neither obvious nor simple. Moreover, how we organize our catalog of Jewish American performance is shaped by existing conceptions about what it means to act Jewish as much as those performances shape the organization of the catalog.

Popular listings such as Darryl Lyman's *Great Jews on Stage and Screen*, Kathryn Bernheimer's *The 50 Greatest Jewish Movies*, and Jewhoo tend to underestimate the anxiety produced by this reflexive loop of thought. For scholars, the problem is more frustrating and becomes almost another level of double bind with which we must contend. On the one hand, *Jewish* is reduced to a label, a flag of convenience with which to mark and delimit our terrain of inquiry. On the other hand, it is our belief that *Jewish* is a more meaningful designation, one that has some essential roots in the real that drives our inquiry in the first place. On yet another hand—we now know why Tevye has so many other hands—shouldn't that essential Jewishness be gleaned from the performances themselves? But on the other hand—and now we're in a full-fledged conversation, rapidly approaching a minyan—we have to decide what performances we're dealing with a priori or the field of inquiry becomes too large to survey.

The anxiety (the term is used loosely rather than indicating a psychoanalytic condition) of this situation is readily discernible in the performative language with which scholars attempt to write through, around, and over the boundaries of their investigations. Our arguments are informed not only by Foucault and other poststructuralist critics' critique of such conventional categories as genre, period, and geographic locus but also by the heated conversation about "Who is a Jew?" that has marked at least the last 150 years of Jewish history. If we are ever to move past the simplest stage of defining our terms, our thoughts and rhetoric must be continually in motion. This leads to apparent contradictions, to the adoption of models freely admitted to be provisional and heuristic rather than definitive, and to the use of quotation marks around the word *Jewish* throughout the literature. Brook, for example, notes in the opening of *Something Ain't Kosher Here* that "quotes around the word 'Jewish' acknowledge the constructed and highly contested nature of Jewish identity generally, as well as the tenuous, largely inferred, and increasingly 'virtual' nature of Jewish televisual representation specifically."[14] Brook's explanation neatly summarizes the challenges to would-be critics of Jewish American popular performance. "Constructed . . . highly contested . . . virtual." These terms, of course, could also be used to characterize the elusive object that is performance itself.[15] My contribution to this conversation, I hope, is to rescue this uncertainty from the fine print of prefaces and footnotes. Rather than perform our anxieties about the instability of Jewishness as a locus of identity formation, this book has tried to demonstrate how that very instability has been, and can continue to be, an opportunity for dialogue, creativity, and positive social change.

Brook, for example, includes in his definition of "Jewish" television shows any program in which the protagonist is "ethnically marked" by means that include surname and explicit textual reference.[16] Both of these identifying traits have a long history in the popular and scholarly discourses of Jewish representation and have been touched on in various ways in the preceding chapters. But Brook extends this definition to include characters who "have been conceived as Jewish by the show's creators although they may not be perceived as such by the show's viewers."[17] The inclusion of the latter category in the list of Jewish sitcoms reflects a provocative turn in a direction taken by the present study: the active vanishing or unmarked presence of Jewishness is considered significant to the reception of a performance by a Jewish audience, and this significance is presented as being equal to, if not greater than, the more easily identifiable performance codes.

If Brook's study moves the scholarship of Jewish American popular culture toward a greater appreciation for who and what is *not* shown on television, Zurawik's *The Jews of Prime Time* provides an example of how the knowledge of that absence can circulate within and without the Jewish audience. Based primarily on interviews conducted with Jewish television writers, producers, actors, and directors, *The Jews of Prime Time* documents dozens of incidents, large and small, of explicitly Jewish content being censored, often at the behest of Jewish network executives. Zurawik, for example, cites Brandon Tartikoff, the former head of programming of NBC television, declaring, "The maxim of show business is, you know: write Yiddish, cast British. Which, you know, was the thing that we always said to Jewish writers."[18]

Taken together, these two books offer a narrative of the Jewish American experience in the television industry that is significantly more complex than conventional studies of minority representation in mass media. But to many of America's Jews, especially those involved in the entertainment industry, this heretofore unexplored area of scholarship is old news. Indeed, a familiarity with the anecdotes, outrages, and urban legends of Jewish censorship and self-censorship is a major part of the process by which reading Jewish is carried out in the popular conversation. Stories of Jewish artists literally or metaphorically changing their names for business purposes function as folklore that helps define the Jewish American community in the absence of Old World traditions.

This phenomenon is often noted in terms of disapproval, disappointment, or crisis. Samuel Freedman, for example, describes a Jewishness grounded in popular entertainment in contrast to the rise of ultra-Orthodox Judaism, which he chronicles in *Jew vs. Jew:* "On one flank, rampant interfaith marriage and declining religious observance leave a plurality of American Jews with that husk of identity that sociologist Herbert Gans has called 'symbolic ethnicity'—'Seinfeld' and a *schmear*, one might say."[19] Less dismayed, but still characterized by the rhetoric of loss, are the comments made by Stephen Whitfield in the provocatively titled *In Search of American Jewish Culture.* He cites "one of the inescapable conditions of American Jewish culture: its bias toward mass entertainment," which he calls "[t]he only culture American Jews have ever known."[20] For Freedman and Whitfield, as for many other critics who write in this mode, American Jews' loss of connection with an older, more traditional Jewish culture is inevitable, caused by the trauma of the Holocaust and the counterpunch of unprecedented acceptance of Jews in all areas of American society. The Holocaust not only annihilated millions of Jews who might have passed their Jewish heritage to the next generation, but it also erased nearly all of the "Old World" in which that heritage was grounded. The acceptance of Jews as business partners, spouses, and politicians by mainstream America has, ironically, diminished the importance of "Jewish" as a significant marker of identity. As Freedman writes:

America has genuinely accepted the Jews—not simply tolerated them as court physicians or expedient bankers who could be jettisoned in times of crisis, but literally loved them to such a degree that the intermarriage rate now stands at 52 percent. The 1998 election left eleven Jews serving in the Senate and twenty-three in the House of Representatives, while two others held lifetime appointments on the Supreme Court. Nothing in the diasporic past of ghettos and oppression, and nothing in the Israeli present of forming a majority culture, has prepared Jews for the phenomenon of being embraced by a diverse society.[21]

The coherence of the Jewish community, Freedman suggests, has historically been linked to Jews' status as different from the mainstream. To be a "chosen people," to be "a light unto nations," requires by definition that Jews be a separate community.

Theater and Its "Doubles"

Although Whitfield acknowledges the enormity of the cultural changes brought about by intermarriage and other social factors in the American Jewish population, *In Search of American Jewish Culture* offers a narrative that would seem to reconcile the "symbolic ethnicity" of reading Jewish with the Jewish theological and intellectual tradition. Specifically, Whitfield argues that "binarism is deeply encoded in historic Judaism."[22] He cites the religious distinctions made by Jews between *kosher* (ritually clean) and *trayf* (ritually impure), between *milchik* (dairy) and *fleichik* (meat), and most significantly between *Jew* and *gentile*. He parallels these ritual binaries with intellectual binaries developed by modern Jewish thinkers—Durkheim's distinction between sacred and profane, Lévi-Strauss's raw and cooked—adding, "A third French Jewish thinker, philosopher Jacques Derrida, has also argued that dichotomies are codependent. Difference is how to begin to understand culture—and indeed to grasp the making of the self, which is formed in relation to the Other."[23] From Whitfield's list of codependent dichotomies, reading Jewish draws primarily on the Jewish-gentile and self-Other formations. But there are other binary pairs—perhaps better understood as poles of a continuum, since performances rarely play themselves out as singular and uncomplicated moments—that come into play when we examine the contemporary fascination with Jewish readings of mass culture. These might include written and oral law, Orthodox and Reform Judaism, Ashkenazic and Sephardic Jew, artist and audience, actor and character, universal and specific, and text and performance. Despite appearances, none of these binaries is truly an either-or proposition; the terms themselves are too unstable, too subject to individual interpretation. It would be better, perhaps, to think of Jewish and goyish (or other codependent dichotomies) as shared possibilities whose exact relationships are determined differently by each reader through the act of interpretation, that moment when a spectator voices his or her answer to the question "Jew/not-a-Jew."[24] The decoding of Jewishness or non-Jewishness is therefore both performative and provisional. When I "read" a character or theme as Jewish I am not describing an existing condition but enacting my own ideology of Jewishness.[25] When I acknowledge a text's universality, I am similarly performing an ideology of universalizing humanism. In either case, my interpretation is subject to debate, deconstruction, and change.

Furthermore, to the degree that I am conscious of the *choices* I make in interpreting a performance, my decoding must be understood as strategic. In choosing the codes that I employ to extract meaning from a performance, I am positioning myself within an imagined community of like-minded decoders. A term coined by the historian Benedict Anderson, *imagined community* refers to the social construction of identity in connection with a nation-state. This national community is imagined, he suggests, "because the members of even the smallest nation will never know most of their fellow-members, meet them, or even hear of them, yet in the minds of each lives the image of their communion."[26] Some of the devices that contribute to this imagination of community include a common language, religion, and folklore. These devices help to turn an area defined arbitrarily by a map into a nation. For Anderson, Jewish identity is conceived racially and therefore imagined differently. Jews are "forever Jews, no matter what passports they carry or what languages they speak or read."[27] Yet this racialized sense of community is one that, as Anderson notes, is imposed from outside. From an in-group perspective, Jews are in a sense the original imagined community, a nation without a country for the last two thousand years. For most of that time, the community of Jews was imagined through religious and linguistic commonality: acceptance of the Torah, which required Hebrew literacy. But the

Enlightenment, the Reform movement, and other forces of seculariza-
tion have removed those points of orientation. The rise of Zionism and
the establishment of the state of Israel has actually divided rather than
united the Jewish community. How does the imagined community of
Jews, especially American Jews, continue (however shakily) to cohere?
It does so in part through the sustained and strategic project of reading
Jewish.

In order to understand the desire to read Jewish, we need to first
acknowledge that Jewish Americans, like other hyphenated groups, are
engaged in two simultaneous "conversations" about what it means to be
(or act) Jewish with the "mainstream" culture of the United States and
with other Jews. As anthropological and sociological studies have
shown, any community or kinship structure is bound up in a concept of
us and them. Thus, the desire to recognize and celebrate Jewish contributions to theater, film, and television carries its own doubled set of
meanings. To the non-Jewish reader, popular and scholarly attention
to Jewishness may evoke a sense of me-tooism: in an era in which multiculturalism is celebrated within and without the economy, where
nearly every identity formation can claim a body of critical literature, a
constellation of university departments, and a field (or at least a
subfield) of its own, why not highlight the cultural achievements of
Jews? Indeed, it would appear that the cultural inferiority complex that
David Mamet identified in "The Decoration of Jewish Houses" has
perhaps abated. "We Jews," wrote Mamet in 1989, "consider it a matter of course, for example, that there has never even been a Jewish can-
didate for *Vice* President."[28]

Since then, the United States has seen Senator Joseph Lieberman of
Connecticut as the Democratic vice presidential nominee in 2000 and
a legitimate contender for the presidential nomination in 2004. Lieberman's presence on the national ticket provides yet another occasion for
representing to the gentile world the question of what Jewish is.
Closely connected to this is the increasingly important and conflicted
role of Israel in U.S. foreign policy. Since 11 September 2001, America's attention to the Middle East has grown exponentially and with it,
perhaps, a greater desire to understand religious and political issues in
Israel. Added to this mix is the phenomenon of millenarian Baptist support for Israel on the grounds that repatriation of the Jews to Jerusalem
is a necessary precursor for the return of Jesus Christ. One might
almost conclude that Jewish has become a hot identity in recent years.[29]
As Andrew Furman asked in *Tikkun* magazine, "Is the Jew in Vogue?"[30]
This is an unusual and perhaps uncomfortable situation for a community that has long imagined itself as eternally "outside."[31] This new

incarnation of the double bind is exemplified by the carefully worded introduction written by Joan Rosenbaum, Helen Goldsmith Menschel Director of the Jewish Museum, to the catalog for the exhibition *Entertaining America.*

> From the first neighborhood nickelodeons to today's mass television programming, Jews have intersected with film and broadcasting in ways that have helped to build the entertainment industry. New Americans of all backgrounds became part of an evolving mass culture, and many first- and second-generation Jews were involved in its emergence and development. . . . National attention and widespread discussion have been generated by some of the issues implicit in this history. Among them are the history of Jewish immigration to this country, experiences of American anti-Semitism, and the creation of a cultural identity. While the focus here is on a Jewish story, the subject illuminates two broader themes: the challenge of becoming fully American while holding on to a specific ethnic or religious identity; and the dynamic and variegated fabric of American popular culture. Thus *Entertaining America* is both celebratory and complex.[32]

Rosenbaum's text moves back and forth across the line between Jewish specificity and American universality. In the same breath, she claims the uniqueness of Jews' history in entertainment and acknowledges the contributions of "new Americans of all backgrounds." She highlights the exhibition's status as "a Jewish story" but maintains its applicability to "broader themes." Unspoken here, but implied by the very nature of a museum exhibition, is the idea that the early history of the moving image in the United States is part of a lost or forgotten Jewish culture. Part of the aim of institutions such as the Jewish Museum is preservation, and the project of preservation depends for its legitimacy on the threat of loss. Here, however, the perceived loss is not of a religious or Old World cultural heritage. What *Entertaining America* seeks to preserve is the "celebratory and complex" respect for Jewish contributions to American popular culture.

Reading Jewish and Religious Judaism

Religious Judaism has traditionally maintained a philosophical dualism with regard to religious and ethnic identity; Jews may be the chosen people, but all human beings are beloved by God and must be treated accordingly. Judaism is the most perfect path to righteousness but not the only path. A page of the Talmud is laid out with a passage from the Torah in the center. Surrounding the passage, in the margins of the page, are various rabbinic commentaries on the text. Although the various long-dead rabbis disagreed on many fine points of interpretation, the structure of the "debate" emphasizes their basic agreement: they shared the Torah as a common point of departure and the common belief that the Torah is the divine word of God.

Reform Judaism, counter to popular opinion, did not abandon this common text. Rather, the Reform movement, through its successive platforms (adopted in Pittsburgh in 1885, Columbus in 1937, and San Francisco in 1976), expanded the range of the conversation to include exegesis of secular texts. For example, the Columbus Platform states:

> Judaism welcomes all truth, whether written in the pages of scripture or deciphered from the records of nature. The new discoveries of science, while replacing the older scientific views underlying our sacred literature, do not conflict with the essential spirit of religion as manifested in the consecration of man's will, heart and mind to the service of God and of humanity.[33]

Membership in this imagined community of Jews, then, is not determined through complete agreement in language, ritual, or ideology. Rather, acting Jewish means performing oneself *as if* there were such agreement. The choice to act Jewish is the choice to behave as if *Jewish* is a meaningful term. Whitfield's project, my own, and those of the many others that insist on Jewishness as an organizing principle represent the natural corollary to this choice: reading Jewish. Though acting Jewish and reading Jewish may be practiced independently, they are mutually dependent. The choice to act Jewish requires the belief that someone (in the most extreme case, only God) is capable of decoding that behavior as Jewish. The choice to read Jewish, if it is to be more than a project of self-amusement, requires the belief that at least some of the time those whose behavior we read as Jewish would proudly acknowledge acting Jewish as their intent.

Through an understanding of the text-performance and artist-audience relationships at play in Jewish-created American popular entertainment, we can discern a "way of being Jewish otherwise than being."[34] This does not mean that the Jewish American community is imagined solely in aesthetic terms, nor that the academy is necessarily the site of the most influential analysis. Rather, the choice to perform oneself as a Jew is the essence of modern Jewish continuity, and, further, the shape this performance takes is less important than the desire to identify it as Jewish. The title of Whitfield's book, *In Search of American Jewish Culture*, is instructive. More than anything else, Jewish American culture is defined, and united, by this search; Whitfield's analysis, like Brook's, Zurawik's, and Hoberman and Shandler's, speaks loudest through his desire to make it at all.

Jewish identity offstage and offscreen is closely linked to the concept of performance. For example, nearly all Jews recognize any child born of a Jewish mother as a Jew. Yet for many the practice of Reform Judaism is not truly Judaism. As Boyarin notes, some Hasidic Jews even go so far as to identify themselves as *yiddishe yidn*, "Jewish Jews."[35] This double appellation denotes those whose claim to Jewish identity goes beyond the accident of birth. The Jewish Jew not only *is* a Jew. He or she has *become* Jewish. This process of making oneself Jewish is rooted in performance, both the performance of religious ritual and the performance of everyday life in accordance with *halacha* (Jewish law). It is this performance-based approach that allows for the formulation "to act Jewish."

Seen in this light, the ongoing debate about who is a Jew and who is not is largely a struggle to define the terms of Jewish performance. For the Orthodox Jew, acting Jewish is clearly defined: adherence to the 613 laws of the Torah.[36] The Torah provides a comprehensive guide to all aspects of ritual and everyday life, covering diet, dress, business transactions, child rearing, and so on. But Orthodox Jews make up a small percentage (less than 10 percent) of Americans who identify as Jewish. For the less observant or nonobservant Jew, the meaning of one's Jewish identity is much more complicated. Is Jewishness something to be hidden or something to take pride in? Is it based on descent (one's parents) or consent (religious choice)? Does it affect which box one checks on a census or affirmative action form?

This contemporary "crisis" in Jewish identity is well documented.[37] From the "double bind" articulated by Gilman to the "Jew vs. Jew" conflict chronicled by Freedman, the religious dilemma identified by Soloveitchik to the conflicted response of Hollywood Jews to the Lieberman vice presidential and presidential candidacies, the question of how to be a Jew, or act Jewish, in America grows ever more complex. The question itself, of course, is hardly new. Indeed, the history of the Jewish people is distinguished in part by a tradition of learned debate on the very questions of what it means to be a Jew and how Jews should relate to the non-Jewish world around them. Nor is this "identity crisis" unique to Jews in our postmodern, postethnic, American culture.

All ethnic, racial, and religious groups are struggling with how to maintain cultural continuity in the face of overwhelming pressures. Unlike an earlier era, however, the pressure that contemporary life places on these groups is less a pressure to assimilate than a disorientation caused by the explosion of opportunities for exploration and experimentation. Thanks to the rapid growth of media outlets, from cable and satellite television to the Internet, all individuals, regardless of race or ethnicity, have access to models of behavior from virtually every culture. Christianity, Judaism, Islam, Hinduism, and all of the other world's religions and value systems are within a single click of the mouse or the remote control. The melting pot has given way to an all you can eat buffet. In the absence of fixed points, hierarchies, and absolute truths, all identities become performative. To be Jewish (or Muslim or Polish) is less about making manifest some already existing internal condition or belief than about the performance of behavior associated (rightly or wrongly) with the idea that ethnic and religious identity is important. This performance is not necessarily false or fake: religion and ethnicity are often performed with the utmost sincerity. The performance becomes a way of repeating and reinforcing the boundaries and values of one's identity. By acting and reading Jewish, we keep alive the belief that Jewish is still a meaningful designation. By the ways in which we act and read Jewish, we argue our case for what that designation in fact designates. This is not an argument that one wins, but rather an ongoing process that itself can be understood as the defining characteristic of all postmodern identity formulations. It is noteworthy, for example, that subsequent to his book *An Empire of Their Own: How the Jews Invented Hollywood* Neal Gabler wrote *Life: The Movie*, an exploration of how Americans of all ethnicities have come to treat their lives as performances to be played out on the "screens" of everyday interaction.[38] The Renaissance concept of *Teatrum Mundi* has returned with a high-tech spin. Surrounded by screens, images, and labels both contested and complex, the search for ethnic and religious identity is dominated by the rhetoric of searching and seeking, exploring and mapping. This is not to suggest that identity has become a free-for-all, that anyone can be anything at any moment. Rather, it recognizes that identity is a negotiation. And to the degree that this negotiation is both public and shaped by cultural contexts the contours of it may be mapped, at least provisionally. Or, to put it another way, theoretically acting Jewish can mean anything. Historically, acting Jewish in American popular entertainment has evolved and developed in particular ways. This evolution has in turn been chronicled, analyzed, and shaped into a narrative.[39] Moreover, a working assumption of reading Jewish is that this narrative illuminates and illustrates a vital part of Jewish American culture, as well as American culture more generally.

In the preceding chapters, I have argued that Jewish continuity can be transmitted through performance via the mechanism of double coding, even when the text of the performance contains little or no Judaic content. In the communicative model proposed in chapter 3, the "message" of a performance is encoded by cultural producers for transmission to a mass audience. It is then decoded by each audience member according to his or her reading position. There is, I suggest, a Jewish audience that may glean Jewish specificity from performances that a general audience decodes as universal. The Jewish reader may decode Jewishness through aural, visual, or emotional/genre signs. As we have seen, speech patterns and accents, an actor's looks or hairstyle, a certain kind of anxiety or neurosis about the conflict between tradition and modernity—all of these things may be, and have been, read as Jewish by critics and audiences inclined to do so. The audience that would read Jewish may even stake its reading on knowledge not obtained from the performance itself but from its folk/popular discourse about the artists who create it.

Only Jews (or those who know the codes) will interpret these elements of performance as Jewish. While general audiences may recognize these performance practices as unusual, urban, or ethnic, they will not necessarily recognize them as indicators of Jewish cultural difference. Thus, these performances implicitly indicate Jewish cultural difference while explicitly projecting a universalist, religiously and ethnically nonspecific vision of American society. Again, how do we know a character is Jewish? He's the one without the beard.

Of course, when the Jewish specificity of a performance is double coded, the amount of Judaic content that can be included is minimized, leaving only Jewish continuity. Moreover, through pervasive repetition and reinscription, double coding itself becomes the most salient indicator of this continuity. The danger (if it is a danger) in double coding is that ultimately Jewish difference is reduced to the idea of Jewish difference. Jews are different because we behave as if we are.

On the other hand, this makes the imagined community of American Jews a unique case for understanding minority representation. "Because of the presence of many Jewish men in the commercial show business industry," writes Harley Erdman, "the Jewish situation in twentieth-century America cannot readily be understood through us-them, insider-outsider, Same-Other, domination-resistance binaries which seem more readily to hold for other groups."[40]

The underpinnings of Jewish theology (both Orthodox and Reform) are useful in understanding the mechanism of double coding. But as audiences of all kinds become more sophisticated decoders the terrain is shifting. The historian Werner Sollors writes, "In America, casting oneself as an outsider may in fact be considered a dominant cultural trait. . . . Every American is now considered a potential ethnic."[41] Identity of all kinds has become a source of both ideology and anxiety. Or perhaps, as Bernard Malamud famously remarked, "All men are Jews."[42]

Are All Men Jews?

To what degree can the theoretical model set forth in this book be applied to identity groups other than Jews? As I near the end of this project, I am tempted to respond, "You don't have to be Jewish . . ." But such a response is too reductive. As laid out in this book, the relationship between acting Jewish and reading Jewish, linked by the concept of double coding, is an ongoing negotiation. What it means to act Jewish is deconstructed and reconstructed in each interaction between performance and audience. In this way, the imagination of a community through reading strategies is consistent with established theory in the matter of audience response. As the theater historian and audience theorist Susan Bennett writes:

> Cultural systems, individual horizons of expectations, and accepted theatrical conventions all activate the decoding process for a specific production, but, in turn, the direct experience of that production feeds back to revise a spectator's expectations, to establish or challenge conventions, and, occasionally, to reform the boundaries of culture.[43]

This book, then, has immediate relevance for understanding the role of popular entertainment in the lives of American Jews but also for understanding theater, film, and television more generally.

Certainly the concept of "acting" as one type of identity formation can be applied to many identities. If we can speak of acting Jewish, we can also speak of acting Irish, female, or queer. However, this formulation of identity is more easily applicable and more immediately useful in the case of identities that are already perceived as performative and unstable.[44] One can act queer, for example, much more intelligibly than one can act African American in our contemporary cultural landscape because the latter is not generally regarded as something that can be hidden.[45] While questions of identity-appropriate behavior certainly divide the African American community, the element of choice in self-identification does not usually apply. Similarly, one could theoretically act Episcopalian, but this religious minority group has never had to contend with the possibility that public assertion of its identity will result in alienation of or censure by the general population.

With regard to double coding, certainly any identity group may apply distinctive cultural codes to extract meaning from a performance. However, to the degree that double coding depends, at least in part, on the desire of the in-group audience to attribute intent to the producers of the performance, there must be some significant access by members of that group to the means of mass cultural production. Because of the large Jewish presence in the American entertainment industry (itself a source of imagined community), this attribution of intent has been possible for Jewish audiences since the early twentieth century. But it would be much harder to establish this part of the double coding model for most other identity groups, especially when considering an era in which American show business was dominated by men who were almost exclusively white and/or Jewish. Thus, many studies have examined what might be called the double coding of queer identity but few have addressed the double coding of Latino identity, though this is changing as more minority groups gain access to the industry.

Finally, the use of reading as a strategy for imagining community is meaningful only in a community that has a strong desire to remain distinct. While this might apply to every identity group in our era of multiculturalism, it does not apply to every group in every time and place. Many European immigrants to the United States in the early twentieth century, for example, quite freely abandoned their ties to the Old World.

That said, I believe that the advantages of this model, where applicable, are considerable. It allows for a fluid, affective understanding of identity, as well as a more nuanced relationship to mass cultural representation than that provided by a conventional ethnic studies model. It requires us to assume neither a sinister culture industry in thrall to an equally sinister dominant culture nor a community imagined on a foundation of shared victimhood. Perhaps most importantly, it offers the reader whom society at large regards as Other to recenter the conversation, to ask if "we" like a performance in a different way from "them," while at the same time challenging and redefining the very category of "we."

Moreover, as performance theorist Richard Schechner notes, performance functions in part as a "restoration of behavior," a continual reclamation project that helps sustain the chain of cultural continuity.[46] Schechner's model is generally understood to apply to the experience of the performers and the meanings produced by the performance. However, as Schechner himself notes, the role of the audience in negotiating the terms and meanings of restored behavior cannot be overlooked. Hence, it is reasonable to suggest that it is the audience's desire to read Jewish into a performance, as much if not more than any single element of the performance itself, that serves as the vehicle for cultural continuity.

Conclusion: On Writing Jewish

From 1947 to the present, and from *Gentleman's Agreement* to *Seinfeld*, this book has attempted to trace the shifting formulation of acting Jewish on the American stage and screen as a continuing and continuous conversation between Jewish particularism and American universalism over the last half century. Through the use of double coding, Jewish American writers, directors, and actors have been able to play out questions of Jewish identity in front of a mainstream audience.

In *Gentleman's Agreement, The Goldbergs,* and *Death of a Salesman,* we see a self-conscious reduction in the overt difference between acting Jewish and, for lack of a better term, acting American. These performances are marked by the absence of Judaic content and the minimization, if not the erasure, of Jewish ethnic and racial difference. However, as the subsequent critical and performance history of these examples shows, this must be understood not as simple invisibility but as an active vanishing, a selective approach to visibility that is consistent with the everyday behavior exhibited by the majority of American Jews during the 1940s and 1950s.[47]

As the example of *Fiddler on the Roof* demonstrates, double coding also helped to package selected aspects of Jewish culture for consumption by a general audience. "They" (the imagined gentile audience) could enjoy the singing and dancing of some generic European peasants, thinking this harmless spectacle to be a full depiction of Jewishness, while "we" (the equally imagined Jewish audience) brought a wealth of culturally informed associations to the performance that provided the Jewish religious and cultural specificity the musical lacked.

In the rise to stardom of Barbra Streisand and Woody Allen, acting Jewish no longer meant acting just like everyone else. Beginning in the late 1960s, as the strength of the melting pot myth waned, performances created by Jewish American artists shifted toward the Jewish-specific end of the spectrum. While still seeking to appeal to a general audience, performances such as *Funny Girl; Play It Again, Sam; The Way We Were;* and *Manhattan* showed Jewish audiences that Jewish men and women could be sexually appealing to each other, and especially to gentiles, while still acting Jewish. In the early 1980s, *Yentl* and *Zelig* played with the idea of passing across the boundaries of female and Jewish subject positions, questioning whether Jewish was still a meaningful designation.

In the 1990s, as anxiety increased in the Jewish community about the future of Jewish identity, *Angels in America, The Sisters Rosensweig*, and *The Old Neighborhood* plumbed the depths of memory in an attempt to establish a new kind of Jewish continuity and community. Although these performances were marked by an assertion of Jewish particularism that was stronger than ever before, they were also marked by the anxieties of a multicultural and "postethnic" age. Thus, their desire to remember what it means to act Jewish remained tantalizingly unfulfilled. *Seinfeld* is perhaps the most provocative example of all, for the show that has spurred unprecedented debate about its Jewishness insisted until the last that it was a show "about nothing."

As the twenty-first century begins, the popular and scholarly discourse around the question "You know who else is Jewish?" is thriving. The conversation—"celebratory and complex"—about Jewishness and American popular entertainment seems unlikely to abate any time soon. Looking at the literature, for all its similarities and differences one is struck by the fact that the desire to catalog and list Jewish artists, characters, and performances has been left relatively unchallenged. Names are named. Boundaries are drawn and then erased. Quotation marks around *Jewish* problematize and provoke.

What all critics who would read Jewish discover is a new way of writing and speaking about Jewishness. This *writing Jewish* is closely parallel to what many contemporary theorists call performative writing, a mode of analysis that can be characterized by desire (after French poststructural theory), affect (after psychoanalysis), or will (after Nietzsche). Regardless of the specific theoretical provenance, performative writing mimics the personal, subjunctive, and multiply encoded nature of performance. Rather than pretending to a definitive authority and an ability to establish truth, such writing seeks to open a space for the uncertainty and conflict that (as in drama) moves a dialogue forward. At the same time, performative writing seeks, through its insistence on the importance of having the conversation at all, to repeat and reinforce the notion that its object of inquiry is made more, rather than less, meaningful and important by this very uncertainty and conflict.

Ultimately, however, the search for American Jewish culture and a way of writing about it comes down to two ways of thinking that are already embedded in the subject of our conversation: the *as if* that characterizes performance, and the *faith* that lies at the heart of Judaism. The "as if," a phrase that harkens back to Stanislavsky, suggests the multiple layers of meaning in a performance, as well as the "willing suspension of disbelief" that serves as its foundation. As a performer, I know that I am not really in Anatevka; I know, in fact, that no such place ever existed. But I act as if it were real and I am there. Simultaneously, I must remember the opposite: I am an actor on a stage, not a dairyman in a shtetl. I must hit certain marks, sing certain notes, respond to prescripted cues. By means of the "as if," I help to create an alternate reality, one that an audience often finds more compelling than its everyday world. This alternate reality feeds back into the everyday life of the culture in ways that, while impossible to predict and difficult to identify, are nonetheless an important part of how a community functions and imagines itself.

By using the term *faith*, I wish to point out the parallel between attempts to articulate a Jewish reading of American popular entertainment and attempts to articulate a meaningful way of acting Jewish in the world beyond stage and screen. Both are fraught with the perils of the double bind: the need to speak to a Jewish and non-Jewish audience, the need to be both "Jewish enough" and not "too Jewish." As a consequence, both are complex, conflicted, and constantly in motion. Both, in short, represent the search for an enactable truth in the face of an ultimate unknowability, which, for lack of a better term, we might call God. So this new mode of writing Jewish is not really new at all but a restoration of behavior familiar to American Jews for all the reasons described and analyzed in the preceding pages.

In the rhetoric of contemporary American Jewish discourse, converts to Judaism are labeled "Jews by choice." But in a sense, all Jews are Jews by choice. While the double bind still haunts the imagined community of Jews, the Jewish American performer, the Jewish American audience, and ultimately the Jewish American person is neither a victim nor a passive subject. Rather, it is the example of Jews and their relationship with American mass culture than may provide the model for community formation in the postethnic millennium. This may not bring about the messianic age of universal brotherhood promised by the Reform movement . . . but it's a start.

Notes

CHAPTER I

1. *Seinfeld,* episode 145, "The Yada Yada," originally aired 24 April 1997.

2. As quoted in Vincent Brook, "From the Cozy to the Carceral: Transformations of Ethnic Space in *The Goldbergs* and *Seinfeld.*" *The Velvet Light Trap* 44 (1999): 66, n. 1.

3. Ibid., 54–67.

4. Jon Stratton, *Coming Out Jewish* (London: Routledge, 2000), 282.

5. Dwight Conquergood, "Performance Studies: Interventions and Radical Research," *TDR* 46, 2 (2002): 146.

6. David Zurawik, *The Jews of Prime Time* (Hanover: University Press of New England, 2003), 5–6.

7. Ibid., 224.

8. See Benedict Anderson, *Imagined Communities,* rev. ed. (London: Verso, 1995).

9. Jeffrey Shandler, "Is There a Jewish Way to Watch Television? Notes from a Tuned-in Ethnographer," *Jewish Folklore and Ethnology Review* 16, 1 (1994): 21.

10. Stephen Steinberg, *The Ethnic Myth* (Boston: Beacon, 1989), 222–23.

11. Ella Shoat, "Ethnicities-in-Relation: Toward a Multicultural Reading of American Cinema," in *Unspeakable Images: Ethnicity and the American Cinema,* ed. Lester Friedman (Urbana: University of Illinois Press, 1991), 215. Note that this reading of the word *ethnic* is ironic, since its etymology derives from the Greek word for *goy* (*ethnikos*)—literally, "a non-Jew"; cf. Werner Sollors, *Beyond Ethnicity: Consent and Descent in American Culture* (New York: Oxford University Press, 1986), 7.

12. See, for example, Mike Hill, ed., *Whiteness: A Critical Reader* (New York: New York University Press, 1997).

13. Cf. J. Hoberman and Jeffrey Shandler, eds., *Entertaining America: Jews, Movies, and Broadcasting* (Princeton: Princeton University Press, 2003), 74–75.

14. See, for example, Ahuva Belkin, "The 'Low' Culture of the *Purimshpil,*" in *Yiddish Theatre: New Approaches,* ed. Joel Berkowitz 29–43. (Oxford: Littman Library of Jewish Civilization, 2003).

15. Cf. Richard Schechner, *Performance Theory* (London: Routledge, 1988).

16. See Brooks McNamara, *The Shuberts of Broadway* (New York: Oxford University Press, 1990).

17. See Jon McKenzie, *Perform or Else* (London: Routledge, 2001), 47–54.

18. See Peggy Phelan, *Unmarked: The Politics of Performance* (New York: Rout-

ledge, 1993); Susan Bennett, *Theatre Audiences*, 2d ed. (London: Routledge, 1997); Marvin Carlson, *Performance: A Critical Introduction* (London: Routledge, 1996); and elsewhere.

19. See Augusto Boal, *Theatre of the Oppressed*, trans. Charles A. McBride and Maria-Odilia Leal McBride (New York: Theatre Communications Group, 1985).

20. See Neil Gabler, *An Empire of Their Own: How the Jews Invented Hollywood* (New York: Anchor, 1989), esp. 187–236.

21. See Steinberg; also see Seymour Martin Lipset and Earl Raab, eds., *Jews and the New American Scene* (Cambridge: Harvard University Press, 1995).

22. See Michel Foucault, *Discipline and Punish*, trans. Alan Sheridan (New York: Vintage, 1977).

23. John Fiske, *Television Culture* (London: Routledge, 1989), 44.

24. Gabler, *Empire*, 6.

25. See Phelan; also see Laura Mulvey, *Visual and Other Pleasures* (Bloomington: Indiana University Press, 1989).

26. Zurawik, 6.

27. Ibid.

28. For a discussion of whether the term *closet* is appropriate in understanding Jewish identity, see Eve Kosofsky Sedgwick, *Epistemology of the Closet* (Berkeley: University of California Press, 1990), 75.

29. See, for example, Jonathan Boyarin and Daniel Boyarin, eds., *Jews and Other Differences: The New Jewish Cultural Studies* (Minneapolis: University of Minnesota Press, 1997).

30. Andrea Most, *Making Americans: Jews and the Broadway Musical* (Cambridge: Harvard University Press, 2004), 308.

31. Alain Finkielkraut, *The Imaginary Jew*, trans. Kevin O'Neill and David Suchoff (Lincoln: University of Nebraska Press, 1994), 15.

32. Joseph Stein, Jerry Bock, and Sheldon Harnick, *Fiddler on the Roof* (New York: Limelight Editions, 1964), 54.

33. Jonathan Boyarin, *Thinking in Jewish* (Chicago: University of Chicago Press, 1996), 170.

34. Ibid.

35. Indeed, throughout *Thinking in Jewish*, Boyarin remarks on his own inability to secure long-term gainful employment in academia.

36. Arnold Eisen, "In the Wilderness: Reflections on American Jewish Culture," *Jewish Social Studies* 5, 1–2 (1999): 26.

37. Stuart Z. Charmé, "Varieties of Authenticity in Contemporary Jewish Identity," *Jewish Social Studies* 6, 2 (2000): 133.

38. Ibid., 144.

39. See J. Boyarin, 174 and elsewhere.

40. Haym Soloveitchik, "Rupture and Reconstruction: The Transformation of Contemporary Orthodoxy," *Tradition* 28, 4 (1994): 90.

41. Stephen J. Whitfield, *In Search of American Jewish Culture* (Hanover: Brandeis University Press, 1999), 59.

42. Egon Mayer, "From an External to an Internal Agenda," in *The Americanization of the Jews*, ed. Robert M. Seltzer and Norman J. Cohen (New York: New York University Press, 1995), 432.

43. Arnold Band, "Popular Fiction and the Shaping of Jewish Identity," in *Jewish Identity in America*, ed. David M. Gordis and Yoav Ben-Horin (Los Angeles: Wilstein Institute of Jewish Policy Studies, 1991), 224–25.

44. Cf. J. Boyarin, 172.

45. See Michael Rogin: *Blackface, White Noise: Jewish Immigrants in the Hollywood Melting Pot* (Berkeley: University of California Press, 1996); Gabler; Norman Kleeblatt, ed., *Too Jewish? Challenging Traditional Identities* (New Brunswick: Rutgers University Press, 1996).

46. J. Boyarin, 170.

47. Dwight Conquergood, "Of Caravans and Carnivals: Performance Studies in Motion," *Drama Review* 39, 4 (1995): 137–38.

48. See also Schechner, *Performance Theory*.

49. Cf. Glazer, "American Jewry or American Judaism?" *Society* 28, 1 (1990): 14–20; Gordis and Ben-Horin; and many others.

50. Charmé, 149.

51. For explanation of consent-based versus descent-based identities, see Sollors, *Beyond Ethnicity*.

52. Sander Gilman, "The Jew's Body: Thoughts on Jewish Physical Difference," in Kleeblatt, 61. Gilman refers here to the work of French poststructuralist philosophers Gilles Deleuze and Felix Guattari, authors of *Anti-Oedipus*, trans. Robert Hurley, Mark Seem, and Helen R. Lane (Minneapolis: University of Minnesota Press, 1983); and *A Thousand Plateaus*, trans. Brian Massumi (Minneapolis: University of Minnesota Press, 1987), among many other works.

53. Judith Butler, "Performative Acts and Gender Constitution: An Essay in Phenomenology and Feminist Theory," *Theatre Journal* 40, 4 (1988): 519–20.

54. See Schechner, *Performance Theory*, 187–206 and elsewhere.

55. Sander Gilman, *The Jew's Body* (New York: Routledge, 1991), 6.

56. See W. E. B. Du Bois, *The Souls of Black Folk* (Chicago: A. C. McClurg, 1903).

57. David Krasner, *Resistance, Parody, and Double-Consciousness in African American Theatre, 1895–1910* (New York: St. Martin's, 1997), 8.

58. Ibid., 77–98 and elsewhere.

59. As Karen Brodkin writes in her influential study *How Jews Became White Folks and What That Says about Race in America* (New Brunswick: Rutgers University Press, 1998):

> Prevailing classifications at a particular time have sometimes assigned us to the white race, and at other times have created an off-white race for Jews to inhabit. Those changes in our racial assignment have shaped the ways in which American Jews who grew up in different eras have constructed their ethnoracial identities. Those changes give us a kind of double vision that comes from racial middleness: of an experience of marginality vis-à-vis whiteness, and an experience of whiteness and belonging vis-à-vis blackness. (1–2)

60. Robert Vorlicky, ed. *Tony Kushner in Conversation* (Ann Arbor: University of Michigan Press, 1998): 217–18.

61. Most, 117, 107.

62. In *The Haunted Stage: The Theatre as Memory Machine* (Ann Arbor: University of Michigan Press, 2001), Marvin Carlson writes, "the 'interpretive community' might in fact be described as a community in which there is a significant overlap of such memory, and the reception process itself might be characterized as the selective application of memory to experience" (5).

63. Richard Schechner, *Between Theatre and Anthropology* (Philadelphia: University of Pennsylvania Press, 1985), 113, emphasis added.

64. Harley Erdman, *Staging the Jew: The Performance of an American Ethnicity, 1860–1920* (New Brunswick, Rutgers University Press, 1997), 145.

65. Technically, according to Jewish law men are not required to wear beards. However, bringing a blade into contact with one's face for cosmetic (rather than medical) purposes is expressly forbidden. The use of depilatory chemicals has a long history among European Jews, and in modern times many rabbis have ruled that some electric razors (which pull facial hairs away from the skin before cutting them so that the blades do not touch the face) may be used.

66. As quoted in William Novak and Moshe Waldoks, eds., *The Big Book of Jewish Humor* (New York: Harper and Row, 1981), 60.

67. The phrase "aesthetics of everyday life" is credited to diverse writers in diverse contexts; my own usage is indebted to the work of Barbara Kirshenblatt-Gimblett.

68. Soloveitchik, 75.

69. Ibid., 77.

70. Steven M. Cohen, "Jewish Continuity over Judaic Content," in Seltzer and Cohen, 396.

71. Felicia Herman, "The Way She *Really* Is: Images of Jews and Women in the Films of Barbra Streisand," in *Talking Back: Images of Jewish Women in American Popular Culture*, ed. Joyce Antler (Hanover: Brandeis University Press, 1998), 173, emphasis in original.

72. Samuel Freedman, *Jew vs. Jew* (New York: Simon and Schuster, 2000), 35.

73. See Steinberg.

74. Kathryn Bernheimer, *The 50 Greatest Jewish Movies* (Secaucus: Birch Lane Press, 1998), 21. According to the World Jewish Congress (1998), this is still the case.

75. See Brooks McNamara, "'A Congress of Wonders': The Rise and Fall of the Dime Museum," *ESQ: A Journal of the American Renaissance* 20, 3 (1974): 216–32. As McNamara notes, however, this does not mean that nineteenth-century Americans did not enjoy popular entertainments. Circuses, museums, and quasi-educational Chatauqua Society shows were among the many diversions they enjoyed. However, theater in the traditional sense was uncommon.

76. Alexis De Tocqueville, "Some Observations on the Drama amongst Democratic Nations," trans. Henry Reeve, in *The Theory of the Modern Stage* ed. Eric Bentley (New York: Penguin, 1976), 483.

77. See Martin Banham, ed., *The Cambridge Guide to Theatre* (Cambridge: Cambridge University Press, 1992), 717.

78. See David Sheward, *It's a Hit: The Backstage Book of Longest Running Broadway Shows, 1884 to the Present* (New York: Backstage Books, 1994).

79. Samson Raphaelson, *The Jazz Singer* (New York: Brentano's, 1925), 9.

80. Bernheimer, 22; see also *The Jazz Singer* dir. Alan Crosland (Culver City, CA: MGM/UA Home Video, 1991).

81. Raphaelson, 152.

82. For an analysis of the role of blackface in configuring ethnic and social mobility in *The Jazz Singer*, see Rogin, 81–90.

83. Bernheimer, 8.

84. As quoted in Gabler, *Empire*, 277.

85. See Bernheimer, 41.

86. For a detailed account of how Jewish studio heads managed the public perceptions of their Jewishness in the 1920s and 1930s, see Gabler, *Empire*, 120–50.

87. Nathan Glazer, *American Judaism*, 2d ed. (Chicago: University of Chicago Press, 1972), 118–19. The first edition was published in 1957 also by the University of Chicago Press.

88. See Seltzer and Cohen; and Lipset and Raab.

89. Barry Gross, "What Shylock Forgot; or Making It and Losing It in America," *Journal of Ethnic Studies* 2, 3 (1974): 51, emphasis in original.

90. Cf. Steinberg; and Shandler, "Jewish Way." See also Joshua Hammer and John Schwartz, "Prime Time Mensch," *Newsweek* 12 October 1992, 88–89.

91. Glazer, "American Jewry," 15. Cf. Shmuel A. Eisenstadt, "The Jewish Experience with Pluralism," *Society* 28, 1 (1990): 21–25; and elsewhere.

92. Stratton, 282–314; Brook, "From the Cozy to the Carceral"; Terry Barr, "Stars, Light, and Finding the Way: The Emergence of Jewish Characters in Contemporary Film and Television," *Studies in Popular Culture* 25, 2 (1993): 87–100.

93. Band, 217–18.

94. See Lipset and Raab.

95. Brook, "From the Cozy to the Carceral."

96. Cf. Ellen Schiff, ed., *Awake and Singing* (New York: Mentor, 1995). See also Lipset and Raab; Glazer, "American Jewry"; and Steinberg.

97. Sollors, *Beyond Ethnicity*, 18.

98. Cf. ibid.

CHAPTER 2

1. See Gabler, *Empire;* Steinberg; and Lipset and Raab.

2. See, for example, Arthur Miller, *Timebends: A Life* (New York: Grove, 1987); and Kirk Douglas, *The Ragman's Son* (New York: Simon and Schuster, 1988).

3. Gilman, *The Jew's Body*, 6.

4. Cf. George Ross, "'Death of a Salesman' in the Original," *Commentary* 11, 2 (1951): 184–86; Enoch Brater, "Ethics and Ethnicity in the Plays of Arthur Miller," in *From Hester Street to Hollywood: The Jewish-American Stage and Screen*, ed. Sarah Blacher Cohen (Bloomington: Indiana University Press, 1983), 123–36; Julius Novick, "Salesman Redivivus," *Threepenny Review* 19 (1985): 18–19; and Michiko Kakutani, "A Salesman Who Transcends Time," *New York Times*, 7 February 1999.

5. Bernheimer, 37.

6. Gabler, 349.

7. Bernheimer, 39.

8. Gabler, 349.

9. Unless otherwise noted, all direct references to and quotations from *Gentleman's Agreement* (including promotional trailers) are drawn from the Twentieth Century-Fox Home Video VHS Edition (Beverly Hills: Fox Video, 1992).

10. Leonard Maltin, ed., *Leonard Maltin's 2001 Movie and Video Guide* (New York: Signet, 2001), 509.

11. Hobson was the daughter of noted Yiddish-language journalist Michael Zametkin, a former editor of the Jewish daily newspaper *Forward* (Bernheimer, 38).

12. Lester Friedman, ed., *Unspeakable Images: Ethnicity and the American Cinema* (Urbana: University of Illinois Press, 1991), 24.

13. Barry Gross, "No Victim, She: Barbra Streisand and the Movie Jew," *Journal of Ethnic Studies* 3, 1 (1975): 33.

14. For the savvy audience member, this revelation is doubly ironic because Havoc herself changed her last name from Hovick when she became an actress (Gabler, 371).

15. Jean-Paul Sartre, *Anti-Semite and Jew*, trans. G. Brecker (New York: Schocken, 1995 [1948]), 109.

16. Cf. Phelan.

17. Elaine K. Ginsberg, ed., *Passing and the Fictions of Identity* (Durham: Duke University Press, 1996), 4, emphasis in original.

18. Kathryn Bernheimer cites an anecdote about the film in which "a stagehand remarked that he had learned a valuable lesson from the movie: From now on he would be nice to Jews because they might turn out to be gentiles" (41).

19. Samuel J. Rosenthal, "John Garfield," in Hoberman and Shandler, 174.

20. Ibid.

21. Ibid.

22. Ibid., 175.

23. Ibid., 173.

24. See Sollors, *Beyond Ethnicity*.

25. Cf. Brater.

26. See Gabler, 301; and Darryl Lyman, *Great Jews on Stage and Screen* (Middle Village, NY: Jonathan David, 1994), 88–89.

27. As quoted in Gabler, 371–72.

28. George Lipsitz, *Time Passages: Collective Memory and American Popular Culture* (Minneapolis: University of Minnesota Press, 1990), 39–75.

29. Donald Weber, "The Jewish-American World of Gertrude Berg: *The Goldbergs* on Radio and Televison, 1930–1950," in *Talking Back: Images of Jewish Women in American Popular Culture*, ed. Joyce Antler (Boston: Brandeis University Press, 1998), 91, emphasis in original.

30. See Donald Weber, "Taking Jewish American Popular Culture Seriously: The Yinglish Worlds of Gertrude Berg, Milton Berle, and Mickey Katz," *Jewish Social Studies* 5, 1–2 (1999): 124–53.

31. Unless otherwise noted, references to and quotations from specific episodes of *The Goldbergs* are based on the author's viewing of videotapes housed by the National Jewish Archive of Broadcasting, New York City. A complete list of the episodes quoted here appears in the bibliography.

32. Vincent Brook, *Something Ain't Kosher Here: The Rise of the "Jewish" Sitcom* (New Brunswick: Rutgers University Press, 2003), 27.

33. Zurawik, 20–26.

34. Ibid., 20.

35. Ibid., 31.

36. As quoted in ibid., 24.

37. Ibid., 24–25.

38. Francine Klagsbrun, "Remembering the Goldbergs," *New York Times*, 8 August 1988.

39. Vincent Brook, "The Americanization of Molly: How Mid-Fifties TV Homogenized *The Goldbergs* (and Got 'Berg-larized' in the Process)," *Cinema Journal* 38, 4 (1999): 58.

40. Sam Levenson, "The Dialect Comedian Should Vanish," *Commenatry* 14, 2 (1952): 169.

41. Ibid.

42. Zurawik, 26.

43. See Brook, "The Americanization of Molly."

44. CBS-TV press release, 19 November 1949, National Jewish Archive of Broadcasting.

45. Cf. Kleeblatt.

46. Cf. Brook, *Something Ain't Kosher*, 33; and Zurawik, 45–47.

47. Brook gives the air date of this episode as 5 April 1954 (*Something Ain't Kosher*, 33). However, the October date cited by Zurawik seems more reliable, both because it is confirmed by other sources and because of its proximity to the Yom Kippur holiday.

48. Zurawik has timed this sequence at six minutes, nine seconds, or more than 20 percent of the half-hour broadcast (47).

49. For an analysis of the "Kol Nidre" scene in *The Jazz Singer*, see chapter 1.

50. Zurawik, 45–47.

51. Berg authored *Molly and Me* (New York: McGraw-Hill, 1961) with the assistance of her son, Cherny Berg.

52. Ibid., 246.

53. CBS-TV press release, 13 January 1949, National Jewish Archive of Broadcasting.

54. See Weber, "Jewish-American World."

55. Klagsbrun.

56. David J. Schneider, Albert H. Hastorf, and Phoebe Ellsworth, *Person Perception* (Reading: Addison-Wesley, 1979), 9.

57. Zurawik, 45.

58. Cf. Klagsbrun; and Levenson.

59. Brook, "From the Cozy to the Carceral," 58.

60. Novick, "Salesman Redivivus."

61. G. Ross, 184.

62. Novick, "Salesman Redivivus."

63. G. Ross, 185.

64. See Arthur Miller, *Death of a Salesman* (New York: Penguin Books, 1949), 129 and elsewhere.

65. Ibid., 56.

66. G. Ross, 185.

67. See, for example, Brater; and Novick, "Salesman Redivivus."

68. Miller makes exactly this point in his *The Theater Essays of Arthur Miller*, ed. Robert A. Martin and Steven R. Centola, rev. and expanded ed. (New York: Da Capo, 1996), 114.

69. George Bernard Shaw, *Four Plays by George Bernard Shaw* (New York: Modern Library, 1953), 213.

70. Steve Vineberg, *Method Actors: Three Generations of an American Acting Style* (New York: Schirmer, 1991), 299.

71. Julius Novick, "Willy Loman's Secret," *Forward*, 8 October 1999.

72. Vineberg, 77.

73. Harold Clurman, *The Fervent Years: The Group Theatre and the 30s* (New York: Knopf, 1975), 4.

74. Nahma Sandrow, *Vagabond Stars: A World History of Yiddish Theater* (Syracuse: Syracuse University Press, 1996), 205.

75. For more on the Group Theater and the psychological aspects of the Method, see Vineberg, esp. 85–113. Not surprisingly, when we acknowledge the historical link between the American Method and the Yiddish theater, critiques of the Method as unrefined, vulgar, neurotic, or overly emotional begin to sound very similar to the charges leveled by anti-Semites against Jews themselves. Compare this to the thinly veiled racism of early invectives against rock and roll.

76. One illustration of class consciousness in the Yiddish theater is the fact that the foundation of its union, the Hebrew Actors Union, predated the foundation of the Actors' Equity Association (AEA) by nearly two decades (and to this day is jointly affiliated with both the AEA and the AFL-CIO).

77. Clurman, 55.

78. As quoted in Brater, 128. See also Miller, *Theater Essays*.

79. See Leslie Fiedler, *Fiedler on the Roof: Essays on Literature and Jewish Identity* (Boston: David R. Godine, 1991).

80. Kakutani.

81. Schechner, *Between Theatre and Anthropology*, 120.

82. José Esteban Muñoz, "Feeling Brown: Ethnicity and Affect in Ricardo Bracho's *The Sweetest Hangover (and Other STD's)*," *Theatre Journal* 52, 1 (March 2000): 69.

83. Ibid., 70.

84. Ibid.

85. Viewed in this light, David Mamet's polemics against Method acting—for example, in his *True and False: Heresy and Common Sense for the Actor* (New York: Pantheon, 1997)—may seem incongruous with his desire for an improved Jewish self-image in performance; however, Mamet's "practical aesthetic" of acting must be understood as a critique not of emotional acting itself but of what he sees as falsely generated emotion. I take up this topic more extensively in another essay (in progress): "The Old Religion, the New Actor: Judaism and David Mamet's Practical Aesthetics."

86. See Miller, *Timebends*; Miller, *Theater Essays*; and elsewhere.

87. Brenda Murphy, *Death of a Salesman* (New York: Cambridge University Press, 1995), 94–5.

88. Phelan.

89. Ibid., 19.

90. As quoted in Novick, "Willy Loman's Secret," 12.

CHAPTER 3

1. Stein is quoted in Peter Stone, Jerry Bock, Sheldon Harnick, and Joseph Stein, "Landmark Symposium: 'Fiddler on the Roof,'" *Dramatists' Guild Quarterly* 20, 1 (1983): 15, 27, respectively.

2. Norman Nadel, "'Fiddler on the Roof' Is Humorous, Tender Musical," *New York Theatre Critics Reviews* 25, 19 (1964): 214.

3. Ibid.

4. Richard Watts Jr., "Two on the Aisle: The Brilliance of Zero Mostel," *New York Theatre Critics Reviews* 25, 19 (1964): 215.

5. Ibid.

6. See Sollors, *Beyond Ethnicity*.

7. Howard Taubman, "Theater: Mostel as Tevye in 'Fiddler on the Roof,'" *New York Theatre Critics Reviews* 25, 19 (1964): 217.

8. This is a fairly basic semiotic model, and it is by no means unique to Hall. I use Hall's essay here because of both its clarity and its canonical status within cultural studies.

9. Stuart Hall, "Encoding and Decoding in Television Discourse," in *The Cultural Studies Reader*, ed. Simon During (London: Routledge, 1993), 93–94.

10. Ibid., 102.

11. Seth Wolitz, "The Americanization of Tevye; or, Boarding the Jewish Mayflower," *American Quarterly* 40, 4 (1988): 530, emphasis in original.

12. Hall, 103.

13. Walter Kerr, Review of "Fiddler on the Roof," *New York Theatre Critics Reviews* 25, 19 (1964): 217.

14. Cf. Wolitz.

15. See, for example, Ruth Wisse, *The Modern Jewish Canon* (New York: Free Press, 2000).

16. See Richard Altman and Mervyn Kaufman, *The Making of a Musical: Fiddler on the Roof* (New York: Crown, 1971); see also Stone et al.

17. Hall, 100.

18. See Stanley Fish, *Is There a Text in This Class?* (Cambridge: Harvard University Press, 1980); and elsewhere.

19. Marvin Carlson, *Theatre Semiotics: Signs of Life* (Bloomington: Indiana University Press, 1990), 13.

20. Ibid., 14.

21. Ibid., 24; cf. Tony Bennett, "Text, Readers, Reading Formations," *Literature and History* 9 (1983): 214.

22. See S. Bennett; Carlson, *Theatre Semiotics*; Fish; and others.

23. See Gordis and Ben-Horin; Whitfield; and Freedman; and Riv-Ellen Prell, *Fighting to Become Americans: Jews, Gender, and the Anxiety of Assimilation* (Boston: Beacon, 1999).

24. J. Boyarin, 170.

25. The act of identifying oneself as a goy or shiksa is itself a remarkable moment, in that the outsider is making a claim (via the use of the insider term) for

at least provisional in-group status. A number of recent popular articles, for example, have addressed the adoption of Yiddish catchphrases by non-Jewish actors, writers, and producers in Hollywood, apparently for the purpose of establishing a connection with Jewish movie moguls.

26. For a discussion of "the absence of a Jewish presence" in the work of Hall and other writers in British cultural studies, see Stratton, 35–52.

27. Boyarin and Boyarin, xii.

28. Carlson, *Theatre Semiotics*, 14.

29. Kerr, "Review of 'Fiddler,'" 217.

30. Taubman, "Theater: Mostel as Tevye," 217.

31. My interpretation of Mostel's musical performance is based on *Fiddler on the Roof: The Original Broadway Cast Recording* (New York: RCA, 1964, compact disc issued 1986).

32. Henry Jenkins, *Textual Poachers* (London: Routledge, 1993), 26.

33. Ibid., 27.

34. Curiously, Jenkins's "ethnographic" analysis of science fiction fandom is silent on the question of ethnicity (and religion), and how this might fit into the equation.

35. Leonard Nimoy, *I Am Spock* (New York: Hyperion, 1995), 67.

36. Cf. Jenkins, 101.

37. Ibid., 11.

38. Jeffrey Shandler, *While America Watches: Televising the Holocaust* (New York: Oxford University Press, 1999), 147–51.

39. Shandler, "Jewish Way," 20.

40. Ibid.

41. Hall, 100.

42. Nadel, "Fiddler," 214. Leonard Dinnerstein (personal communication, 1999) has pointed out that Nadel's statement is likely a parodic reference to a New York–based advertising slogan of the period: "You don't have to be Jewish to love Levy's Real Jewish Rye." However, Nadel's appropriation of the slogan does not diminish the significance of the example; rather, it shows that a similar ambivalence about Jewish identity is at work in the advertising industry.

43. The reason critics don't declare "You don't have to be Danish to love Hamlet" is because it is not in any significant way important to *Hamlet* that the characters are Danish.

44. Cf. Umberto Eco, "The Semiotics of Theatrical Performance," *Drama Review* 21, 1 (1977): 113.

45. For more on *Fiddler* as popular ethnography, see Barbara Kirshenblatt-Gimblett, "Imagining Europe: The Popular Arts of American Jewish Ethnography," in *Divergent Centers: Shaping Jewish Cultures in Israel and America*, ed. Deborah Dash Moore and Ilan Troen (New Haven: Yale University Press, 2001), 155–91.

46. Wolitz, 516.

47. Ibid., 530.

48. For his description of this production, see Nimoy, 147.

49. Unless otherwise noted, biographical information concerning Mostel is drawn from Jared Brown, *Zero Mostel* (New York: Atheneum, 1989).

50. Ibid., 128.

51. Stone et al., 18.

52. Watts, 215.

53. John McClain, "Mostel Makes Musical Tick," *New York Theatre Critics Reviews* 25, 19 (1964): 215.

54. Taubman, "Theater: Mostel as Tevye," 217–18.

55. Stone et al., 22.

56. Brett M. Rhyne, "'Fiddler on the Roof' Lyricist Featured in New Musical," *Jewish Journal*, 28 February 2003, retrieved 12 January 2004 from http://www.jewishjournal.org/archives.

57. Stone et al., 22.

58. Brown, 32.

59. Kerr, "Review of 'Fiddler,'" 215.

60. Carlson, *The Haunted Stage*, 53.

61. Ibid., 59.

62. Wolitz, 525.

63. Stone et al., 27.

64. Ibid.

65. The Anti-Defamation League published a strong condemnation of *Jesus Christ Superstar* in 1974 on the grounds that the film allegedly perpetuates the "blood libel" that the Jews bear responsibility for Jesus' crucifixion.

66. All references to the film version of *Fiddler*, dir. Norman Jewison, are drawn from the CBS/Fox Video VHS edition (Farmington Hills, MI: CBS/Fox Video, 1984).

67. Carlson, *The Haunted Stage*, 66; see also Joseph Roach, *Cities of the Dead* (New York: Columbia University Press, 1996).

68. Though no video recording of Mostel's performance is publicly available, his accent and speech patterns can be discerned from the sound recording: *Fiddler on the Roof: The Original Broadway Cast Recording* (New York: RCA, 1964, compact disc issued 1986).

69. I am indebted to a number of acting and voice teachers at New York University for confirming this observation.

70. This and subsequent quotations from Canby, unless otherwise noted, are drawn from Vincent Canby, "Life-Style of Aleichem Characters Is Missing amid Production's Grandeur," *New York Times*, 4 November 1971.

71. Vincent Canby, "Is 'Fiddler' More DeMille Than Sholem Aleichem?" *New York Times*, 28 November 1971.

72. Ibid.

73. Ibid.

74. Stone et al., 21.

75. Ibid., 27.

76. Michael Feingold, "Introduction," in Donald Margulies, *Sight Unseen and Other Plays* (New York: Theatre Communications Group, 1995), xi.

77. Ben Brantley, "A Cozy Little McShtetl," *New York Times*, 27 February 2004.

78. Thane Rosenbaum, "A Legacy Cut Loose," *Los Angeles Times*, 15 February 2004.

79. Caleb Ben-David, "Tevye's Happy Ending," *Jerusalem Post,* 22 September 2004.

80. John Heilpern, "New-ish, but Still Jew-ish: *Fiddler* Breaks Tradition," *New York Observer,* 8 March 2004.

81. Mark Kennedy, "Alfred Molina Scales New Heights in 'Fiddler on the Roof,'" Associated Press wire report, 25 February 2004.

82. As quoted in Alisa Solomon, "Fiddling with 'Fiddler,'" *Village Voice,* 21 January 2004.

83. Elysa Gardner, "'Fiddler' Again Plays Its Magic," *USA Today,* 27 February 2004.

84. "Nowadays," writes theater critic Alisa Solomon in "Fiddling," "lesbians get married under the chupah, boys talk baseball at their bar mitzvahs, and Passover Seders proclaim the rights of Palestinians. But one Jewish text has remained resistant to renovation, with strict prohibitions against any alterations to the practice it originally laid out. Call it the 11th Commandment: Don't fuck with Fiddler."

85. Jeremy McCarter, "The Musical to Start All Musicals," *New York Sun,* 27 February 2004.

86. John Lahr, "Bittersweet," *New Yorker,* 8 March 2004, 89.

87. McCarter.

CHAPTER 4

1. *Playboy,* October 1977.

2. The claim that Streisand was "the first female celebrity in 24 years" to appear on the cover of *Playboy* was made in an unsigned editorial note in the magazine's table of contents.

3. John Chapman, "'Wholesale' Depressing Musical," *New York Theatre Critics Reviews* 23, 9 (1962): 316; Walter Kerr, "First Night Report: 'I Can Get It for You Wholesale,'" *New York Theatre Critics Reviews* 23, 9 (1962): 314; Howard Taubman, "Theatre: 'I Can Get It for You Wholesale' Opens," *New York Theatre Critics Reviews* 23, 9 (1962): 316.

4. John McClain, "Even at Retail, It's No Bargain," *New York Theatre Critics Reviews* 23, 9 (1962): 317.

5. See Jerome Weidman and Harold Rome, *I Can Get It for You Wholesale* (New York: Random House, 1962), pls. 1–3.

6. See, for example, Sander Gilman, *Jewish Self-Hatred: Anti-Semitism and the Hidden Language of the Jews* (Baltimore: Johns Hopkins University Press, 1986); and Annette Wernblad, *Brooklyn Is Not Expanding: Woody Allen's Comic Universe* (Rutherford, NJ: Fairleigh Dickinson University Press, 1992).

7. Robert Leslie Liebman, "Rabbis or Rakes, Schlemiels or Supermen? Jewish Identity in Charlie Chaplin, Jerry Lewis, and Woody Allen," *Literature/Film Quarterly* 12, 3 (1984): 199.

8. Bernheimer, 33.

9. Cf. ibid.; and Herman.

10. Herman, 172.

11. Letty Cottin Pogrebin, *Deborah, Golda, and Me: Being Female and Jewish in America* (New York: Crown, 1991), 267 (as referenced in Herman).

12. The casting of Sharif as a Jewish character (and Streisand's love interest) caused significant uproar from Jewish organizations and the Egyptian government, though this controversy was largely ignored by the mainstream film press (Bernheimer, 35).

13. Unless otherwise noted, references to and quotations from the 1968 film version of *Funny Girl*, dir. William Wyler, are based on the RCA/Columbia Pictures Home Video edition (Burbank, CA: RCA/Columbia Pictures Home Video, 1985).

14. Whether Ziegfeld was in fact Jewish is somewhat disputed. His biographer, Charles Higham, relates that the Ziegfeld family was Lutheran (*Ziegfeld* [Chicago: H. Regnery, 1972], 1). However, Bernheimer identifies him as Jewish, and he is listed in several Jewish biographical dictionaries, including American Jewish Historical Society, *The American Jewish Desk Reference* ([New York: Random House, 1999], 427–28); Jacob R. Marcus ed., *The Concise Dictionary of American Jewish Biography* ([Brooklyn: Carlson, 1994], 708); and Isaac Landman, ed., *The Universal Jewish Encyclopedia*, which notes, "Ziegfeld had no formal connections with Jewish life; but among his benefactions were his contributions to the Israel Orphan Asylum of New York" ([New York: Universal Jewish Encyclopedia Co., 1948], 642).

15. Norman Nadel, "'Funny Girl' Is Just This Side of Paradise," *New York Theatre Critics Reviews* 25, 9 (1964): 314.

16. Herman, 175.

17. Gilman, "The Jew's Body," 61.

18. Joshua Halberstam, *Schmoozing: The Private Conversations of American Jews* (New York: Perigree, 1997), 78.

19. Judith Butler, *Gender Trouble* (New York: Routledge, 1990), 272. For a discussion of how Butler's own Jewishness informs her theory, see Naomi Seidman, "Fag-Hags and Bu-Jews: Toward a (Jewish) Politics of Vicarious Identity," in *Insider/Outsider: American Jews and Multiculturalism*, ed. David Biale, Michael Galchinsky, and Susan Heschel (Berkeley: University of California Press, 1998), 254–68.

20. See Erving Goffman, *The Presentation of Self in Everyday Life* (Woodstock: Overlook, 1959).

21. Halberstam, 76–77.

22. Erdman, 6.

23. Schneider, Hastorf, and Ellsworth, 14.

24. Halberstam, 78.

25. Woody Allen, *Play It Again, Sam* (New York: Random House, 1971), 3.

26. Ibid., 5.

27. Ibid., 10.

28. David Biale, *Eros and the Jews: From Biblical Israel to Contemporary America* (New York: Basic Books, 1992), 205–6.

29. Ibid., 205. For a more thorough history of the schlemiel, see Ruth Wisse, *The Schlemiel as Modern Hero* (Chicago: University of Chicago Press, 1971).

30. Biale, 206, emphasis added.

31. Allen, *Play It Again, Sam*, 85.

32. Liebman, 198.

33. "The main characters I always try to name before I begin anything," Allen

told Stig Björkman. "It's always important to me what I name them." See Woody Allen, *Woody Allen on Woody Allen*, ed. Stig Björkman (New York: Grove, 1993), 135.

34. Allen, *Play It Again, Sam*, 11.

35. Biale, 206.

36. It should be noted that the film version of *Play It Again, Sam* includes one brief explicit reference to Allan Felix's Jewishness. Explaining why he identifies with Bogart, Allan asks, "Who'm I gonna pick, my rabbi?" This and other references to or quotations from the film version of *Play It Again, Sam*, dir. Herbert Ross, are drawn from the Paramount Studio VHS edition (Hollywood, CA: Paramount Home Video, 1991).

37. As quoted in Allen, *Play It Again, Sam*, book jacket copy.

38. Schneider, Hastorf, and Ellsworth, 14, emphasis added.

39. Unless otherwise noted, all references to and quotations from *The Way We Were*, dir. Sydney Pollack, are drawn from the Columbia Tristar Home Video VHS edition (New York: Columbia Tristar Home Video, 2001).

40. Herman, 179.

41. Vincent Canby, Review of *The Way We Were*, *New York Times*, 18 October 1973.

42. Ibid.

43. Lawrence Grobel, "Playboy Interview: Barbra Streisand," *Playboy*, October 1977, 80.

44. David Desser, "The Cinematic Melting Pot: Ethnicity, Jews, and Psychoanalysis," in Friedman, 390.

45. See Zurawik, 78–103; and Brook, *Something Ain't Kosher*, 48–54.

46. See Rogin; and Brodkin.

47. Cf. Maltin; Wernblad; and Allen, *Woody Allen*.

48. Bernheimer, 29, italics in original.

49. Cf. Biale; Wernblad; Stratton. Unless otherwise noted, all references to and quotations from *Annie Hall*, dir. Woody Allen, are drawn from the MGM DVD edition (Santa Monica: MGM Home Entertainment, 2000).

50. See Eco, 113.

51. Bernheimer, 32.

52. Biale, 207.

53. Cf. Gilman, *The Jew's Body*.

54. Biale, 207.

55. See Gilman, *The Jew's Body*; Rogin; and Boyarin and Boyarin.

56. Gilman, "The Jew's Body," 61.

57. Cf. Kleeblatt; Herman; Bernheimer, and others.

58. Grobel, 98.

59. Ibid.

60. Ibid., 81.

61. Elsewhere in the interview, Streisand makes clear that she considers anti-Semitism a problem, speculating that the reason she was turned down for a Manhattan co-op apartment was that she was Jewish (ibid., 92).

62. Vivian Sobchak, "Postmodern Modes of Ethnicity," in Friedman, 332–33.

63. Allen also directed *Interiors* (1978), but this film was already in production

when *Annie Hall* was released. Unless otherwise noted, all references to and quotations from *Manhattan* are drawn from the MGM Home Entertainment VHS edition (Culver City, CA: MGM Home Entertainment, 2000).

64. Allen played a brief and explicit pastiche of *A Streetcar Named Desire* in an earlier film, *Sleeper* (1973).

65. The character names here suggest competing archetypes of Jewish masculinity. Jeremiah, the prophet, represents the Jew as mystical and exotic, as played out in his inexplicable sexual mastery. Isaac, the patriarch, represents the Jew as stable and paternal.

66. Unless otherwise noted, all references to and quotations from *Yentl*, dir. Barbra Streisand, are drawn from the MGM/UA Home Video VHS edition (Culver City, CA: MGM/UA Home Video, 1989).

67. Unless otherwise noted, all references to and quotations from *Zelig*, dir. Woody Allen, are drawn from the MGM Home Entertainment VHS edition (Santa Monica: MGM Home Entertainment, 2001).

68. Ginsberg, 4.

69. Gilman, *The Jew's Body*, 353; Whitfield, 29.

70. Alison Fernley and Paula Maloof, "*Yentl*," *Film Quarterly* 38 (spring 1985): 43.

71. Allen, *Woody Allen*, 141.

72. Rex Reed, "Review of *Yentl*." *Film Review Annual* (1983): 1436–37. For Nadel's comments on *Fiddler*, see chapter 3.

CHAPTER 5

1. Cf. Lipset and Raab; Steinberg; and S. Cohen.

2. Hammer and Schwartz, 88.

3. See Albert Auster, "'Funny, You Don't Look Jewish': The Image of Jews on Television," *Television Quarterly* 26, 3 (1993): 65–74; and Barr, 87–100.

4. *Jewish Folklore and Ethnology Review* 16, 1 (1994).

5. David Mamet, "The Decoration of Jewish Houses," in David Mamet, *Some Freaks* (New York: Viking, 1989), 7.

6. "The Decoration of Jewish Houses" first appeared in *Penthouse*; "A Plain Brown Wrapper" first appeared in *Tikkun*.

7. Wendy Wasserstein, *Shiksa Goddess; or, How I Spent My Forties* (New York: Knopf, 2001), 4.

8. Page numbers cited parenthetically for *The Sisters Rosensweig* refer to Wendy Wasserstein, *The Sisters Rosensweig* (San Diego: Harcourt Brace, 1993).

9. Norman J. Cohen, "Wrestling with Angels," in Vorlicky, 220.

10. J. Boyarin, 170.

11. Eisenstadt, 25.

12. Cf. David A. Hollinger, *Postethnic America: Beyond Multiculturalism* (New York: Basic Books, 1995).

13. Kirshenblatt-Gimblett, 181.

14. David Savran, "Ambivalence, Utopia, and a Queer Sort of Materialism: How *Angels in America* Reconstructs the Nation," in *Approaching the Millennium: Essays on* Angels in America, ed. Deborah Geis and Steven Kruger (Ann Arbor: University of Michigan Press, 1997), 13.

15. Part 1 opened at the end of the 1992–93 award season, and part 2 was added to the repertory at the start of the 1993–94 season.

16. Geis and Kruger, 2.

17. N. Cohen, 220.

18. Page numbers cited parenthetically for *Angels in America* refer to Tony Kushner, *Angels in America*, part 1: *Millennium Approaches* (New York: Theatre Communications Group, 1993); and *Angels in America*, part 2: *Perestroika* (New York: Theatre Communications Group, 1993). The roman numeral preceding the page number indicates the part from which the quotation is drawn.

19. John Simon, Review of *Angels in America*, *New York Theatre Critics Reviews* 54, 11 (1993): 207.

20. John Lahr, "Angels on Broadway," *New York Theatre Critics Reviews* 54, 11 (1993): 208.

21. Ward Morehouse II, "'Angels in America' Remains Earthbound," *New York Theatre Critics Reviews* 54, 11 (1993): 215–16; David Patrick Stearns, "Soaring 'Angels in America,'" *New York Theatre Critics Reviews* 54, 11 (1993): 219.

22. Clive Barnes, "Angelically Gay about Our Decay," *New York Theatre Critics Reviews* 54, 11 (1993): 210.

23. Michael Feingold, "Building the Monolith," *New York Theatre Critics Reviews* 54, 11 (1993): 218.

24. Alisa Solomon, "Wrestling with *Angels:* A Jewish Fantasia," in Geis and Kruger, 125.

25. Wasserstein, *Shiksa Goddess*, 4. This specific code, as we shall see, is a significant trope in *The Sisters Rosensweig*.

26. Solomon, "Wrestling," 124.

27. Sedgwick, 75. For a discussion of how Sedgwick's ambivalent relationship with her own Jewishness informs this argument, see Seidman, 261–65.

28. As quoted in N. Cohen, 217.

29. Frank Rich, "Embracing All Possibilities in Art and Life," *New York Theatre Critics Reviews* 54, 11 (1993): 214.

30. N. Cohen, 220.

31. Testimony by an ex-KGB officer suggests that Julius, at least, did act as a Soviet agent, but this information was not revealed until 1997, five years after the Los Angeles premiere of *Angels in America*.

32. See Nicholas von Hoffman, *Citizen Cohn* (New York: Doubleday, 1988).

33. Lahr, "Angels," 208.

34. Simon, 207.

35. See Erdman; Gilman, *Jewish Self-Hatred;* and elsewhere.

36. Solomon, "Wrestling," 126.

37. Feingold, "Building," 219.

38. Solomon, "Wrestling," 126.

39. Linda Winer, "Pulitzer-Winning 'Angels' Emerges from the Wings," *New York Theatre Critics Reviews* 54, 11 (1993): 209.

40. Jeremy Girard, Review of *Angels in America*, *New York Theatre Critics Reviews* 54, 11 (1993): 212.

41. See, for example, Clive Herschorn, Review of *Angels in America*, *Theatre Record* 13, 24 (1993): 1358; Louise Doughty, Review of *Angels in America*, *Theatre Record* 13, 24 (1993): 1359–60; Paul Taylor, Review of *Angels in America*, *Theatre*

Record 13, 24 (1993): 1357; Michael Billington, Review of *Angels in America, Theatre Record* 13, 24 (1993): 1357; and others.

42. Winer, 209.

43. Rich, 214.

44. Stephen J. Bottoms, "Re-staging Roy: Citizen Cohn and the Search for Xanadu," *Theatre Journal* 48 (1996): 167.

45. Solomon, "Wrestling," 129.

46. Rich, 386.

47. An earlier version had been presented the previous April as part of the Seattle Repertory Theatre's New Plays Reading Series.

48. Unless otherwise noted, all references to *The Sisters Rosensweig* are drawn from the 1993 trade edition by Wendy Wasserstein, published by Harcourt Brace under its Harvest Book imprint.

49. Robert Brustein, Review of *The Sisters Rosensweig, New York Theatre Critics Reviews* 54, 4 (1993): 79; Doug Watt, "Wasserstein Pens a Pointed Drawing-Room Comedy," *New York Theatre Critics Reviews* 54, 4 (1993): 77.

50. Mel Gussow, "Wasserstein: Comedy, Character, Reflection," *New York Theatre Critics Reviews* 54, 4 (1993): 80.

51. William Henry III, Review of *The Sisters Rosensweig, New York Theatre Critics Reviews* 54, 4 (1993): 83.

52. Howard Kissell, "Sharpened 'Sisters' Act," *New York Theatre Critics Reviews* 54, 4 (1993): 74.

53. Brustein, 79.

54. See chapter 2.

55. In *Fiddler on the Roof*; see chapter 3.

56. See chapter 4.

57. Wasserstein's fictive invention, *Pimpernel* the musical, predates by five years the Broadway musical *The Scarlet Pimpernel* (1997).

58. Michael Feingold, Review of *The Sisters Rosensweig, New York Theatre Critics Reviews* 54, 4 (1993): 84.

59. Jeremy Girard, Review of *The Sisters Rosensweig, New York Theatre Critics Reviews* 54, 4 (1993): 70.

60. David Patrick Stearns, "'Sisters' Is a Kind, Clever, Wasserstein Chronicle," *New York Theatre Critics Reviews* 54, 4 (1993): 75.

61. Brustein, 79.

62. Clive Barnes, "'Sisters' Makes the Big Move to B'way," *New York Theatre Critics Reviews* 54, 4 (1993): 72; Brustein, 79; Gussow, 80.

63. Feingold, "Review of *Sisters*," 84, italics in original.

64. Howard Kissell, "Family Circus," *New York Theatre Critics Reviews* 54, 4 (1993): 73.

65. Winer, 76.

66. See the following section.

67. Gussow, 81.

68. Jan Stuart, "If Chekhov Sisters Had Lived in Brooklyn," *New York Theatre Critics Reviews* 54, 4 (1993): 75; Kissell, "Family Circus," 73; Simon, 82.

69. David Mamet, *Three Jewish Plays* (New York: Samuel French, 1987).

70. Leslie Kane, *Weasels and Wisemen: Ethics and Ethnicity in the Works of David Mamet* (New York: St. Martin's/Palgrave, 1999), 227.

71. Page numbers cited parenthetically for *The Old Neighborhood* refer to David Mamet, *The Old Neighborhood* (New York: Vintage, 1998).

72. See Finkielkraut, 1–56.

73. Ibid., 7.

74. Kane, 237.

75. Shandler, "Jewish Way," 21.

76. Geoffrey Norman and John Rezek, "*Playboy* Interview: David Mamet," *Playboy*, April 1995, 149.

77. Mamet, "Decoration," 9.

78. Kane, 247.

79. For a fuller discussion of Jewish speech patterns in Mamet's work, see Toby Silverman Zinman, "Jewish Aporia: The Rhythm of Talking in Mamet," *Theatre Journal* 44 (1992): 207–15.

80. As quoted in John Heilpern, *How Good Is David Mamet, Anyway?* (New York: Routledge, 2000), 225.

81. Ben Brantley, "A Middle-Aged Man Goes Home, to Mametville," *New York Times*, 20 November 1997.

82. Ibid.

83. Heilpern, *How Good Is David Mamet?* 227.

84. For a fuller discussion of the way ritual performance produces *communitas*, see Victor Turner, *The Ritual Process: Structure and Anti-Structure* (Ithaca: Cornell University Press, 1977), esp. chap. 3, "Liminality and Communitas."

CHAPTER 6

1. Hoberman and Shandler, 12.

2. See Brook, *Something Ain't Kosher*; Eliot Gertel, *Over the Top Judaism: Precedents and Trends in the Depiction of Jewish Beliefs and Observances in Film and Television* (Lanham, MD: University Press of America 2003); and Zurawik.

3. See Most; Paul Buhle, *From the Lower East Side to Hollywood: Jews in American Popular Culture* (New York: Verso, 2004); and Jack Gottlieb, *Funny, It Doesn't Sound Jewish: How Yiddish Songs and Synagogue Melodies Influenced Tin Pan Alley, Broadway, and Hollywood* (Albany: State University of New York Press, 2004).

4. Stratton, 310; Mamet, *The Old Neighborhood*, 26.

5. Hoberman and Shandler, 11.

6. Joseph Hanania, "Playing Princesses, Punishers, and Prudes: Jewish Women on Television," *New York Times*, 7 March 1999.

7. Matt Mendres, "How Can You Tell?" *New York Times*, 21 March 1999 (letter to the editor).

8. Stratton, 304.

9. This quotation, and subsequent quotations from Jewhoo were retrieved 12 February 2004 from http://www.Jewhoo.com.

10. Davida Bloom, "White but Not Quite: The Jewish Character and Anti-Semitism—Negotiating a Location in the Gray Zone between Other and Not," *Journal of Religion and Theatre* 1, 1 (2002), online journal, retrieved 2 February 2004 from http://www.fa.mtu.edu/~dlbruch/rtjournal.

11. See Hoberman and Shandler, 151–204.

12. See Brook, *Something Ain't Kosher*, 1–7.

13. Michel Foucault, *The Order of Things* (New York: Vintage, 1994).

14. Brook, *Something Ain't Kosher*, 1.

15. See Schechner, *Between Theatre and Anthropology*, 113, and elsewhere.

16. Brook, *Something Ain't Kosher*, 1.

17. Ibid.

18. Zurawik, 53.

19. Freedman, 25.

20. Whitfield, 51.

21. Freedman, 28.

22. Whitfield, 12.

23. Ibid.

24. For a brief history of *Saturday Night Live*'s infamous "Jew/Not-a-Jew" sketch, see Zurawik, 2–3.

25. It may be ideologically attractive to act "as if" this Jewishness is immanent in the performance.

26. Anderson, 6.

27. Ibid., 149.

28. Mamet, "Decoration," 9, emphasis in original.

29. The highly publicized dabbling in cabala by Madonna and other non-Jewish celebrities would seem to support this view.

30. Andrew Furman, "Is the Jew in Vogue?" *Tikkun* 15, 6 (November-December 2000), retrieved 4 February 2004 from http://www.tikkun.org.

31. See Freedman; Furman; Zurawik; and others.

32. Hoberman and Shandler, 8.

33. Central Conference of American Rabbis Columbus Platform, 1937, as quoted in Michael A. Meyer, *Response to Modernity: A History of the Reform Movement in Judaism* (Detroit: Wayne State University Press, 1988), 389.

34. J. Boyarin, 170.

35. Ibid., 174.

36. It should be noted that even within this strict definition there are virtually infinite debates over interpretation of specific laws.

37. See Charmé; Freedman; and others.

38. See Neal Gabler, *Life: The Movie* (New York: Knopf, 1998).

39. Or, more properly, it has been shaped into many narratives.

40. Erdman, 160.

41. Werner Sollors, ed., *The Invention of Ethnicity* (New York: Oxford University Press, 1989), 31, 33.

42. See Furman.

43. S. Bennett, 207.

44. As Jeffrey Shandler writes, "[I]n the case of Jews—a group whose existence in the modern era is so infused with discussions of identity and difference—the issue of identity is something else again, as it is for other identities that can be hidden, or whose definition is seen as problematic, or for whom the act of identification has a history of being dangerous" ("Jewish Way," 19).

45. Cf. Sedgwick, 75.

46. See Schechner, *Between Theatre and Anthropology*, 113–14.

47. See Glazer, *American Judaism*; Glazer, "American Jewry"; and elsewhere.

Bibliography

Allen, Woody, dir. *Annie Hall*. Santa Monica: MGM Home Entertainment, 2000. DVD, 94 min.

———. *Manhattan*. Culver City, CA: MGM Home Entertainment, 2000. Videocassette, 96 min.

———. *Zelig*. Santa Monica: MGM Home Entertainment, 2001. Videocassette, 79 min.

Allen, Woody. *Play It Again, Sam*. New York: Random House, 1971.

———. *Woody Allen on Woody Allen*. Ed. Stig Björkman. New York: Grove, 1993.

Altman, Richard, and Mervyn Kaufman. *The Making of a Musical: Fiddler on the Roof*. New York: Crown, 1971.

American Business Consultants. *Red Channels: The Report of Communist Influence in Radio and Television*. New York: Counterattack, 1950.

American Jewish Historical Society. *The American Jewish Desk Reference*. New York: Random House, 1999.

Anderson, Benedict. *Imagined Communities*. Rev. ed. London: Verso, 1995.

Auster, Albert. "'Funny, You Don't Look Jewish': The Image of Jews on Television." *Television Quarterly* 26, 3 (1993): 65–74.

Band, Arnold. "Popular Fiction and the Shaping of Jewish Identity." In *Jewish Identity in America*, ed. David M. Gordis and Yoav Ben-Horin, 215–26. Los Angeles: Wilstein Institute of Jewish Policy Studies, 1991.

Banham, Martin, ed. *The Cambridge Guide to Theatre*. Cambridge: Cambridge University Press, 1992.

Barnes, Clive. "Angelically Gay about Our Decay." *New York Theatre Critics Reviews* 54, 11 (1993): 210.

———. "'Sisters' Makes the Big Move to B'way." *New York Theatre Critics Reviews* 54, 4 (1993): 72.

Barr, Terry. "Stars, Light, and Finding the Way: The Emergence of Jewish Characters in Contemporary Film and Television." *Studies in Popular Culture* 25, 2 (1993): 87–100.

Belkin, Ahuva. "The 'Low' Culture of the *Purimshpil*." In *Yiddish Theatre: New Approaches*, ed. Joel Berkowitz, 29–43. Oxford: Littman Library of Jewish Civilization, 2003.

Ben-David, Caleb. "Tevye's Happy Ending." *Jerusalem Post*, 22 September 2004.

Bennett, Susan. *Theatre Audiences*. 2d ed. London: Routledge, 1997.

Bennett, Tony. "Text, Readers, Reading Formations." *Literature and History* 9 (1983): 214–27.

Berg, Gertrude, with Cherny Berg. *Molly and Me*. New York: McGraw-Hill, 1961.

Bernheimer, Kathryn. *The 50 Greatest Jewish Movies*. Secaucus: Birch Lane Press, 1998.

Biale, David. *Eros and the Jews: From Biblical Israel to Contemporary America*. New York: Basic Books, 1992.

Billington, Michael. Review of *Angels in America*. *Theatre Record* 13, 24 (1993): 1357–58.

Bloom, Davida. "White but Not Quite: The Jewish Character and Anti-Semitism—Negotiating a Location in the Gray Zone Between Other and Not." *Journal of Religion and Theatre* 1, 1 (2002). Online journal. Retrieved 2 February 2004 from http://www.fa.mtu.edu/~dlbruch/rtjournal.

Boal, Augusto. *Theatre of the Oppressed*. Trans. Charles A. McBride and Maria-Odilia Leal McBride. New York: Theatre Communications Group, 1985.

Bock, Jerry, comp., and Sheldon Harnick, lyr. *Fiddler on the Roof: The Original Broadway Cast Recording*. New York: RCA, 1964. Compact disc issued 1986.

Bottoms, Stephen J. "Re-staging Roy: Citizen Cohn and the Search for Xanadu." *Theatre Journal* 48 (1996): 157–84.

Boyarin, Jonathan. *Thinking in Jewish*. Chicago: University of Chicago Press, 1996.

Boyarin, Jonathan, and Daniel Boyarin, eds. *Jews and Other Differences: The New Jewish Cultural Studies*. Minneapolis: University of Minnesota Press, 1997.

Brantley, Ben. "A Cozy Little McShtetl." *New York Times*, 27 February 2004.

———. "A Middle-Aged Man Goes Home, to Mametville." *New York Times*, 20 November 1997.

Brater, Enoch. "Ethics and Ethnicity in the Plays of Arthur Miller." In *From Hester Street to Hollywood: The Jewish-American Stage and Screen*, ed. Sarah Blacher Cohen, 123–36. Bloomington: Indiana University Press, 1983.

Brodkin, Karen. *How Jews Became White Folks and What That Says about Race in America*. New Brunswick: Rutgers University Press, 1998.

Brook, Vincent. "The Americanization of Molly: How Mid-Fifties TV Homogenized *The Goldbergs* (and Got 'Berg-larized' in the Process)." *Cinema Journal* 38, 4 (1999): 45–67.

———. "From the Cozy to the Carceral: Trans-formations of Ethnic Space in *The Goldbergs* and *Seinfeld*." *The Velvet Light Trap* 44 (1999): 54–67.

———. *Something Ain't Kosher Here: The Rise of the "Jewish" Sitcom*. New Brunswick: Rutgers University Press, 2003.

Brown, Jared. *Zero Mostel*. New York: Atheneum, 1989.

Brustein, Robert. Review of *The Sisters Rosensweig*. *New York Theatre Critics Reviews* 54, 4 (1993): 79–80.

Buhle, Paul. *From the Lower East Side to Hollywood: Jews in American Popular Culture*. New York: Verso, 2004.

Butler, Judith. *Gender Trouble*. New York: Routledge, 1990.

———. "Performative Acts and Gender Constitution: An Essay in Phenomenology and Feminist Theory." *Theatre Journal* 40, 4 (1988): 519–31.

Canby, Vincent. "Is 'Fiddler' More DeMille than Sholem Aleichem?" *New York Times*, 28 November 1971.

———. "Life-Style of Aleichem Characters Is Missing amid Production's Grandeur." *New York Times*, 4 November 1971.

———. Review of *The Way We Were*. *New York Times*, 18 October 1973.

Carlson, Marvin. *The Haunted Stage: The Theatre as Memory Machine.* Ann Arbor: University of Michigan Press, 2001.

———. *Performance: A Critical Introduction.* London: Routledge, 1996.

———. *Theatre Semiotics: Signs of Life.* Bloomington: Indiana University Press, 1990.

CBS-TV. Press release, 13 January 1949. National Jewish Archive of Broadcasting.

———. Press release, 19 November 1949. National Jewish Archive of Broadcasting.

Chapman, John. "'Wholesale' Depressing Musical." *New York Theatre Critics Reviews* 23, 9 (1962): 316.

Charmé, Stuart Z. "Varieties of Authenticity in Contemporary Jewish Identity." *Jewish Social Studies* 6, 2 (2000): 133–55.

Clurman, Harold. *The Fervent Years: The Group Theatre and the 30s.* New York: Knopf, 1975.

Cohen, Rabbi Norman J. "Wrestling with Angels." In *Tony Kushner in Conversation,* ed. Robert Vorlicky, 217–30. Ann Arbor: University of Michigan Press, 1998.

Cohen, Stephen M. "Jewish Continuity over Judaic Content." In *The Americanization of the Jews,* ed. Robert M. Seltzer and Norman J. Cohen, 395–416. New York: New York University Press, 1995.

Conquergood, Dwight. "Of Caravans and Carnivals: Performance Studies in Motion." *Drama Review* 39, 4 (1995): 137–41.

———. "Performance Studies: Interventions and Radical Research." *TDR* 46, 2 (2002): 145–56.

Crosland, Alan, dir. *The Jazz Singer.* Culver City, CA: MGM/UA Home Video, 1991. Videocassette, 89 min.

De Tocqueville, Alexis. "Some Observations on the Drama amongst Democratic Nations." Trans. Henry Reeve. In *The Theory of the Modern Stage,* ed. Eric Bentley, 479–85. New York: Penguin, 1976.

Deleuze, Gilles, and Félix Guattari. *Anti-Oedipus.* Trans. Robert Hurley, Mark Seem, and Helen R. Lane. Minneapolis: University of Minnesota Press, 1983.

———. *A Thousand Plateaus.* Trans. Brian Massumi. Minneapolis: University of Minnesota Press, 1987.

Desser, David. "The Cinematic Melting Pot: Ethnicity, Jews, and Psychoanalysis." In *Unspeakable Images: Ethnicity and the American Cinema,* ed. Lester Friedman, 353–403. Urbana: University of Illinois Press, 1991.

Doughty, Louise. Review of *Angels in America. Theatre Record* 13, 24 (1993): 1359–60.

Douglas, Kirk. *The Ragman's Son.* New York: Simon and Schuster, 1988.

Du Bois, W. E. B. *The Souls of Black Folk.* Chicago: A. C. McClurg, 1903.

Eco, Umberto. "The Semiotics of Theatrical Performance." *Drama Review* 21, 1 (1977): 107–17.

Eisen, Arnold. "In the Wilderness: Reflections on American Jewish Culture." *Jewish Social Studies* 5, 1–2 (1999): 26–33.

Eisenstadt, Shmuel A. "The Jewish Experience with Pluralism." *Society* 28, 1 (1990): 21–25.

Erdman, Harley. *Staging the Jew: The Performance of an American Ethnicity, 1860–1920.* New Brunswick: Rutgers University Press, 1997.

Feingold, Michael. "Building the Monolith." *New York Theatre Critics Reviews* 54, 11 (1993): 218.

———. "Introduction." In Donald Margulies, *Sight Unseen and Other Plays*, ix–xv. New York: Theatre Communications Group, 1995.

———. Review of *The Sisters Rosensweig*. *New York Theatre Critics Reviews* 54, 4 (1993): 84.

Fernley, Alison, and Paula Maloof. "*Yentl.*" *Film Quarterly* 38 (spring 1985): 38–45.

Fiedler, Leslie. *Fiedler on the Roof: Essays on Literature and Jewish Identity*. Boston: David R. Godine, 1991.

Finkielkraut, Alain. *The Imaginary Jew*. Trans. Kevin O'Neill and David Suchoff. Lincoln: University of Nebraska Press, 1994.

Fish, Stanley. *Is There a Text in This Class?* Cambridge: Harvard University Press, 1980.

Fiske, John. *Television Culture*. London: Routledge, 1989.

Foucault, Michel. *Discipline and Punish*. Trans. Alan Sheridan. New York: Vintage, 1977.

———. *The Order of Things*. New York: Vintage, 1994.

Freedman, Samuel. *Jew vs. Jew*. New York: Simon and Schuster, 2000.

Friedman, Lester, ed. *Unspeakable Images: Ethnicity and the American Cinema*. Urbana: University of Illinois Press, 1991.

Furman, Andrew. "Is the Jew in Vogue?" *Tikkun* 15, 6 (November-December 2000). Retrieved 4 February 2004 from http://www.tikkun.org.

Gabler, Neal. *An Empire of Their Own: How the Jews Invented Hollywood*. New York: Anchor, 1989.

———. *Life: The Movie*. New York: Knopf, 1998.

Gardner, Elysa. "'Fiddler' Again Plays Its Magic." *USA Today*, 27 February 2004.

Geis, Deborah, and Steven Kruger, eds. *Approaching the Millennium: Essays on Angels in America*. Ann Arbor: University of Michigan Press, 1997.

Gertel, Elliot B. *Over the Top Judaism: Precedents and Trends in the Depiction of Jewish Beliefs and Observances in Film and Television*. Lanham, MD: University Press of America, 2003.

Gilman, Sander. *Jewish Self-Hatred: Anti-Semitism and the Hidden Language of the Jews*. Baltimore: Johns Hopkins University Press, 1986.

———. *The Jew's Body*. New York: Routledge, 1991.

———. "The Jew's Body: Thoughts on Jewish Physical Difference." In *Too Jewish*, ed. Norman Kleeblatt, 60–73. New Brunswick: Rutgers University Press, 1996.

Ginsberg, Elaine K., ed. *Passing and the Fictions of Identity*. Durham: Duke University Press, 1996.

Girard, Jeremy. Review of *Angels in America*. *New York Theatre Critics Reviews* 54, 11 (1993): 212.

———. Review of *The Sisters Rosensweig*. *New York Theatre Critics Reviews* 54, 4 (1993): 70.

Glazer, Nathan. "American Jewry or American Judaism?" *Society* 28, 1 (1990): 14–20.

———. *American Judaism*. 2d ed. Chicago: University of Chicago Press, 1972.

Goffman, Erving. *The Presentation of Self in Everyday Life*. Woodstock: Overlook, 1959.

The Goldbergs. "08–29–1949." 1949. National Jewish Archive of Broadcasting.
———. "09–05–1949." 1949. National Jewish Archive of Broadcasting.
———. "Ann Bancroft." 1949. National Jewish Archive of Broadcasting.
———. "Molly's Wedding Plans." 1955. National Jewish Archive of Broadcasting.
———. "Rosie's Nose." 1955. National Jewish Archive of Broadcasting.
———. "Sammy Gets Married." 1955. National Jewish Archive of Broadcasting.
Gottlieb, Jack. *Funny, It Doesn't Sound Jewish: How Yiddish Songs and Synagogue Melodies Influenced Tin Pan Alley, Broadway, and Hollywood.* Albany: State University of New York Press, 2004.
Grobel, Lawrence. "*Playboy* Interview: Barbra Streisand." *Playboy,* October 1977, 79–106, 193–200.
Gross, Barry. "No Victim, She: Barbra Streisand and the Movie Jew." *Journal of Ethnic Studies* 3, 1 (1975): 28–40.
———. "What Shylock Forgot; or Making It and Losing It in America." *Journal of Ethnic Studies* 2, 3 (1974): 50–57.
Gussow, Mel. "Wasserstein: Comedy, Character, Reflection." *New York Theatre Critics Reviews* 54, 4 (1993): 80.
Halberstam, Joshua. *Schmoozing: The Private Conversations of American Jews.* New York: Perigree, 1997.
Hall, Stuart. "Encoding and Decoding in Television Discourse." In *The Cultural Studies Reader,* ed. Simon During, 90–103. London: Routledge, 1993.
Hammer, Joshua, and John Schwartz. "Prime Time Mensch." *Newsweek,* 12 October 1992, 88–89.
Hanania, Joseph. "Playing Princesses, Punishers, and Prudes: Jewish Women on Television." *New York Times,* 7 March 1999.
Heilpern, John. *How Good Is David Mamet, Anyway?* New York: Routledge, 2000.
———. "New-ish, but Still Jew-ish: *Fiddler* Breaks Tradition." *New York Observer,* 8 March 2004.
Henry, William, III. Review of *The Sisters Rosensweig. New York Theatre Critics Reviews* 54, 4 (1993): 83.
Herman, Felicia. "The Way She *Really* Is: Images of Jews and Women in the Films of Barbra Streisand." In *Talking Back: Images of Jewish Women in American Popular Culture,* ed. Joyce Antler, 171–90. Hanover: Brandeis University Press, 1998.
Herschorn, Clive. Review of *Angels in America. Theatre Record* 13, 24 (1993): 1358.
Higham, Charles. *Ziegfeld.* Chicago: H. Regnery, 1972.
Hill, Mike, ed. *Whiteness: A Critical Reader.* New York: New York University Press, 1997.
Hoberman, J., and Jeffrey Shandler, eds. *Entertaining America: Jews, Movies, and Broadcasting.* Princeton: Princeton University Press, 2003.
Hollinger, David A. *Postethnic America: Beyond Multiculturalism.* New York: Basic Books, 1995.
Jenkins, Henry. *Textual Poachers.* London: Routledge, 1993.
Jewhoo. Anonymously edited Web site. http://www.jewhoo.com.
Jewison, Norman, dir. *Fiddler on the Roof.* Farmington Hills, MI: CBS/Fox Video, 1984. 2 videocassettes, 3 hrs.

Kakutani, Michiko. "A Salesman Who Transcends Time." *New York Times*, 7 February 1999.

Kane, Leslie. *Weasels and Wisemen: Ethics and Ethnicity in the Work of David Mamet.* New York: St. Martin's/Palgrave, 1999.

Kazan, Elia, dir. *Gentleman's Agreement.* Beverly Hills: Fox Video, 1992. Videocassette, 118 min.

Kennedy, Mark. "Alfred Molina Scales New Heights in 'Fiddler on the Roof.'" Associated Press wire report, 25 February 2004.

Kerr, Walter. "First Night Report: 'I Can Get It for You Wholesale.'" *New York Theatre Critics Reviews* 23, 9 (1962): 314.

———. Review of "Fiddler on the Roof." *New York Theatre Critics Reviews* 25, 19 (1964): 217.

Kirshenblatt-Gimblett, Barbara. "Imagining Europe: The Popular Arts of American Jewish Ethnography." In *Divergent Centers: Shaping Jewish Cultures in Israel and America*, ed. Deborah Dash Moore and Ilan Troen, 155–91. New Haven: Yale University Press, 2001.

Kissell, Howard. "Family Circus." *New York Theatre Critics Reviews* 54, 4 (1993): 73.

———. "Sharpened 'Sisters' Act." *New York Theatre Critics Reviews* 54, 4 (1993): 74.

Klagsburn, Francine. "Remembering the Goldbergs." *New York Times*, 8 August 1988.

Kleeblatt, Norman, ed. *Too Jewish? Challenging Traditional Identities.* New Brunswick: Rutgers University Press, 1996.

Krasner, David. *Resistance, Parody, and Double-Consciousness in African American Theatre, 1895–1910.* New York: St. Martin's, 1997.

Kushner, Tony. *Angels in America.* Part 1: *Millennium Approaches.* New York: Theatre Communications Group, 1993.

———. *Angels in America.* Part 2: *Perestroika.* New York: Theatre Communications Group, 1993.

Lahr, John. "Angels on Broadway." *New York Theatre Critics Reviews* 54, 11 (1993): 208.

———. "Bittersweet." *New Yorker*, 8 March 2004, 89.

Landman, Isaac, ed. *The Universal Jewish Encyclopedia.* New York: Universal Jewish Encyclopedia Co., 1948.

Levenson, Sam. "The Dialect Comedian Should Vanish." *Commentary* 14, 2 (1952): 168–70.

Liebman, Robert Leslie. "Rabbis or Rakes, Schlemiels or Supermen? Jewish Identity in Charlie Chaplin, Jerry Lewis, and Woody Allen." *Literature/Film Quarterly* 12, 3 (1984): 195–201.

Lipset, Seymour Martin, and Earl Raab, eds. *Jews and the New American Scene.* Cambridge: Harvard University Press, 1995.

Lipsitz, George. *Time Passages: Collective Memory and American Popular Culture.* Minneapolis: University of Minnesota Press, 1990.

Lyman, Darryl. *Great Jews on Stage and Screen.* Middle Village, NY: Jonathan David, 1994.

Maltin, Leonard, ed. *Leonard Maltin's 2001 Movie and Video Guide.* New York: Signet, 2001.

Mamet, David. *The Old Neighborhood.* New York: Vintage, 1998.

————. *Some Freaks.* New York: Viking, 1989.

————. *Three Jewish Plays.* New York: Samuel French, 1987.

————. *True and False: Heresy and Common Sense for the Actor.* New York: Pantheon, 1997.

Marcus, Jacob R., ed. *The Concise Dictionary of American Jewish Biography.* Brooklyn: Carlson, 1994.

Mayer, Egon. "From an External to an Internal Agenda." In *The Americanization of the Jews,* ed. Robert M. Seltzer and Norman J. Cohen, 417–35. New York: New York University Press, 1995.

McCarter, Jeremy. "The Musical to Start All Musicals." *New York Sun,* 27 February 2004.

McClain, John. "Even at Retail, It's No Bargain." *New York Theatre Critics Reviews* 23, 9 (1962): 317.

————. "Mostel Makes Musical Tick." *New York Theatre Critics Reviews* 25, 19 (1964): 215.

McKenzie, Jon. *Perform or Else.* London: Routledge, 2001.

McNamara, Brooks. "'A Congress of Wonders': The Rise and Fall of the Dime Museum." *ESQ: A Journal of the American Renaissance* 20, 3 (1974): 216–32.

————. *The Shuberts of Broadway.* New York: Oxford University Press, 1990.

Mendres, Matt. "How Can You Tell?" Letter to the editor. *New York Times,* 21 March 1999.

Meyer, Michael A. *Response to Modernity: A History of the Reform Movement in Judaism.* Detroit: Wayne State University Press, 1988.

Miller, Arthur. *Death of a Salesman.* New York: Penguin, 1949.

————. *The Theater Essays of Arthur Miller.* Rev. and expanded ed. Ed. Robert A. Martin and Steven R. Centola. New York: Da Capo, 1996.

————. *Timebends: A Life.* New York: Grove, 1987.

Morehouse, Ward, II. "'Angels in America' Remains Earthbound." *New York Theatre Critics Reviews* 54, 11 (1993): 215–16.

Most, Andrea. *Making Americans: Jews and the Broadway Musical.* Cambridge: Harvard University Press, 2004.

Mulvey, Laura. *Visual and Other Pleasures.* Bloomington: Indiana University Press, 1989.

Muñoz, José Esteban. "Feeling Brown: Ethnicity and Affect in Ricardo Bracho's *The Sweetest Hangover (and Other STD's)." Theatre Journal* 52, 1 (March 2000): 67–79.

Murphy, Brenda. *Death of a Salesman.* New York: Cambridge University Press, 1995.

Nadel, Norman. "'Fiddler on the Roof' Is Humorous, Tender Musical." *New York Theatre Critics Reviews* 25, 19 (1964): 214.

————. "'Funny Girl' Just This Side of Paradise." *New York Theatre Critics Reviews* 25, 9 (1964): 314.

Nimoy, Leonard. *I Am Spock.* New York: Hyperion, 1995.

Norman, Geoffrey, and John Rezek. "*Playboy* Interview: David Mamet." *Playboy,* April 1995, 51–60, 148–50.

Novak, William, and Moshe Waldoks, eds. *The Big Book of Jewish Humor.* New York: Harper and Row, 1981.

Novick, Julius. "Salesman Redivivus." *Threepenny Review* 19 (1985): 18–19.

———. "Willy Loman's Secret." *Forward*, 8 October 1999.

Phelan, Peggy. *Unmarked: The Politics of Performance*. New York: Routledge, 1993.

Pogrebin, Letty Cottin. *Deborah, Golda, and Me: Being Female and Jewish in America*. New York: Crown, 1991.

Pollack, Sydney, dir. *The Way We Were*. New York: Columbia Tristar Home Video, 2001. Videocassette, 118 min.

Prell, Riv-Ellen. *Fighting to Become Americans: Jews, Gender, and the Anxiety of Assimilation*. Boston: Beacon, 1999.

Raphaelson, Samson. *The Jazz Singer*. New York: Brentano's, 1925.

Reed, Rex. Review of *Yentl*. *Film Review Annual* (1983): 1436–37.

Rhyne, Brett M. "'Fiddler on the Roof' Lyricist Featured in New Musical." *Jewish Journal*, 28 February 2003, retrieved 12 January 2004 from http://www.jewishjournal.org/archives.

Rich, Frank. "Embracing All Possibilities in Art and Life." *New York Theatre Critics Reviews* 54, 11 (1993): 214.

Roach, Joseph. *Cities of the Dead*. New York: Columbia University Press, 1996.

Rogin, Michael. *Blackface, White Noise: Jewish Immigrants in the Hollywood Melting Pot*. Berkeley: University of California Press, 1996.

Rosenbaum, Thane. "A Legacy Cut Loose." *Los Angeles Times*, 15 February 2004.

Rosenthal, Samuel J. "John Garfield." In *Entertaining America: Jews, Movies, and Broadcasting*, ed. J. Hoberman and Jeffrey Shandler, 173–75. Princeton: Princeton University Press, 2003.

Ross, George. "'Death of a Salesman' in the Original." *Commentary* 11, 2 (1951): 184–86.

Ross, Herbert, dir. *Play It Again, Sam*. Hollywood, CA: Paramount Home Video, 1991. Videocassette, 85 min.

Sandrow, Nahma. *Vagabond Stars: A World History of Yiddish Theater*. Syracuse: Syracuse University Press, 1996.

Sartre, Jean-Paul. *Anti-Semite and Jew*. Trans. G. Brecker. New York: Schocken, 1995.

Savran, David. "Ambivalence, Utopia, and a Queer Sort of Materialism: How *Angels in America* Reconstructs the Nation." In *Approaching the Millennium: Essays on* Angels in America, ed. Deborah Geis and Steven Kruger, 13–39. Ann Arbor: University of Michigan Press, 1997.

Schechner, Richard. *Between Theatre and Anthropology*. Philadelphia: University of Pennsylvania Press, 1985.

———. *Performance Theory*. London: Routledge, 1988.

Schiff, Ellen, ed. *Awake and Singing*. New York: Mentor, 1995.

Schneider, David J., Albert H. Hastorf, and Phoebe Ellsworth. *Person Perception*. 2d Edition. Reading, MA: Addison-Wesley, 1979.

Sedgwick, Eve Kosofsky. *Epistemology of the Closet*. Berkeley: University of California Press, 1990.

Seidman, Naomi. "Fag-Hags and Bu-Jews: Toward a (Jewish) Politics of Vicarious Identity." In *Insider/Outsider: American Jews and Multiculturalism*, ed. David Biale, Michael Galchinsky, and Susan Heschel, 254–68. Berkeley: University of California Press, 1998.

Seinfeld. "The Yada Yada." Episode 145, originally aired 24 April 1997.

Shandler, Jeffrey. "Is There a Jewish Way to Watch Television? Notes from a Tuned-in Ethnographer." *Jewish Folklore and Ethnology Review* 16, 1 (1994): 19–22.

———. *While America Watches: Televising the Holocaust.* New York: Oxford University Press, 1999.

Shaw, George Bernard. *Four Plays by George Bernard Shaw.* New York: Modern Library, 1953.

Sheward, David. *It's a Hit: The Backstage Book of Longest Running Broadway Shows, 1884 to the Present.* New York: Backstage Books, 1994.

Shoat, Ella. "Ethnicities-in-Relation: Toward a Multicultural Reading of American Cinema." In *Unspeakable Images: Ethnicity and the American Cinema,* ed. Lester Friedman, 215–50. Urbana: University of Illinois Press, 1991.

Simon, John. Review of *Angels in America. New York Theatre Critics Reviews* 54, 11 (1993): 207.

Sobchak, Vivian. "Postmodern Modes of Ethnicity." In *Unspeakable Images: Ethnicity and the American Cinema,* ed. Lester Friedman, 329–52. Urbana: University of Illinois Press, 1991.

Sollors, Werner. *Beyond Ethnicity: Consent and Descent in American Culture.* New York: Oxford University Press, 1986.

Sollors, Werner, ed. *The Invention of Ethnicity.* New York: Oxford University Press, 1989.

Solomon, Alisa. "Fiddling with 'Fiddler.'" *Village Voice,* 21 January 2004.

———. "Wrestling with *Angels*: A Jewish Fantasia." In *Approaching the Millennium: Essays on* Angels in America, ed. Deborah Geis and Steven Kruger, 118–33. Ann Arbor: University of Michigan Press, 1997.

Soloveitchik, Haym. "Rupture and Reconstruction: The Transformation of Contemporary Orthodoxy." *Tradition* 28, 4 (1994): 64–130.

Stearns, David Patrick. "'Sisters' Is a Kind, Clever, Wasserstein Chronicle." *New York Theatre Critics Reviews* 54, 4 (1993): 75.

———. "Soaring 'Angels in America.'" *New York Theatre Critics Reviews* 54, 11 (1993): 219.

Stein, Joseph, Jerry Bock, and Sheldon Harnick. *Fiddler on the Roof.* New York: Limelight Editions, 1964.

Steinberg, Stephen. *The Ethnic Myth.* Boston: Beacon, 1989.

Stone, Peter, Jerry Bock, Sheldon Harnick, and Joseph Stein. "Landmark Symposium: 'Fiddler on the Roof.'" *Dramatists' Guild Quarterly* 20, 1 (1983): 10–29.

Stratton, Jon. *Coming Out Jewish.* London: Routledge, 2000.

Streisand, Barbra, dir. *Yentl.* Culver City, CA: MGM/UA Home Video, 1989. Videocassette, 134 min.

Stuart, Jan. "If Chekhov Sisters Had Lived in Brooklyn." *New York Theatre Critics Reviews* 54, 4 (1993): 75.

Taubman, Howard. "Theater: Mostel as Tevye in 'Fiddler on the Roof.'" *New York Theatre Critics Reviews* 25, 19 (1964): 217–18.

———. "Theatre: 'I Can Get It for You Wholesale' Opens." *New York Theatre Critics Reviews* 23, 9 (1962): 316.

Taylor, Paul. Review of *Angels in America. Theatre Record* 13, 24 (1993): 1357.

Turner, Victor. *The Ritual Process: Structure and Anti-Structure*. Ithaca: Cornell University Press, 1977.

Vineberg, Steve. *Method Actors: Three Generations of an American Acting Style*. New York: Schirmer, 1991.

von Hoffman, Nicholas. *Citizen Cohn*. New York: Doubleday, 1988.

Vorlicky, Robert, ed. *Tony Kushner in Conversation*. Ann Arbor: University of Michigan Press, 1998.

Wasserstein, Wendy. *Shiksa Goddess; or, How I Spent My Forties*. New York: Knopf, 2001.

———. *The Sisters Rosensweig*. San Diego: Harcourt Brace, 1993.

Watt, Doug. "Wasserstein Pens a Pointed Drawing-Room Comedy." *New York Theatre Critics Reviews* 54, 4 (1993): 77.

Watts, Richard, Jr. "Two on the Aisle: The Brilliance of Zero Mostel." *New York Theatre Critics Reviews* 25, 19 (1964): 215.

Weber, Donald. "The Jewish-American World of Gertrude Berg: *The Goldbergs* on Radio and Televison, 1930–1950." In *Talking Back: Images of Jewish Women in American Popular Culture*, ed. Joyce Antler, 85–99. Boston: Brandeis University Press, 1998.

———. "Taking Jewish American Popular Culture Seriously: The Yinglish Worlds of Gertrude Berg, Milton Berle, and Mickey Katz." *Jewish Social Studies* 5, 1–2 (1999): 124–53.

Weidman, Jerome, and Harold Rome. *I Can Get It for You Wholesale*. New York: Random House, 1962.

Wernblad, Annette. *Brooklyn Is Not Expanding: Woody Allen's Comic Universe*. Rutherford, NJ: Fairleigh Dickinson University Press, 1992.

Whitfield, Stephen J. *In Search of American Jewish Culture*. Hanover: Brandeis University Press, 1999.

Winer, Linda. "Pulitzer-Winning 'Angels' Emerges from the Wings." *New York Theatre Critics Reviews* 54, 11 (1993): 209.

Wisse, Ruth. *The Modern Jewish Canon*. New York: Free Press, 2000.

———. *The Schlemiel as Modern Hero*. Chicago: University of Chicago Press, 1971.

Wolitz, Seth. "The Americanization of Tevye; or, Boarding the Jewish Mayflower." *American Quarterly* 40, 4 (1988): 514–36.

Wyler, William, dir. *Funny Girl*. Videocassette, 165 min. Burbank, CA: RCA/Columbia Pictures Home Video, 1985.

Zinman, Toby Silverman. "Jewish Aporia: The Rhythm of Talking in Mamet." *Theatre Journal* 44 (1992): 207–15.

Zurawik, David. *The Jews of Prime Time*. Hanover: University Press of New England, 2003.

Index

visibility, 10, 17–19, 35, 57–58, 131,
135, 143–44, 152

Waltons, The, 46
Warner, Harry, 39. *See also* Warner
Brothers Studio
Warner Brothers Studio, 25, 38, 132
Wasserstein, Wendy, 5, 108–10, 113,
119–29, 136
Watt, Doug, 120
Watts, Richard, Jr., 60, 78, 94
Way We Were, The, 27, 94–97, 102,
108, 156
Weber, Donald, 41, 47
Weidman, Jerome, 86
whiteness, 7, 56
Whitfield, Stephen, 13, 105, 144–45,
149–50
Williams, Robin, 71
Willis, Carl, 135
Winer, Linda, 117
Wolfe, George C., 113
Wolitz, Seth, 62, 72–73, 82

Woods, James, 94
World of Sholem Aleichem, The, 61, 74
Wyler, William, 87–88

Yentl, 27, 87, 102, 104–6, 156
Yiddish: accent/dialect, 41–45, 48, 79,
84, 126, 134; language, 49–50, 58,
113, 119, 124, 134–36; linguistic patterns, 49–51, 54, 58, 134–35; theater, 49–50, 52–53
Yiddishkeit, 21–22, 38, 84
Yom Kippur, 24–25, 45–46
Young Lions, The, 40

Zangwill, Israel, 23
Zanuck, Daryl F., 31
Zelig, 28, 87, 104–6, 156
Ziegfeld, Florenz, 89
Zigler, Scott, 129
Zionism, 11, 23, 28, 147
Zukor, Adolph, 26
Zurawik, David, 3, 10, 42–44, 46–48,
137, 140–42, 144, 150